CHILDREN'S

W🌻RLD

Encycl🌀pedia

CHILDREN'S

WORLD

Encyclopedia

Sean Connolly

This edition published in 2003
by Miles Kelly Publishing Ltd
Bardfield Centre, Great Bardfield, Essex, CM7 4SL

First published in 2002
by Machaon Publishing
7/1, 2-nd Khoroshevsky proezd
Moscow 123007, Russia

24681097531

Project Manager: Ian Paulyn
Design: Gill Mumford / Starry Dog
Picture Research: Liberty Newton
Production: Estela Godoy

British Library Cataloguing-in-Publication Data
A catalogue record for this book is available from the British library

ISBN 1-84236-343-3

Printed in Singapore

CONTENTS

HOW TO USE

The *Children's World Encyclopedia* offers you the chance to discover hundreds of facts about the world around you and the people who live in it. Each page unlocks new secrets and gives you an inside view of how things work, where people live, how plants grow and what lies beyond even the stars we see in the night sky. Illustrations and pictures dot these pages, making it easy to grasp even the most complicated ideas.

Eight sections give you a sense of direction, so that you can find out information quickly and easily. These sections are Space, Planet Earth, Science and Technology, Plants, Animals, Ancient History, Modern History and the Atlas.

Coloured bands

Each section of the encyclopedia has its own colour, making it quick and easy to navigate.

HOW PLANTS F

IMAGINE being able to feed yourself j all types of weather. Most plants are a called photosynthesis. 'Photo' means 'lig 'making', which is exactly what plants ar using light. Photosynthesis takes place in leaves. These parts are called chloroplast chlorophyll, a green colouring that takes

INGREDIENT

While chloroplast of the leaf take i are two of the photosynthesis parts of the pla through a series other parts of the Once the three in plant can get to we photosynthesis is glucose is absor as phloem, whic the plant. One oxygen gas, is re leaves. Animals need oxygen to of oxygen from helps all living

▲ Roots extend far out beneath a plant. They act as anchors and also gather water and minerals from the soil.

ener
s
ot

▲ The Amazon region of South America has a warm climate and constant rain, supporting a vast expanse of rainforest. This produces the widest variety of plants in any one area of the world.

water
from
roots

104

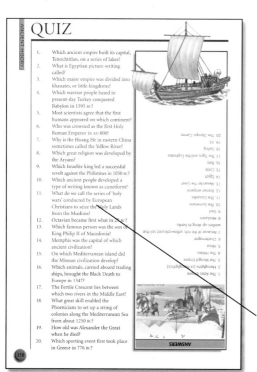

QUIZ

1. Which ancient empire built its capital, Tenochtitlan, on a series of lakes?
2. What is Egyptian picture-writing called?
3. Which major empire was divided into khanates, or little kingdoms?
4. Which warrior people based in present-day Turkey conquered Babylon in 1595 BC?
5. Most scientists agree that the first humans appeared on which continent?
6. Who was crowned as the first Holy Roman Emperor in AD 800?
7. Why is the Huang He in eastern China sometimes called the Yellow River?
8. Which great religion was developed by the Aryans?
9. Which Israelite king led a successful revolt against the Philistines in 1050 BC?
10. Which ancient people developed a type of writing known as cuneiform?
11. What do we call the series of 'holy wars' conducted by European Christians to seize the Holy Lands from the Muslims?
12. Octavian became first what in 27 BC?
13. Which famous person was the son of King Philip II of Macedonia?
14. Memphis was the capital of which ancient civilization?
15. On which Mediterranean island did the Minoan civilization develop?
16. Which animals, carried aboard trading ships, brought the Black Death to Europe in 1347?
17. The Fertile Crescent lies between which two rivers in the Middle East?
18. What great skill enabled the Phoenicians to set up a string of colonies along the Mediterranean Sea from about 1250 BC?
19. How old was Alexander the Great when he died?
20. Which sporting event first took place in Greece in 776 BC?

20. The Olympic Games
19. 33
18. Sailing
17. The Tigris and the Euphrates
16. Rats
15. Crete
14. Egypt
13. Alexander the Great
12. Roman emperor
11. The Crusades
10. The Sumerians
9. Saul
8. Hinduism
7. Because of the rich, yellow-coloured soil that washes up along its banks.
6. Charlemagne
5. Africa
4. The Hittites
3. The Mongol Empire
2. Hieroglyphs (or hieroglyphics)
1. The Aztec Empire

ANSWERS

158

Quiz pages

There are quiz pages at the beginning of each section to test your knowledge before and after reading it. You will be amazed how much you learn.

Illustrations

There are photographs and illustrations on every spread to help you visualise the subject matter.

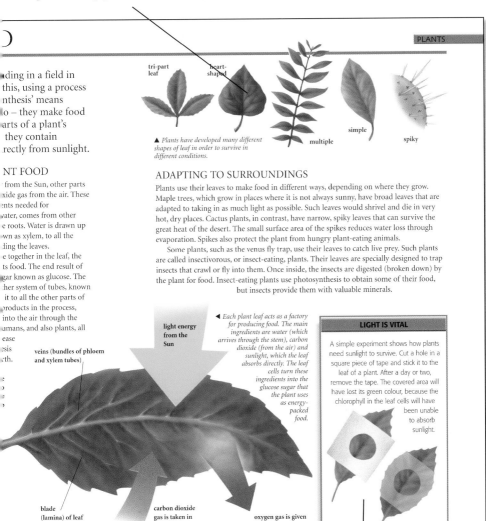

ding in a field in
this, using a process
nthesis' means
o – they make food
arts of a plant's
they contain
rectly from sunlight.

tri-part
leaf

heart-
shaped

simple

spiky

multiple

▲ Plants have developed many different
shapes of leaf in order to survive in
different conditions.

NT FOOD

from the Sun, other parts
xide gas from the air. These
ents needed for
vater, comes from other
e roots. Water is drawn up
wn as xylem, to all the
ding the leaves.
e together in the leaf, the
ts food. The end result of
gar known as glucose. The
her system of tubes, known
it to all the other parts of
products in the process,
into the air through the
umans, and also plants, all
ease
esis
th.

ADAPTING TO SURROUNDINGS

Plants use their leaves to make food in different ways, depending on where they grow. Maple trees, which grow in places where it is not always sunny, have broad leaves that are adapted to taking in as much light as possible. Such leaves would shrivel and die in very hot, dry places. Cactus plants, in contrast, have narrow, spiky leaves that can survive the great heat of the desert. The small surface area of the spikes reduces water loss through evaporation. Spikes also protect the plant from hungry plant-eating animals.

Some plants, such as the venus fly trap, use their leaves to catch live prey. Such plants are called insectivorous, or insect-eating, plants. Their leaves are specially designed to trap insects that crawl or fly into them. Once inside, the insects are digested (broken down) by the plant for food. Insect-eating plants use photosynthesis to obtain some of their food, but insects provide them with valuable minerals.

light energy
from the
Sun

◀ Each plant leaf acts as a factory
for producing food. The main
ingredients are water (which
arrives through the stem), carbon
dioxide (from the air) and
sunlight, which the leaf
absorbs directly. The leaf
cells turn these
ingredients into the
glucose sugar that
the plant uses
as energy-
packed
food.

veins (bundles of phloem
and xylem tubes)

blade
(lamina) of leaf

carbon dioxide
gas is taken in
from the air

oxygen gas is given
off to the air

LIGHT IS VITAL

A simple experiment shows how plants need sunlight to survive. Cut a hole in a square piece of tape and stick it to the leaf of a plant. After a day or two, remove the tape. The covered area will have lost its green colour, because the chlorophyll in the leaf cells will have been unable to absorb sunlight.

Labels

Detailed illustrations are labelled to help explain the individual parts of the artwork.

Panels

Panels give fascinating facts for you to digest, to help you learn about the subject.

QUIZ

1. What is a chunk of frozen gas and dust with a long, bright tail called?
2. What causes a solar eclipse?
3. What is the name of the chemical process that turns hydrogen into helium in the Sun, releasing vast amounts of energy?
4. Why can we not see a black hole?
5. What is the name given to the massive, bright explosion of a red giant star?
6. What type of telescope 'looks' for light and visible images, rather than 'listening' for radio waves?
7. What is the difference between a meteor and a meteorite?
8. What is the photosphere?
9. What is special about Proxima Centauri in relation to Earth?
10. Who was the first person to orbit Earth in a spacecraft?
11. Which four planets are sometimes called the 'gas giants'?
12. Astronauts on the 1993 space shuttle *Endeavor* mission conducted an important repair to what?
13. What is another name for Polaris?
14. How long ago do scientists think the Big Bang took place?
15. Why could you probably still see the footprints left by visitors to the Moon?
16. What do the initials SETI stand for?
17. What is the name of the constellation that appears on the flags of Australia and New Zealand?
18. Which two planets in our Solar System do not have moons?
19. Which 17th-century scientist explained how the planets and the Moon move through space?
20. Ganymede, the largest moon in the Solar System, orbits which planet?

ANSWERS

20. Jupiter
19. Sir Isaac Newton
18. Mercury and Venus
17. Crux Australis, or the Southern Cross
16. The Search for Extra-Terrestrial Intelligence
15. Because the Moon has no atmosphere and there is no wind or rain to wipe the footprints away.
14. About 15 billion years ago
13. The North Star
12. The Hubble Space Telescope
11. Jupiter, Saturn, Uranus and Neptune
10. Yuri Gagarin of the Soviet Union, in 1961.
9. It is the nearest star to Earth, after our own Sun.
8. The visible surface of the Sun.
7. A meteor is a small chunk of rock travelling at high speed through space. A meteorite is a meteor that has crashed to Earth.
6. An optical telescope
5. A supernova
4. Because this type of massive dying star pulls everything towards it, including light.
3. Fusion
2. The Moon passing directly in front of the Sun, blocking our view of it for a short time.
1. A comet

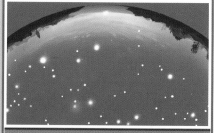

SPACE

IF YOU look up at the night sky, you will see thousands of stars twinkling against a blue-black background. A few of these 'stars' are planets like our own Earth. Some of the other sparkling lights are groups of stars, many millions of kilometres away from us. All these stars and planets, including our own Earth and Sun, and the space between them, make up the Universe.

The Universe is far larger than we can ever imagine. The numbers of stars are almost countless. Even the star nearest to us, Proxima Centauri, is about 40 million million kilometres away. Telescopes on Earth and up in space continue to find stars that are farther away than we could ever imagine.

BIG BANG

HOW did the Universe begin? Indeed, did it have a beginning, or has it always been there? To appreciate the immense spans of time involved, we have to look back a long, long way. Recognisable human beings have probably been around on Earth for less than 200,000 years. Life on our planet started more than 3,000 million years ago. The Earth itself, along with the Sun and the rest of the Solar System, is about 4,600 million years old. Yet the estimated age of the Universe is much greater, perhaps three or four times older than the Solar System. What was there before the Universe began? Possibly there was nothing – no space and no time.

THE SIZE OF SPACE

Astronomers measure the enormous distances in the Universe in light-years. A light-year is the distance that light travels in one year: 9,460,000,000,000 kilometres.

◆

There are special names for the tiniest fractions of seconds (during which so much to happened in the Big Bang). A microsecond is a millionth of a second, and a nanosecond is a billionth of a second.

▲ *The Big Bang, shown here as a flash in the centre of the picture, was enormously powerful. Although it took place in just a fraction of a second, the explosion was strong enough to send energy and matter flying out at great speed in all directions.*

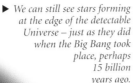

▶ *We can still see stars forming at the edge of the detectable Universe – just as they did when the Big Bang took place, perhaps 15 billion years ago.*

BLOWING UP A HUGE BALLOON

Astronomers, the scientists who study space, have discovered that everything in space is moving away from everything else at high speed. Imagine everything in the Universe was lying on the surface of a balloon. As the balloon is blown up, objects move farther apart from each other, and from the centre. Astronomers think that if the Universe is still expanding, it must have started very small – and could have been formed in one big event, like a huge explosion. The explosion is called the 'Big Bang'.

THE FIRST STARS

By examining what makes up distant stars, and judging their speed and direction, astronomers have been able to work out a theory as to what might have happened during the Big Bang. Most astronomers believe that the Universe was once a tiny, extremely hot ball. They estimate that, about 15 billion years ago, this ball exploded, sending energy and material shooting out in all directions. The material cooled as it sped away, allowing the first stars to form. Huge changes took place within the first millionths of a second, and within just three minutes, all of the Universe's hydrogen (the main chemical substance in stars) was created.

11

HOW STARS FORM

WHEN most people talk about 'stars', they tend to mean the many objects we see sparkling in the night sky. Many of these may not, in fact, be stars at all. Some are planets, others are groups of stars or simply clouds of gas.

A star is a ball of gas so hot that it burns and glows. Stars range in temperature from 2,100°C to about 50,000°C. The colour of a star is an indication of how hot it is. Think of a piece of metal being heated in a fire. At first, it glows a strong red. Then, as it becomes hotter, it turns white, and is described as being 'white-hot'. White stars are hotter than red ones, but some stars become even hotter and shine with a blue light.

▲ *Pleiades is a cluster, or group, of more than 100 stars that are close together. They are so far away that to the unaided eye they look like pale mist.*

THE BIRTH OF A STAR

Scientists have spent many years trying to find answers to the question: 'how do stars form?'. Stars come in different sizes, and how they behave – including how long they burn – depends on their size. A star that is about the same size as our Sun starts to form when a large cloud of gas floating in space begins to gather in on itself, becoming more and more massive. This gathering process causes the baby star to get hotter and hotter, reaching perhaps 15 million °C at the centre. The intense heat triggers major changes in the gases of the star. Hydrogen fuses to form helium. At the same time it releases enough energy to prevent the star's gravity from making it collapse into itself. A new star has formed.

▶ *3. High-temperature chemical action inside a star sends energy outwards. This energy stops the star from being pulled inwards any further.*

3

▶ 1. Stars start to form when a mass of gas and dust begins to pull in on itself, by the force known as gravity. The gas heats up and begins to glow.

▲ 2. The gas continues to heat up and the young star glows even more brightly. At this point it blows away any remaining dust, leaving behind only very hot gas.

A LONG LIFE

The same energy that keeps a star from collapsing also causes it to shine – for a very long time. A star that is about the size of the Sun usually burns for about 10 billion years. Much bigger stars tend to burn up their gas far more quickly – they might last only 100,000 years. The smallest stars remain cooler and they may survive for 50 billion years or more.

BORN AS TWOS

Two stars sometimes develop alongside each other, like twins. Even when fully formed, they spend their lives circling each other in the way that the Moon goes around Earth. These twins are called binary stars. More than half the stars in the night sky are binaries. If there are more than two stars in the group, they are called multiple stars. Astronomers compare the strength and brightness of such stars by watching them as they block or reinforce each other's light. They become brighter, then less bright, in regular patterns. Some single stars show a similar rise and fall. These are called variable stars.

◀ Our own star, the Sun, has reached the third stage of a star's life. It will continue to use up its gases for another five billion years.

THE MILKY WAY

O N a clear, dark night, a faint band of misty light is often visible stretching across part of the sky. Called the Milky Way, because of its whitish colour, this band of light is a galaxy of dust, gas and billions of stars floating in the vastness of space. Astronomers estimate that there are about 200 billion stars in the Milky Way. Our Sun is just one of the many stars. The Milky Way is also known just as 'the Galaxy'.

▲ *A nebula is a mass of gas and dust where very young stars are forming. This is the Orion Nebula.*

GALAXIES – LOOKING BACK IN TIME

There are millions of galaxies in the Universe, with immense, empty, expanding gaps between them. The Milky Way, with its 200 billion stars, is just one of many.
One of the nearest galaxies to the Milky Way is the Andromeda Galaxy, visible with the naked eye. It appears as a faint, whitish blur in the night sky. The Andromeda Galaxy is 2.2 million light-years away. When you look at it, in a way you are looking back in time, because the light you can see has been travelling across the Universe for more than two million years.

Like the Milky Way, the Andromeda Galaxy is a 'spiral' galaxy. It has a roughly ball-shaped centre, or nucleus, and curved, spider-like 'arms' that spiral outwards. In the nucleus, the oldest part of a galaxy, the stars are closer together.

▶ *Viewed from above, the Milky Way looks like a spinning Catherine-wheel firework. It measures about 100,000 light-years across, and the central bulge, or nucleus, is some 2,000 light-years thick. What we see as the Milky Way when we look at the sky are the stars in the arm where Earth is situated.*

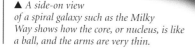

▲ *A side-on view of a spiral galaxy such as the Milky Way shows how the core, or nucleus, is like a ball, and the arms are very thin.*

▶ *The 'milky' look of the Milky Way comes from the large number of stars that appear close together. Away from this pale band in the night sky are darker areas lying beyond our Galaxy.*

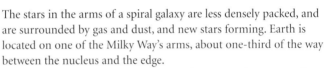

The stars in the arms of a spiral galaxy are less densely packed, and are surrounded by gas and dust, and new stars forming. Earth is located on one of the Milky Way's arms, about one-third of the way between the nucleus and the edge.

Older galaxies do not have 'arms'. Instead, they have a round or oval shape, like a ball or an egg. Called 'elliptical' galaxies, they have used up all of their spare gas and dust to create stars. Sometimes an elliptical galaxy forms when two galaxies collide. Other galaxies, known as 'irregular' galaxies, have no defined shape at all.

MAGELLANIC CLOUDS

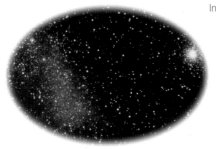

In the night sky of Earth's Southern Hemisphere, two blurry shapes can be seen with the naked eye. These are the Magellanic Clouds – small galaxies lying relatively near to our own Galaxy, the Milky Way. The Magellanic Clouds are irregular galaxies, having no distinct pattern or shape.

DEATH OF A STAR

AFTER A STAR is born from a cloud of gas, it burns fiercely for millions of years, then dies. Some stars gradually fade away, others go out with a huge bang. The way a star dies depends partly on the size of the star, and partly on what other objects there are nearby in space.

BURNING OUT

The glow of an active star comes from massive amounts of hydrogen being converted into helium, by the process of nuclear fusion (joining together). Eventually all the hydrogen burns away. The helium at the heart of the star collapses in on itself, while the outer layers expand and cool down, their colour changing from white to red. This type of enlarged, cooling star is called a red giant. The cooled, reddish layers then drift off into space, leaving behind the centre – a smaller, hotter star, known as a white dwarf. This also cools and eventually releases no light at all. It has become a black dwarf.

▲ *The Crab Nebula is actually the remains of a supernova, or exploded star. People on Earth noticed it blow up in AD1054. Since then, it has grown dimmer.*

A SPECTACULAR FINISH

Stars that start off very big – much bigger than our Sun – often end their lives dramatically. After becoming red giants, they keep on expanding until they have become red supergiants. Finally they explode, destroying themselves completely in the process. Such an explosion is called a supernova, and is billions of times brighter than our Sun. All that is left is a tiny pulsar, or neutron star.

▼ *The 'life cycle' of a star: gases and dust collect (1) and form a hot core, a new star (2). A 'main sequence' star (3), like our Sun, shines for 10 billion years. This cools to a red giant (4), which leaves a smaller, hotter white dwarf (5).*

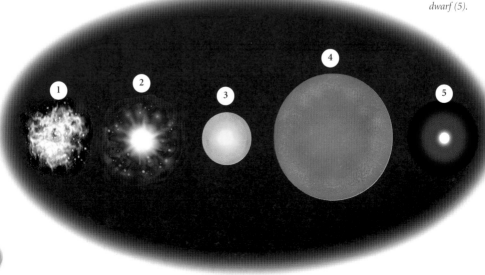

16

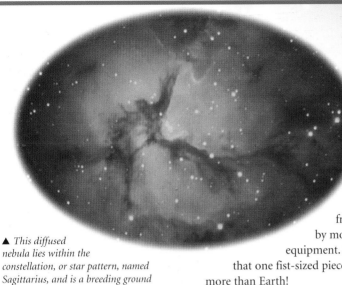

▲ This diffused nebula lies within the constellation, or star pattern, named Sagittarius, and is a breeding ground for new stars. Nebulae, or 'sky clouds', can give us valuable information about the birth and death of stars.

PULSARS

A pulsar is an incredibly dense, fast-spinning remnant of an almost-dead star. It gives off sharp pulses of radio waves as it spins, detectable from deep space by modern scientific equipment. Pulsars are so dense that one fist-sized piece of one would weigh more than Earth!

BLACK HOLES

Just as dramatic as exploding stars, although invisible, are black holes. These are created when a really massive dying star drags everything back towards itself, including light waves. Nothing can escape its gravitational pull. Various sizes of black holes have now been identified. Scientists believe that near some of them strange things occur with time. Understanding more about black holes might one day point the way to making time travel possible.

nearby star being drawn into black hole

▼ No light can escape from a black hole, but scientists can still tell where they are. The gravitational pull from a black hole sucks the gas from a star into a disc around the black hole. As the gas swirls, it heats up and emits X-rays, which can be detected from Earth.

CONSTELLATIONS

▶ *In the northern night sky, you can see all of the ancient constellations, including the 12 that are named after the signs of the zodiac. Polaris, the North Star, lies at the end of the* constellation Ursa Minor *(the Little Bear).*

E VEN without binoculars or a telescope, we can see thousands of stars in the night sky – especially when the Moon is new or old (not full). Look more closely and you will begin to see patterns among the stars. Some seem to form lines. Others make giant shapes, such as rectangles and triangles. Bright stars catch the eye and seem to lead from one shape to another. These patterns of stars are called constellations.

ASTRONOMERS IN ANCIENT TIMES

Thousands of years ago, astronomers in China and Greece saw the constellations and named each one after characters in their own myths and legends. Today we still know many of the constellations by these old names: *Leo* (the Lion), *Ursa Major* (the Great Bear), and so on. People in ancient times also used the constellations to help them find their way when they were travelling long distances, especially by sea. They noticed that all the stars seemed to move in circles around a single star, Polaris.

▶ Crux Australis *(the Southern Cross)* is the smallest constellation, and one of the most distinctive. *Proxima Centauri, just to its left, is the closest star to Earth – after the Sun.*

Polaris seemed to remain in one place directly above the North Pole, so it helped sailors to work out where south, west and east lay. The main feature of the southern night sky is the constellation *Crux Australis*, or Southern Cross. The flags of Australia and New Zealand show this famous constellation. Constellations always stay the same shape. The planets, however, move through the constellations to slightly new positions each night. Ancient astronomers noticed this, hence the word 'planet', which comes from a Greek word meaning 'wanderer'.

CONSTELLATIONS

Sometimes it takes a great deal of imagination to recognize in a constellation the shape that ancient people saw. Can you see the shape of an archer drawing a bow in this pattern of stars?

◀ *The three great pyramids of ancient Egypt, at Giza, are positioned in such a way as to mirror the pattern of the three bright stars in the constellation Orion.*

19

THE SUN

THE Sun is the nearest star to Earth. It is roughly 150 million kilometres away from us, and measures about 1,392,000 kilometres across. In terms of volume, about 1,300,000 Earths would fit inside the Sun. The Sun is some 333,000 times heavier than Earth. It spins around once every 25 days, 9 hours.

'MAIN SEQUENCE' STARS

All these huge numbers make the Sun seem remarkable, but in relation to the other stars it is quite a small-to-normal size. Its size places it in a large group of star types that astronomers call 'main sequence' stars. Most of these stars, including the Sun, will burn for about 10 billion years before expanding and cooling to become red giants, ultimately using up all their fuel. The Sun is about halfway through its lifetime.

Like all stars, the Sun is a ball of gas. Two gases – hydrogen and helium – make up nearly all of the Sun. The real 'action' takes place in the Sun's core, where a chemical process known as fusion turns the hydrogen into helium. This releases enormous amounts of energy, causing the Sun to shine and making the temperature of the core about 15 million °C. Energy is carried up through the radiative zone and the convective zone to the chromosphere. The visible surface, which can be seen through special solar telescopes, is the photosphere.

convective zone

radiative zone

core

▲ *The Sun's energy is released in its core. It flows out as radiations, passing through several layers before leaving the Sun as heat, light and other forms of electromagnetic radiation.*

chromosphere

photosphere

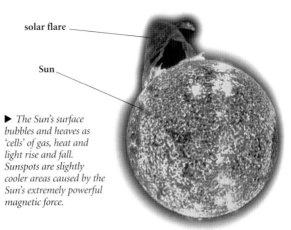

solar flare

Sun

▶ *The Sun's surface bubbles and heaves as 'cells' of gas, heat and light rise and fall. Sunspots are slightly cooler areas caused by the Sun's extremely powerful magnetic force.*

CENTRAL HEATING

The Sun's surface, or photosphere, has a relatively 'cool' temperature of about 6,000°C. This intense heat and other radiation spreads outwards into space at the speed of light. It takes about eight minutes to reach Earth. Astronomers have learned much about the activity of the Sun's core by studying the photosphere. There they have seen dark areas called sunspots, which seem to be caused by intense magnetic activity. Solar flares may burst from the surface near sunspots. Great leaps of flame, called prominences, loop out into space for thousands of kilometres and back again. All these events can emit radiation and particles that disrupt our electrical supplies, radio and TV.

COOLER SUNSPOTS

Astronomers viewing the Sun through special filters can detect dark spots called sunspots on the Sun's surface. The sunspots are caused by changes to the magnetic field surrounding the Sun. As the Sun spins round, the magnetic field becomes tangled. Sunspots develop in places where the magnetic force has become up to 3,000 times stronger than normal. The Sun's surface is cooler at these places, so the sunspots appear darker than the surrounding surface.

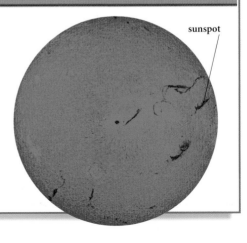

sunspot

OUR SOLAR SYSTEM

NINE large objects called planets orbit, or revolve around, our Sun. One of these is Earth, the third planet out from the Sun. Together the Sun and its nine planets are known as the Solar System (solar means 'to do with the Sun'). All nine planets move around the Sun in the same direction: anti-clockwise, as viewed from above. It takes Earth one year (365 days) to complete one full circuit of the Sun. The two planets nearer the Sun take less time – a year on Mercury lasts only 88 Earth days; 225 on Venus. The other six planets are farther from the Sun than Earth. Because of this increased distance, they are much colder than our planet, and a year lasts a very long time. On Pluto, for example, a year equals nearly 250 Earth years.

▲ *Detailed photographs of Venus show that its surface is covered by a thick layer of swirling clouds, which keep in the heat. The clouds and mist are carbon dioxide and sulphuric acid, which would kill a living thing instantly.*

THE INNER PLANETS

The four planets closest to the Sun (Mercury, Venus, Earth and Mars) are made up mainly of different types of rocks. Mercury, the second-smallest planet, is too small to have an atmosphere (surrounding gases). Its surface is dotted with large pits, or craters, made by the impact from lumps of rock, metal or other debris (meteorites), hitting the planet from space. Venus is only slightly smaller than Earth and has a thick atmosphere. The gases in this atmosphere trap sunlight, making Venus the hottest planet – temperatures reach 447°C on its surface. Mars – known as the red planet because of its red-brown soil – is about half the diameter of Earth,

▼ *The four inner planets look tiny when compared with the four gassy giants that lie beyond. Jupiter, the largest planet, is so big that it could contain all the other eight planets within it.*

Sun

Venus

Earth

Mars

Mercury

Jupiter

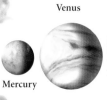

◄ *Mars is cold and forbidding, but some scientists believe that it was once much warmer than it is now, and maybe even supported some forms of life.*

▼ *All nine planets orbit (move around) the Sun. The outermost planet, Pluto, follows an unusual path that sometimes takes it closer to the Sun than the eighth planet, Neptune.*

and has a thin atmosphere. Strong winds blow on Mars, causing huge dust storms that make it hard for astronomers to see the rocky Martian surface for several weeks at a time.

GASSY GIANTS

Jupiter, Saturn, Uranus and Neptune are often called 'gas giants', after their size and mainly gaseous make-up. Jupiter is the largest of the nine planets. Like the other three giants, it has a thick atmosphere (mainly hydrogen and helium), although it probably has a small core of rock and ice. Saturn is known for its colourful rings, made up of tiny rocks orbiting the planet. Uranus and Neptune also have rings. Pluto is the smallest and most distant planet – a dark, deep-frozen world of rock and ice.

Pluto

Neptune

Uranus

Saturn

SATELLITES OF MARS

Deimos and Phobos are the two satellites (moons) that orbit Mars. They are named after the two companions of the Roman war god, Mars.

Deimos Phobos

THE MOON

MANY objects, in addition to the planets, travel around the Solar System. One of the most important to us is the Moon. Astronomers call the Moon a satellite because it goes around Earth. It is our nearest traveller, and our only natural satellite.

CONDITIONS ON THE MOON

▲ *Ganymede, the largest of Jupiter's moons, is the largest among the moons of other planets. It is bigger than the planets Mercury and Pluto.*

Unlike Earth, the Moon is not surrounded by gases – it has no atmosphere. This means there is no wind or rain, so the footprints of the first men to walk on the Moon in 1969 remain undisturbed. The Moon takes about 27 days to orbit Earth. As it travels, it spins on its own axis, so the same side of the Moon is always facing Earth. The Moon shines because it reflects light from the Sun. Depending on where the Moon is in its journey around Earth, different amounts of its surface are visible to us. These are the Moon's phases – New Moon, Crescent Moon, Half Moon and Full Moon. Sometimes the Moon passes directly across our view of the Sun, blocking it out briefly in a solar eclipse. Total solar eclipses are rare, and some astronomers will travel around the world to see one.

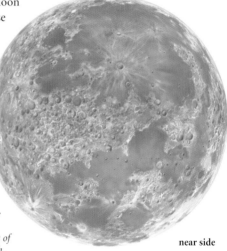

▶ *This is the view of the Moon that we see from Earth (at Full Moon). The clearer parts of its surface are huge, flat plains, called 'seas'. Early astronomers thought the seas were actually oceans of water, like those on Earth.*

near side

▲ *A solar eclipse happens when the Moon passes directly in front of the Sun, as seen from Earth. In this close-up, the Moon's dark edge is about to block out the last bit of the Sun's bright disc, to make the eclipse total. (Note: never look directly at the Sun.)*

OUR MOON: THE FACTS

Diameter: 3,476 kilometres

◆

Average distance from Earth:
384,400 kilometres

◆

Surface temperature:
100°C maximum; -170°C minimum

◆

Length of day:
29 days, 12 hours, 44 minutes

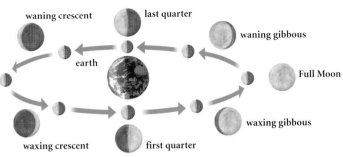

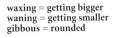

waxing = getting bigger
waning = getting smaller
gibbous = rounded

sunlight

New Moon

waxing crescent

waning crescent

last quarter

waning gibbous

earth

Full Moon

waxing gibbous

first quarter

▲ *The Moon's phases are shown here. Half the Moon always faces, and is lit up by, the Sun. But for much of the time only part of the lit side can be seen from Earth.*

Lunar eclipses, which occur when Earth's shadow passes across the face of the Moon, are much more common.

OTHER MOONS

Every planet in the Solar System, except Mercury and Venus, has at least one moon. Jupiter, Saturn and Uranus all have over a dozen main moons. At last count there were more than 70 moons, including Earth's, in the Solar System. As well as the nine planets and their moons, there are many other travellers in the Solar System. Thousands of rocks, called asteroids, orbit the Sun, mainly between Mars and Jupiter. Asteroids may once have been pieces from a planet that broke apart. Sometimes they are described as 'minor planets'. Most are only one kilometre or so across, but the largest, named Ceres, measures 1,025 kilometres across.

far side

▲ *No one knew what the far side of the Moon looked like until space probes travelled there in the 1960s. Its surface, like the near side, is covered with craters of all sizes. Without an atmosphere to burn them up, even the tiniest meteor is free to crash into the Moon's surface, making a crater.*

HOW OUR MOON FORMED

Some scientists think that four billion years ago Earth was hit by a body called a planetesimal. The impact from the blow blasted bits off Earth. These then orbited Earth, perhaps drawing together into a bigger body – the Moon.

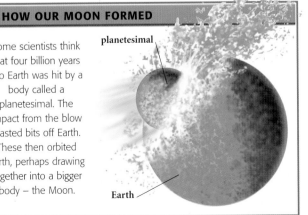

planetesimal

Earth

COMETS AND METEORS

THE night sky is sometimes lit up by the bright tails of comets and meteors hurtling through space. Much smaller than planets, moons or asteroids, comets have been described as 'dirty snowballs'. They are made from chunks of frozen gases mixed with dust. Scientists believe that comets and meteors are formed in a huge cloud thought to surround the whole Solar System. They orbit the Sun, but their paths are elliptical, or shaped like a flattened egg.

A COMET'S TAIL

A comet can take anything from 3 to 2,000 years to make a full orbit of the Sun. During that time, most comets behave in a similar way. As they approach the Sun, their gases begin to evaporate (like water turning into steam). The evaporating gases become very bright and form a long tail extending up to 100 million kilometres away from the Sun.
The brightest comets are visible with the

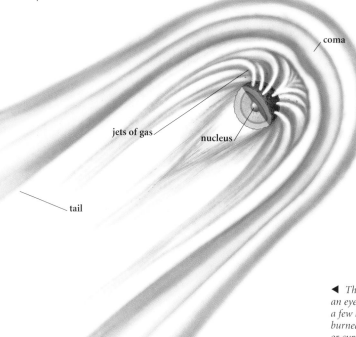

coma

jets of gas

nucleus

tail

▲ *A comet gains its long tail as it is heated by the Sun's warmth. The heat makes the comet's gases and dust evaporate. The tail always trails away from the Sun, not out behind the nucleus.*

◄ *The nucleus of a comet (resembling an eye in this diagram) is usually just a few kilometres across. Jets of gas burned off by the Sun form the coma, or curved front, and the tail.*

naked eye. Comet Hale-Bopp, for example, made a spectacular appearance in 1997.

SHOOTING STARS

What we sometimes call 'shooting stars' are really meteors, which are composed of small chunks of stone and iron. Most are very small, no more than about 30 metres across. Meteors are probably chunks of asteroids and comets that have broken away. Without a powerful telescope, we can only see a meteor once it has entered Earth's atmosphere, where it heats up, leaving a bright tail glowing in the sky for an instant before burning away. Not all meteors burn up fully in the atmosphere, however. They come crashing down and strike Earth's surface. A meteor that hits Earth is called a meteorite. The impact made by the meteorite can create a huge hole, or crater. Scientists believe that a huge meteorite, possibly as large as an asteroid, crashed to Earth 65 million years ago, sending up a huge dust cloud that killed off the dinosaurs.

▲ *Meteors often appear in groups, or swarms, which can be a serious danger to spacecraft or satellites.*

▲ *Most meteors are either stony, containing minerals such as olivine, or metallic, containing lots of metals, mainly iron.*

▶ *The Barringer Crater in Arizona, USA, is 1,200 metres wide. It was formed when a meteorite hit Earth about 25,000 years ago.*

MILESTONES IN ASTRONOMY

ASTRONOMY is the study of space and everything it contains. Every year we learn more about the Solar System, our galaxy the Milky Way, and the many other objects in the Universe. Astronomers, working on their own or in teams, use all sorts of equipment to build up this knowledge. Because of their work, many people now have a good understanding of how the Solar System works.

▲ *Nicolaus Copernicus (1473–1543) showed how Earth moves around the Sun, an idea that contradicted the previous view that the Sun orbited Earth.*

FEARS AND SUPERSTITIONS

Many people in ancient times studied the movements of the stars and knew when they would appear in different places in the sky, but they had little idea of how

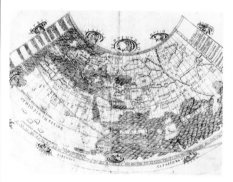

▲ *The famous Mappa Mundi ('Map of the World') was drawn in the 1200s, in England. It shows the world as a round plate, with Jerusalem at its centre.*

or why things moved. Most people believed that everything in the sky – including the Sun – circled Earth. They came to fear events such as a solar eclipse – which occurs when the Moon passes directly in front of the Sun – believing it was a sign that Earth was about to end. Some people prayed each night for the Sun to rise the next morning.

In time, a number of great thinkers began to consider the heavens carefully. More than 2,300 years ago, a Greek astronomer named Aristarchus came to the conclusion that Earth moved around the Sun. Another famous Greek thinker, Aristotle, disagreed, and for 1,800 years

TIMELINE	300 BC		AD 1600

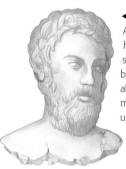

◀ The Greek thinker Aristotle (384–322 BC) helped to develop science in many ways, but his mistaken views about the heavens misled people's understanding of astronomy for a long time.

◀ The Italian mathematician and astronomer Galileo Galilei (1564–1642) used a telescope to discover the moons of other planets, and argued that Earth was not the centre of the Universe. These views were not popular with the Church, and Galileo spent his last years under arrest.

people continued to believe Aristotle's view that Earth was the centre of the Universe. In the 1500s, a Polish astronomer named Nicolaus Copernicus declared that Aristarchus had been right. About 100 years later, around 1608–09, the Italian astronomer Galileo Galilei used one of the first telescopes to help prove this.

FOLLOWING THE RULES

Using telescopes and other equipment, scientists began to get a clearer picture of our Universe. People could see how the planets move around the Sun and how moons move around the planets. Just as important was the work of scientists such as Sir Isaac Newton, who explained not only how things moved in the sky, but also why. Newton's work, in the 1600s, as well as that of later great scientists such as Albert Einstein (1879–1955), made it possible for people to do more than just study the heavens. In the past 40 years space probes and astronauts have begun to explore space and find direct evidence of what makes the Universe tick.

▼ *Today, we have a much better idea of what makes up our Universe, and how it is changing. Astronomers have a wide range of tools at their disposal, such as the Hubble Space Telescope, which took this deep-field view of space. They work closely with chemists, physicists and other scientists, sharing knowledge and ideas.*

AD 1700	AD 2000

▶ Scientist Sir Isaac Newton (1643–1727) outlined the principles of gravity – the force that makes things on Earth fall to the ground, and that keeps the planets attracted to the Sun. He also explained how the planets and the Moon move through space.

▶ Stephen Hawking (born 1942) is a British physicist who helped to explain black holes – collapsing stars that pull everything, including light, into themselves.

STUDYING THE SKY

THE human eye was the only 'tool' that ancient people had to observe the skies. Today, the most familiar tool for an astronomer – or anyone who is interested in the stars – is a telescope. The first telescope was invented in 1608.

TELESCOPES

A refracting telescope consists of a long tube with two or more lenses (curved pieces of glass) lined up carefully along the tube. Light passes into the tube through the lenses, making what you see appear much larger.

A simple, inexpensive telescope can reveal a great deal that cannot be seen with the unaided eye – such as hundreds of craters on the Moon's surface, made by meteors that have crashed into it over the years. A telescope will also enable you to see at least four of Jupiter's moons and Saturn's rings. All telescopes, however, even the most powerful ones on Earth, have to contend with Earth's surrounding atmosphere, which blurs images

TYPES OF TELESCOPE

reflecting telescope

refracting telescope

There are two main types of optical telescope – refracting and reflecting. A refracting telescope uses a series of lenses (pieces of curved glass) to magnify what the viewer can see. The outer lens collects and focuses light, while a smaller lens at the other end acts as an eyepiece, through which the viewer looks. A reflecting telescope collects light on a curved mirror at the base. The light is focused onto a smaller, angled mirror that directs it to the eyepiece.

▼ A radio telescope detects radio signals given off by objects in space. The large, dish aerials collect the waves and bounce them into a receiver, which converts them into electrical signals. These can give a more accurate picture of, for example, a galaxy than the image received by an optical (light-receiving) telescope.

▶ Voyager 2, *launched in 1977, was sent to study four of the outer planets – Jupiter, Saturn, Uranus and Neptune. Its cameras beamed images back to Earth as radio signals.*

of space, even on clear nights. Outside, or beyond, Earth's atmosphere, a telescope's vision is unimpeded, and much clearer images can be obtained. For this reason, the Hubble Space Telescope, an artificial satellite, is positioned out in space. It circles Earth and sends clear pictures back, in the form of coded radio signals, to astronomers on the ground.

'LISTENING' TO THE STARS

A radio telescope 'listens' to the sky. It picks up radio signals, just as a TV satellite dish picks up radio signals from a TV satellite far above Earth. Everything in the Universe gives off various types of waves; radio telescopes pick up radio waves from some of the most distant parts of the Universe. Other specialized telescopes and sensors, both on the ground and in space, pick up microwaves, X-rays and gamma rays from deep space.

▲ *The images received from* Voyager 2 *helped astronomers learn a great deal more about the largest planets in the Solar System. This photograph of Jupiter shows the bands of brownish and yellowish clouds that make up its atmosphere. At the bottom left is the Great Red Spot, a huge storm of whirling clouds.*

A CLEARER VIEW

The largest optical telescopes are mostly housed in dome-shaped observatories. They are generally sited on high hilltops above the layers of atmospheric dust and gas, and away from the blazing artificial lights of cities.

RACE TO THE MOON

HUMANS have always been curious about the stars and space. But it was only in the 1900s that scientists developed equipment advanced enough – and powerful enough – to go beyond Earth's atmosphere and into space. Scientists in two countries, the United States and Russia, spent much of the 1950s building space rockets. These two countries were great rivals in the field of space exploration, and their competition for supremacy became known as the 'Space Race'.

▲ Sputnik, *which means 'traveller' in Russian, was the first artificial satellite to be launched into space.*

EARLY SUCCESSES

Russia (or the Soviet Union as it was then known) had the first success. On October 4, 1957, it launched the first artificial satellite into space. A year later the United States launched one too, and over the next few years many satellites were sent into space. They were used to predict the weather, to study the atmosphere and to help with communications back on Earth.

Both countries then tackled the challenge of sending humans into space. Once again, Russia succeeded first, sending Yuri Gagarin around Earth safely in April 1961. Just one month later, the United States followed suit with Alan Shepard's mission.

▶ *The US* Titan *and the Soviet* Vostok *rockets sent manned capsules into orbit around Earth. The similar-sized* Ariane, *launched by the European Space Agency, sends satellites and other equipment into orbit. The bulkier* Energiya *launched the Soviet* Buran *space shuttle into orbit. The much larger* Saturn V *sent US spacecraft to the Moon. A rocket, or launch vehicle, needs enough fuel and power to reach escape velocity (40,000 km/h), in order to break free of Earth's gravitational pull.*

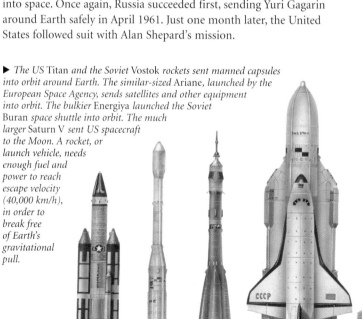

Titan 3   Ariane   Vostok   Energiya launcher / Buran shuttle   Saturn V

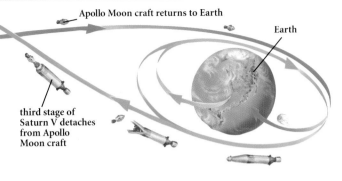

Apollo Moon craft returns to Earth

Earth

Moon

third stage of
Saturn V detaches
from Apollo
Moon craft

▶ *The* Saturn V *rocket that took US astronauts Neil Armstrong, 'Buzz' Aldrin and Michael Collins into space circled Earth first before speeding off towards the Moon. This loop gave the spacecraft the extra speed it needed to 'catapult' it towards the Moon.*

▲ *Yuri Gagarin became a national hero when he returned to Earth after completing the first space flight, in 1961.*

SENDING HUMANS TO THE MOON

Having successfully sent men into space, Russia and the United States began to explore the possibility of sending men to the Moon. During the 1960s, both countries sent spacecraft on longer missions into space. They needed to test equipment carefully to prepare for the 770,000-kilometre journey to the Moon and back. They also needed to see if astronauts (the American term for space travellers) and cosmonauts (the Russian term) could survive such a voyage. Russia's cosmonauts undertook many important space missions, but it was the United States that won the race to set foot on the Moon. On July 20, 1969, Americans Neil Armstrong and 'Buzz' Aldrin became the first humans to walk on the Moon. Their craft was *Apollo 11*. Armstrong's first words when he stepped onto the Moon's surface were: "That's one small step for (a) man, one giant leap for mankind".

▲ *Astronauts from six* Apollo *missions to the Moon took photographs, collected rocks and set up equipment that sent information back to Earth.*

ONE SMALL STEP

The first 'Moon walk' (shown here) was made in 1969. Because there is no air or wind on the Moon, the US flag was held at the top by a rod to make it look as if it were flying.

LIVING IN SPACE

A FTER the triumphant Moon landing in 1969, the United States sent five more missions to the Moon over the next three years. Scientists joined the astronauts on several of these trips, finding out more about the Moon and its history. The missions led people to hope that it might be possible one day to build long-term stations in space, on the Moon, or perhaps even on another planet. But first scientists had to find out if people could survive life in space.

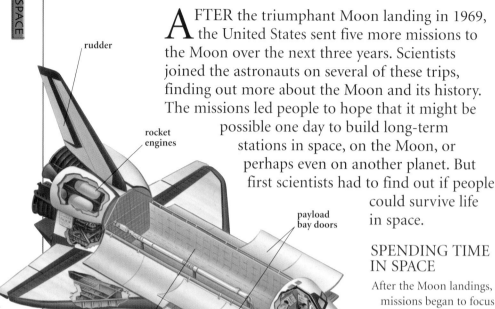

rudder

rocket engines

payload bay doors

payload bay

▲ *The US space shuttles can take humans and cargo into orbit around Earth, and then return home again. Although launched by rockets, shuttles land like planes. The first shuttle orbiter,* Columbia, *blasted off in April 1981.*

flightdeck

SPENDING TIME IN SPACE

After the Moon landings, missions began to focus on living and working for long periods in space. During the 1970s, American *Skylab* and Russian *Salyut* space stations orbited Earth for months on end. People spent long periods of time on board, being replaced at intervals. The crews had regular medical checks as doctors back on Earth monitored their health and fitness. A new science of space medicine was born to study problems such as space sickness, feelings of isolation, and the wasting of the body's muscles due to the cramped conditions, lack of gravity and limited exercise.

SHUTTLING INTO SPACE

Important space missions undertaken towards the end of the last century included those by US space shuttles. The space shuttle orbiter is a re-useable craft, like a huge spaceplane, able to land on a runway and then blast off again on another mission. Astronauts from many countries have worked together on these missions. They launch, repair and retrieve satellites, take images of the ground below and deep space above, carry out experiments, study animals along for the ride, and even test-grow food.

▲ *Astronauts have left footprints on the Moon. One day they may yet explore planets other than Earth on foot.*

REPAIRS IN SPACE

The Hubble Space Telescope was launched from a US space shuttle into Earth orbit in 1990. But scientists soon noticed that one of its mirrors needed a repair. In 1993, astronauts from the *Endeavour* space shuttle made a daring space walk to carry out the work. These pictures show on-site repairs being done.

SPACE STATIONS

The Russian space station *Mir* was launched in 1986. Some inhabitants spent more than a year on board. The station had its share of troubles, including power failures and crashes with ferry craft bringing supplies. *Mir* was finally abandoned in 1999. It re-entered Earth's atmosphere and burned up in 2001. Since 1999, craft and crews from several nations have been working together to build a huge new 'hotel' in space – the International Space Station (ISS). The main structure should be complete by the year 2006, after more than 40 missions.

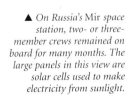

▲ *On Russia's* Mir *space station, two- or three-member crews remained on board for many months. The large panels in this view are solar cells used to make electricity from sunlight.*

◄ *If humans were ever to set up a permanent settlement on another planet, Mars would be the likely choice. Special insulation would be needed to protect humans against the low temperatures. The journey from Earth to Mars would take at least six months – one way.*

IS ANYBODY OUT THERE?

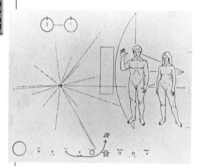

▲ *The US* Pioneer *spacecraft, which was sent deep into space in 1972, carries diagrams of humans and of our Solar System, in the hope that intelligent beings may find them.*

PEOPLE have been asking the question 'is anybody out there?' since earliest times. Some ancient peoples believed that there was a Man in the Moon, perhaps because when the Moon is full, its craters resemble a face. In about 1900, it was popularly believed that Martians (life-forms on Mars) had built huge, water-carrying irrigation canals across their planet. Nowadays, however, it seems clear that there is no other intelligent life in our Solar System. But there may be some form of primitive life (such as tiny cells) somewhere among the planets – or perhaps on one of the moons. It is impossible to tell how many planets like Earth there may be in the Universe – we simply don't know.

▶ *The Hubble Space Telescope (HST) is smaller than some Earth-based telescopes. But it can detect clearer images of fainter objects from deeper in space because it is above Earth's atmosphere. It orbits at an average height of about 600 km.*

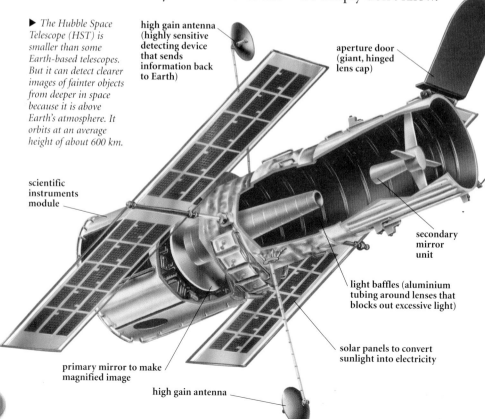

high gain antenna (highly sensitive detecting device that sends information back to Earth)

aperture door (giant, hinged lens cap)

scientific instruments module

secondary mirror unit

light baffles (aluminium tubing around lenses that blocks out excessive light)

primary mirror to make magnified image

solar panels to convert sunlight into electricity

high gain antenna

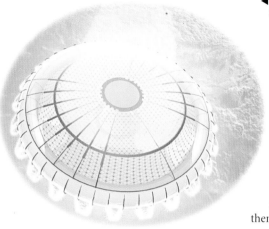

◀ *People who think they have seen Unidentified Flying Objects (UFOs) believe they are proof that creatures from other star systems have visited Earth. UFOs are often reported as being discs, or 'flying saucers'.*

GOING FARTHER...

On March 2, 1972, the United States launched an unmanned spacecraft, called *Pioneer 10*, on a path to Jupiter. The craft successfully sent back to Earth information about the huge planet. It then went on to become the first craft to cross the orbit of Pluto and leave our Solar System, in June 1983.

The *Pioneer* probes were followed by two US *Voyager* probes, launched in 1977. These visited the outer giant planets and are now speeding through interstellar space. Like *Pioneer, Voyager* carries messages for any beings that may find them in the distant future.

LISTENING FOR LIFE

The world's largest radio telescope, which has a dish measuring 305 metres across, is called the Arecibo telescope. It lies in a natural hollow on the Caribbean island of Puerto Rico. The telescope is a vital tool for finding out about the history and appearance of the Universe, but it also has another important job. In 1992, NASA, the organization in charge of US Space Programs, set up the Search for Extra-Terrestrial Intelligence (SETI) project. This aims to examine radio signals coming from 1,000 nearby stars that resemble the Sun. The huge radio telescope 'listens' for signs of life elsewhere in the Universe. So far, there has been no sign of intelligent life, but the telescope continues to search.

THE ARECIBO TELESCOPE

Unlike smaller radio telescopes, the Arecibo telescope (above), in Puerto Rico, cannot be moved around and aimed at a certain point in space. Instead, it uses Earth's rotation to listen to a broad band of sky. The huge dish has nearly 40,000 reflecting panels attached to a network of steel cables. Radio waves from outer space are reflected off these panels onto a detecting platform suspended above the dish. The information collected then passes through a powerful computer before being studied by astronomers.

QUIZ

1. How many continents are there?
2. Long-distance aircraft usually fly through which layer of the atmosphere?
3. What is the 'Ring of Fire'?
4. Which type of rock often has horizontal stripes running through it?
5. Where on Earth would you be able to find the 'Midnight Sun'?
6. A typhoon is another name for which type of weather condition?
7. Which type of landscape has the widest range of plant life?
8. Which continent takes up about one-third of all the land area on Earth?
9. How was the Grand Canyon formed?
10. Why do we need the ozone layer in our atmosphere?
11. How far down would you need to dig through the ice at the North Pole until you reached the ground?
12. What do scientists call a small earthquake that can sometimes only be detected with special equipment?
13. Where is Earth's crust thinnest?
14. How much of the Earth's surface is covered by the oceans?
15. India was once linked to which continent before it joined Asia?
16. What was Pangaea?
17. Which two gases make up most of the air we breathe?
18. Which fault runs through California?
19. Which continent does not have a major mountain range?
20. What is the name given to molten rock beneath Earth's crust?

ANSWERS

1. Seven
2. The stratosphere, because the lower layer (the troposphere) has rougher weather.
3. A string of volcanoes and faults around the edge of the Pacific Ocean.
4. Sedimentary rock, which is made up of layers of once-living things.
5. Near either of the two poles during summertime, when the pole would be tilted towards the Sun.
6. A hurricane
7. A tropical rainforest
8. Asia
9. The rushing waters of the Colorado River ate their way downwards through many layers of rock.
10. Because it filters out harmful radiation from the Sun.
11. You would never reach ground. The ice at the North Pole is the frozen top of the Arctic Ocean.
12. A tremor
13. Beneath the floor of the oceans
14. 71 percent
15. Australia
16. The 'supercontinent' that existed about 300 million years ago.
17. Nitrogen and oxygen
18. The San Andreas Fault
19. Australia
20. Magma

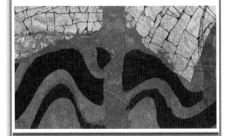

SECTION
2

PLANET EARTH

LONG AGO, people had very different ideas about our world, compared to the understanding we have today. They thought that Earth was flat, and that if you went too near the edge you would fall into a vast, dark void. They believed that Earth was quite young – perhaps just a few thousand years old. They also thought that Earth was solid and unchanging, and would remain as it is for ever.

Now we know that Earth is a globe with no edges, and that it was formed thousands of millions of years ago. We also know that through its long history, it has continually changed. Huge forces have built new mountains, altered the global climate and changed the shapes of the oceans. Earth is restless, and will probably continue to be so for a very long time.

OUR HOME PLANET

OUR Earth is one of nine planets that move around the Sun, which is about 150 million kilometres away from us. Like the other planets, Earth is shaped rather like a huge ball, though it bulges slightly around its middle, which is known as the Equator. The distance around Earth measured at the Equator is 40,075 kilometres, while the distance around Earth measured at the Poles is slightly less, at 40,008 kilometres. Earth has a hard, rocky outer 'shell', called the crust. Beneath the crust Earth is made up of layers. At the centre is an inner core, made from iron and nickel.

SPINNING THROUGH SPACE

As Earth moves through space, it travels around the Sun at an average speed of 30 kilometres a second. Earth takes 365 days (one year) to go once around the Sun. Its path takes it closest to the Sun on January 3 each year (the orbital perihelion) and farthest away on July 4 (the aphelion). As Earth travels around, or orbits, the Sun, it spins on its own centre line, or axis. It takes almost 24 hours – a full day – to make a complete spin. Daytime is on the side of Earth facing the Sun, and night on the other side.

The Equator is the part of Earth closest to the Sun, so it is the warmest part. The areas around the North Pole and the South Pole are never as close to the Sun, so they

▼ Earth is constantly changing. Tall, jagged mountains are worn down into rounded hills by natural forces such as wind and rain.

EARTH'S TILT

northern summer

axis

Sun

southern summer

For the six months of the year that the North Pole tilts towards the Sun, there is a northern summer. For the six months that it tilts away from the Sun, there is a northern winter. When it is summer in the north, it is winter in the south.

remain cold throughout the year. Other parts of Earth become warmer or cooler depending on the time of year. The seasons (spring, summer, autumn and winter) change because Earth is not positioned perfectly upright as it journeys around the Sun. Its centre line, or axis, tilts at an angle of 23.5 degrees.

The overall length of a day is 23 hours, 56 minutes and 4 seconds, and this remains the same throughout the year. At the Equator, which is always close to the Sun, night-time and daytime are always about 12 hours long. But in the regions near the two poles, the length of night and day change dramatically depending on the time of year. For a few weeks in summer, the Sun never sets at the pole – people call this the 'Midnight Sun'. And every winter, there are weeks of almost total darkness, or constant night.

▲ *Viewed from space, Earth – which is mainly covered by oceans – appears mainly blue. Cloud formations swirl above the familiar shapes of the continents.*

▼ *Vast rainforests grow in the hot, humid conditions along the Equator. Rivers such as the Amazon in South America and the Congo in Africa help drain these forests.*

▲ *Oceans cover more than two-thirds of Earth's surface. They shape the coastal landscape, creating rocky cliffs with their constant pounding.*

THE BIRTH OF EARTH

Earth probably formed some 4,500 million years ago (about 10,500 million years after the Universe was formed in the massive explosion of energy called the 'Big Bang'). It was formed as matter clumped together and became hotter and hotter. The matter melted into a ball of molten (liquid) rock. After millions more years, the outer layer of rock began to cool and harden. Deep inside Earth, it is still incredibly hot, and some parts are still molten.

EARTH'S STRUCTURE

Earth consists of layers of rock, rather like the layers of an onion. We live on the outer layer, called the crust, which is the thinnest layer. The crust is thickest (about 50 kilometres) under the continents or landmasses. It is less thick (only 8 kilometres) under the oceans. The distance from Earth's crust to the centre of the core is just over 6,370 kilometres.

INNER LAYERS

Beneath the crust lie several layers of rock, each one hotter the nearer it is to the centre. The layer immediately beneath the crust is the mantle. It is about 2,900 kilometres thick. Some rock in the outer mantle is semi-molten (partially melted), and it can seep up through cracks in the crust and erupt as a volcano. The inner mantle is solid rock.

The innermost part of Earth is the core. Like the mantle, it has an outer layer and an inner layer. The outer core is 2,250 kilometres thick, and is made of molten iron and nickel. The inner core, which is about 1,220 kilometres in radius, is mainly iron. It is solid because of the intense pressure bearing down on it.

THE ATMOSPHERE

Layers of gases surround Earth in a 'blanket', called the atmosphere. This protects us from the heat of the Sun. The atmosphere extends outwards from Earth's surface until it fades away into space. It is held

EARTH'S MAGNETISM

A magnetic field around our planet is generated by the flow of iron-rich material in Earth's core. Migrating birds are able to use the magnetic north and south poles in this field to guide them on long journeys.

▼ *Extra-strong bursts of energy from the Sun causes particles in the sky to become charged with electricity near Earth's magnetic poles. The bright particles put on a colourful display known as the aurora – or the Northern and Southern Lights.*

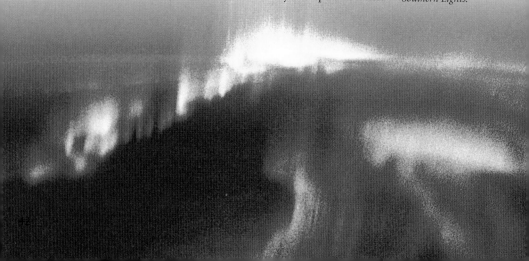

in place by a force called gravity. Gravity gives things weight and pulls them towards Earth.

The air that we breathe is compressed into the lowest layer of the atmosphere, called the troposphere. It is made up of a mixture of gases – mainly nitrogen and oxygen. The troposphere is where the majority of clouds form and where most weather takes place. It contains almost three-quarters of all the gas in the atmosphere. The next layer out from Earth is the stratosphere, which extends to about 50 kilometres above Earth's surface. Most long-distance aircraft fly in this layer, above the rough weather of the troposphere. Near the top of the stratosphere is the ozone layer, which absorbs harmful radiation from the Sun.

▲ *Dust and other particles in the sky scatter sunlight and make it appear reddish-gold at sunset.*

There are three more layers above the stratosphere. The air in each layer becomes progressively thinner, because the force of gravity is weaker farther away from Earth. The most distant layer from Earth's surface is the exosphere, which starts about 480 kilometres above Earth. The thin air at this height gradually blends into empty space.

exosphere

thermosphere

mesosphere

stratosphere

troposphere

▲ *Air becomes thinner the farther away it is from Earth. Generally, the temperature also falls with height, but it rises to several thousand degrees in parts of the exosphere.*

crust

outer mantle

inner mantle

outer core

inner core

◀ *Earth was an enormously hot ball of rock when it was formed more than 4 billion years ago. Some of this heat remains, while more heat is generated by the pressure the rocks are under. As the hot material in the mantle slowly moves, the 'plates' that make up Earth's crust also slowly move, carrying the landmasses with them.*

CONTINENTS

LESS than one-third of Earth's surface is covered by areas of land – landmasses. The rest is covered by water, mainly from the world's great oceans. Most of the land forms seven main masses, called continents. These seven continents are Europe, North America, South America, Africa, Asia, Australia and Antarctica (around the South Pole). The Arctic region, around the North Pole, has no solid land. It is a great raft of ice made from frozen sea water. The continents rest on top of the outer layer of Earth – the crust. The crust under the continents is thicker and stronger than the crust under the oceans.

▲ *Great forests once covered most of Europe, which has a temperate climate – warm summers, cool or cold winters and regular rainfall.*

North America

South America

Antarctica

▲ *Huge grasslands cover the central areas of most continents. Low rainfall in these areas means that only tough grasses can survive. North America's grasslands are the Great Plains and prairies.*

◀ *The Amazon Basin in South America supports the largest rainforest in the world. Because it is near the Equator, it has constant high temperatures and steady rainfall, allowing a huge variety of plants to thrive.*

▶ *Antarctica is the southernmost – and coldest – of all the continents. More than 95 percent of Antarctica is covered in ice that, in places, is over 4,500 m thick.*

▲ *The northernmost fringes of Europe, Asia and North America are covered in tundra, a mossy marshland that only thaws for about eight weeks each year.*

FLOATING PLATES

Earth's crust is cracked and made up of several giant pieces called plates (their full name is 'lithospheric' plates). The plates move on Earth's surface, floating on the partly melted rock (magma) in the outer part of the mantle. As the magma moves, the plates move with it, and the continents – which form part of the plates – move too.

Asia is the largest continent. It has an area of 44 million square kilometres and makes up nearly one-third of all the world's landmass. The smallest continent is Australia, with an area of about 7.7 million square kilometres.

Parts of Africa, South America and Asia straddle the Equator. These continents have the warmest weather. The coldest place on Earth is Antarctica. Different climates attract and support different types of animals and plant life.

Europe   Asia

ica

Australia

▲ *In Asia, rice is grown in flooded fields called paddies. The rich soil and mild climate in eastern Asia are ideal for growing this crop.*

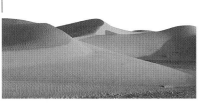

▲ *Shifting sands form huge dunes in Africa's Sahara Desert. The highest-ever temperature on Earth, 58°C, was recorded in the Sahara.*

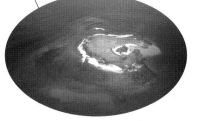

▲ *Ring-shaped reefs known as atolls are dotted across the Pacific Ocean. Atolls are the remains of volcanic islands that have sunk into the ocean.*

CONTINENTAL DRIFT

On a map of the world, the Eastern edge of South America and the western edge of Africa seem as if they could fit together, like two pieces of a giant jigsaw puzzle. This is because they were once joined together. Many millions of years ago, all the continents were part of a single, huge landmass. Over time, this 'supercontinent' broke up and the separate continents drifted apart.

▲ 1) About 300 million years ago, all of the world's continents were joined together in a single landmass called Pangaea.

▲ 2) About 200 million years ago Pangaea began to split in two, forming Laurasia in the north and Gondwanaland in the south.

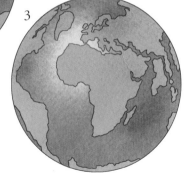

▲ 3) These two great landmasses divided, and 65 million years ago the seven continents had begun drifting to the positions they are in today.

HOW DID THE CONTINENTS SEPARATE?

The many curved plates that make up Earth's crust are moving very slowly all the time, carrying with them the continents that sit on top of them. Molten rock from beneath the crust seeps up through cracks between the plates. This forces the plates apart. The movement of the continents is called continental drift. It amounts to no more than several centimetres per year, but over millions of years this means that the continents have moved great distances. Some, like South America and Africa, have drifted far apart. Others have been pushed closer together. North and South America, for example, were separated for many millions of years. They joined up again about 3 million years ago, which is recent in terms of Earth's history – Earth is about 4,600 million years old.

◀ Magma (melted rock) forces its way through cracks in the thin ocean crust. It hardens along these cracks, forming ridges on the ocean floor.

THE BIG BREAK-UP

Most scientists now believe that about 300 million years ago all of the continents were joined together as one great continent.

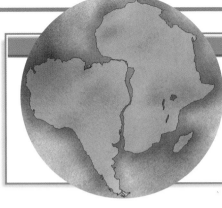

CONTINENTAL DIVISION

The continents of South America and Africa lie on different plates, which have drifted apart. Between them now is the Atlantic Ocean. Along the sea bed in the middle of the Atlantic Ocean, magma oozes up through a crack. It sets solid in the cold ocean, forming a chain of undersea hills called the Mid Atlantic Ridge.

This landmass was called Pangaea, and it was surrounded by a huge ocean called Panthalassa. Pangaea lasted for about 100 million years. Then the movements of the plates split it into two landmasses: Laurasia in the north and Gondwanaland in the south. The Tethys Sea separated these two masses. Over time, Laurasia and Gondwanaland broke up into the seven continents that we know today.

TESTING THE EVIDENCE

A German scientist named Alfred Wegener first proposed the idea of continental drift in about 1912. At first many scientists did not support his ideas. But some took Wegener's ideas more seriously and began to look for evidence. They tried to match up the shape of one continent with the shape of another – like pieces of a jigsaw. Scientists have found rocks in Antarctica that match those in Australia and South America. There are similar matches between eastern North America and western Europe. The process that pushes continents around the globe was gradually worked out in detail, and is called plate tectonics.

▲ *Fossils provide evidence of how the world once looked. They show that similar living things developed at the same time in continents that are now separate. This suggests that the continents were once joined.*

ANIMAL CLUES

Evidence of continental drift can be found in the living world, too. Fossils show that long ago there were marsupials (animals with pouches) on continents other than Australia. They faded out as their place was taken by mammals without pouches. But pouchless mammals never reached Australia, because the continent had moved away and become an island, which it remains today.

◀ *The opossums of North and South America are among the few marsupials – mammals with pouches – outside Australia. Other mammals took the place of marsupials in most places except Australia, which a long time earlier had drifted away from the other continents.*

47

VOLCANOES AND EARTHQUAKES

THE giant curved plates that make up Earth's crust are constantly rubbing and pressing against each other very slowly. Normally we do not notice this movement. But sometimes the powerful forces that cause plate motion can produce great destruction. Two of the world's most dramatic and frightening natural events, volcanic eruptions and earthquakes, are linked to these forces. Somewhere on Earth, there is an eruption or an earthquake happening at this very moment.

FORCES OF DESTRUCTION

The place where two neighbouring plates or sections of plate meet is called a fault. Sometimes hot, liquid rock known as magma seeps up from Earth's mantle through a fault. If the steady flow of magma is blocked by the rock of Earth's crust, pressure can build up as the magma tries to find a way through. If the pressure becomes too great, the magma can

▲ *The San Andreas Fault, which runs through California, USA, is unstable and the site of many earthquakes. It is clearly visible from the air.*

▼ *Rock that has been heated to melting point below Earth's surface comes gushing out in a volcanic eruption. Called lava, it flows like a river down the slope of the volcano, causing great damage before it cools and hardens into solid rock.*

burst through in a volcanic eruption. Magma, ash, gases and rocks blast into the air with tremendous force. Magma that erupts from a volcano is called lava. As the lava flows out and cools, it hardens into rock, forming a mountain around the opening in Earth's crust.

Plates can get 'stuck' as they try to move past each other. This causes pressure to build up along the fault line, until suddenly the crust breaks and the pressure is abruptly released as an earthquake. Small earthquakes create tremors. Some are so small that scientists need special instruments to detect them. Other earthquakes are more severe, causing enormous damage for a great distance around the area of the fault.

▶ *Most active volcanoes are found around the edges of the Pacific Ocean, an area called the 'Ring of Fire'.*

🏛 active volcano

'RING OF FIRE'

Most volcanoes and earthquake zones are found along the join, or fault line, between Earth's plates. The world's most active zone is called the 'Ring of Fire'. It is created by the Pacific plate (which lies beneath most of the Pacific Ocean) constantly rubbing against the continental plates of Asia to the west and North and South America to the east. Many areas around the Pacific experience earthquakes, particularly Japan and the Far East (in Asia) to the west, and Alaska and California (in North America) to the east. One of the most famous faults on the Pacific rim is the San Andreas Fault, which runs close to the city of San Francisco in California, USA. The Ring of Fire has dozens of active volcanoes dotted along its path. Japan's tallest mountain, Mount Fuji, is a volcano, as is Mount St Helens in the American state of Washington. Mount St Helens blew itself apart in a massive volcanic eruption in 1980.

▲ *The force of a powerful earthquake is enough to rip apart Earth's surface, creating a huge chasm.*

▼ *A powerful earthquake in 1989 destroyed many buildings around San Francisco, which lies near the San Andreas Fault in California, USA.*

49

MOUNTAINS AND VALLEYS

T HERE are long 'ranges', or lines, of mountains on nearly all Earth's continents. Extremely high mountains are covered in snow all year round, even if they are in tropical regions, because at greater heights the air is very cold, however warm the ground may be. A mountain's melting snow forms streams, which run into rivers. The land between two mountains is called a valley or, if very steep-sided, a gorge.

▼ *The Himalayas were created by the process called 'folding', after a collision between two of Earth's plates. Millions of years ago, India was a huge island that crashed into the southern edge of the Asian plate. The rock between them was thrust upwards as the northern edge of India was forced under the Asian plate.*

AFFECTING WEATHER

Air moving over the ocean becomes filled with invisible water vapour, which forms clouds. As clouds from the ocean meet high mountains, the moist air rises. Once the clouds reach a certain height, their droplets enlarge and fall as rain. So the side of a mountain range facing the ocean receives a great deal of rain, while the other side is often dry.

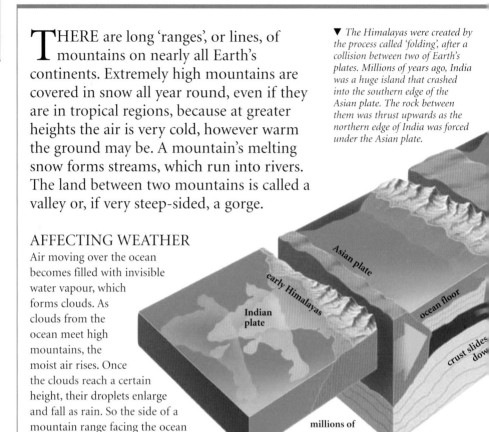

HOW DO MOUNTAINS FORM?

Most mountains are created by the same forces that cause earthquakes and volcanic eruptions. The process begins when magma (molten rock inside Earth) oozes through a crack between the ocean plates (the parts of Earth's crust found under the sea). The force of the magma pushes the ocean plates away from each other and towards the edge of continental plates (the plates found under land). Ocean plates are thinner than those under the continents. So when a thinner ocean

▼ *Fold mountains form when two of Earth's plates collide. Under the immense pressure, a region of rock crumples or 'folds' into mounds (1). This folded rock is thrust upwards (2), sometimes for thousands of metres. It can even fold back on itself (3).*

1

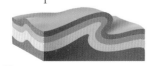

2

3

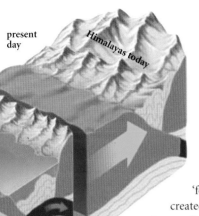

present day
Himalayas today

▶ The Andes of South America began to form 60 million years ago, when one of the Pacific plates pushed into the edge of South America.

plate meets a thicker continental plate, some of the ocean plate is forced under the continental plate and pushed down into the mantle. Other parts of the plates become 'folded' into high mountains. Mountains that are created in this way are jagged when they are first formed. But over millions of years, wind and water wear them down, making them lower and more rounded. The Andes mountains in South America are a recent, pointed range, whereas the Appalachians, in North America are older and less jagged.

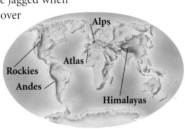

▲ The major mountain ranges in the world are shown here. Every continent except Australia has at least one huge range. Australia's have been worn down over time.

DEEP VALLEYS

Sometimes two continental plates, or parts of them, are forced apart. When this happens, huge blocks of crust may simply tumble into the gap, creating a steep-sided valley. One of the world's largest valleys, the Great Rift Valley in Africa, was created in this way about 50 million years ago. Other valleys are formed by running water, which over time wears away rock. Valleys may also be created by massive, slow-moving blocks of ice, called glaciers.

▲ Britain's highest mountain, Ben Nevis (1,343 m), was once much higher. It has been worn down by ice, wind and rain.

◀ Africa's Great Rift Valley was formed when the plate beneath Africa was bent or bowed upwards. This caused Earth's crust to split, and large chunks of land sank into the gap.

51

EARTH'S ROCKS

STUDYING the rocks that make up Earth's crust helps us to find out about our planet's history and about the forces that shaped it, and continue to shape it today. Rocks are also valuable resources – we use them to make many things, from buildings to jewels. Geologists – scientists who study rocks – divide Earth's rocks into different kinds, depending on the shape of their crystals. A crystal is the shape formed by minerals, which are the building blocks of rocks. The shape of a crystal indicates which minerals make up the rock. Individual minerals sometimes occur on their own, in pure form. But in most rocks different minerals are combined. Geologists group rocks into three main types: igneous, sedimentary and metamorphic. Each is formed in a different way.

▲ *The Giant's Causeway in Ireland formed when a lava flow cooled and hardened into unusual shapes.*

IGNEOUS ROCK

Most of Earth's surface, and nearly all of the ocean floor, is made up of rock that was once molten (melted). This is known as igneous rock –

vent

chimney

magma chamber

▼ *Igneous rocks are created by volcanic eruptions. Magma (hot melted rock) collects and builds up pressure in a chamber below the volcano. It eventually blows through the vent at the top in an eruption, and flows down the slopes as lava, which hardens into igneous rock.*

the word 'igneous' means 'coming from flames'. It forms when hot molten rock (magma) erupts from a volcano as lava, which then cools. The minerals in the cooling lava crystallize and bind together to form igneous rock.

SEDIMENTARY ROCK

The action of wind, rain and water continually wears away tiny fragments of rocks. These fragments are often carried by rivers to the ocean floor or to the bed of a lake, where they settle as sediments. Plant and animal matter may also settle in layers in this way.

▲ *The white cliffs of Dover, England, are made from the remains of tiny marine animals such as shellfish. These remains settled on the sea bed long ago, and gradually became compressed into a form of soft limestone, called chalk.*

Over many years, the weight of each new layer of sediment presses down on the layers beneath, making them harder, until they turn into rock. Many sedimentary rocks have 'stripes', called strata, which are the visible layers of the sediments.

CARBON

cut and polished diamond

coal

Many useful rocks and minerals are made mostly of carbon, a natural element found in all living things. Coal, for example, is formed when plant remains are compressed and exposed to heat for millions of years. Some types of carbon are subjected to much greater pressure and heat. They become far harder and eventually form diamonds.

METAMORPHIC ROCK

'Metamorphosis' is the word for a dramatic change, and that is exactly what creates this type of rock. Metamorphic rocks are igneous or sedimentary rocks, whose composition has been changed by great heat and/or pressure. Marble, a well-known metamorphic rock, for example, is simply limestone (a sedimentary rock) that has been exposed to very high temperatures.

USEFUL ROCKS

We value certain minerals very highly, because they are either useful or beautiful. Pure minerals, known as gemstones, are used for jewellery. Rubies and emeralds are typical gemstones. Other minerals, called ores, contain metals such as copper, tin, iron and lead, which are removed from their ore and used to make all kinds of useful and decorative objects. Miners dig deep into Earth's crust to remove both gemstones and metal-containing ores.

RIVERS OF ICE

Earth has changed temperature many times during its long history. Sometimes it has warmed up, and at other times it has cooled down. When the temperature drops over a long period, much of the water on Earth freezes. These long, cold periods are called ice ages, and they can last for thousands, or even millions, of years.

ICE CAPS

During an ice age, the ice caps – huge areas of ice – that cover the North and South Poles become larger and spread out towards the Equator. The most recent ice age reached a peak about 20,000 years ago, when much of Europe and North America was covered by vast sheets of ice. Gradually, Earth's temperature rose again and much of the ice melted. A new landscape emerged, carved out by the solid slabs of moving ice. Cape Cod, near Boston in the eastern United States, for

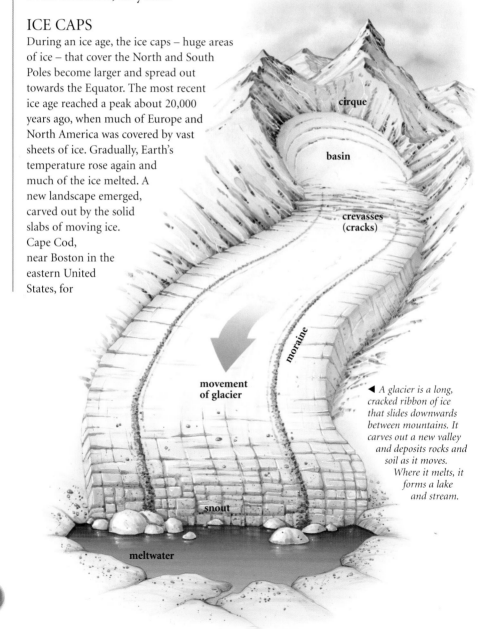

cirque

basin

crevasses (cracks)

moraine

movement of glacier

snout

meltwater

◄ A glacier is a long, cracked ribbon of ice that slides downwards between mountains. It carves out a new valley and deposits rocks and soil as it moves. Where it melts, it forms a lake and stream.

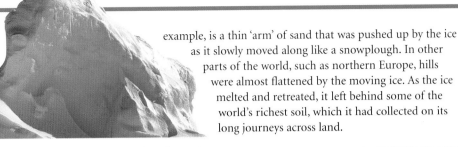

example, is a thin 'arm' of sand that was pushed up by the ice as it slowly moved along like a snowplough. In other parts of the world, such as northern Europe, hills were almost flattened by the moving ice. As the ice melted and retreated, it left behind some of the world's richest soil, which it had collected on its long journeys across land.

▲ *Icebergs are huge chunks of free-floating ice that have broken off glaciers and ice caps. Up to 90 percent of an iceberg lies under water.*

MODERN REMINDERS

Some scientists say that we are still near the end of the recent ice age, because the great ice sheets have not entirely disappeared. The polar ice caps still cover large areas of the globe, and huge icebergs – chunks broken away from the cap – float in the oceans nearby. On land, the main proof of a recent ice age is provided by glaciers. These are large 'rivers' of ice, which form high up in mountains, where it is cold throughout the year. Glaciers slide very slowly down between mountains, carving out distinctive U-shaped valleys. Many of the steep, narrow valleys in the Alps were created by moving glaciers, and are still being shaped today. When glaciers reach lower levels, where it is warmer, they melt, forming lakes and rivers.

GLOBAL WARMING

'Global warming' is a slight increase in Earth's overall temperature, perhaps by just a degree or two. Warming and cooling has occurred naturally many times in the past. But rapid global warming may be due to human activities, such as burning coal and oil, and releasing harmful chemicals into the air. These destroy the ozone layer in the atmosphere that protects us from the Sun's radiation.

PUSHING AHEAD

The huge glaciers (top) that moved through Europe during the most recent ice age loosened tonnes of sand, clay and rocks. The glaciers pushed this material ahead of them. When the glaciers melted, they left behind piles of rubble called moraine and distinctive rocks such as the Sarcen stones in England (above).

◄ *This view of the North Pole shows the island of Greenland in white. Nearly all Greenland lies beneath an ice cap up to 3,000 m thick.*

55

RIVERS AND LAKES

MANY living things, including people, are made mainly from water. All forms of life on Earth rely on water to survive. Fresh water is found in ponds, streams, rivers and lakes. Unlike sea (or salt) water, it contains few dissolved salts and minerals. Fresh water is far less common than salt water, which covers more than two-thirds of Earth's surface. Only about two percent of all the fresh water in the world is on the surface. The rest lies underground.

THE LIFE OF A RIVER

Small streams collect water from three main sources: rain water, the water that melts from glaciers or snowfields, and water that bubbles up from underground springs. The streams join together to form a river. A river empties into a larger body of water, either an ocean or a lake.

How big the river becomes, and how fast it flows, depends on the steepness of the land and the type of rock and soil it passes over. A mountain river tumbles quickly downhill, gradually carving out narrow, V-shaped valleys. As it reaches more level ground, it widens and slows down, creating broader valleys. Because it is now travelling more slowly, it can deposit soil and rocks that it has picked up along the way.

SALTY LAKES

Very few lakes contain salty water. But Great Salt Lake, in northwestern Utah, USA, is eight times saltier than the oceans. The rivers that empty water into this lake have been rich in dissolved mineral salts since earliest times. As the water evaporates from the lake, it leaves the salts behind, making the remaining water even saltier.

meltwaters   tributary

lake

▶ *At the end of its journey a river flows into the sea or sometimes into a large lake. It deposits silt, or soil, as it slows down.*

◀ *Lake Baikal in Russia is the deepest freshwater lake in the world, at 1,640 m.*

Lake Superior

Lake Huron

Lake Michigan

Lake Ontario

Lake Erie

▲ *The five Great Lakes of North America together make up the largest body of fresh water in the world.*

▼ *Most rivers begin when rain and snow falls on uplands. The water flows downhill and is joined by tributaries (other streams and rivers), before flowing through broad valleys.*

meander

oxbow lake

sand bar

estuary (river mouth)

sea

Valleys often have fertile soil, because of the rich deposits left by the river. On flatter ground, a river may meander – twist and turn – as it makes its way around obstacles in its path.

CREATING LAKES

Lakes hold the largest amounts of fresh water on Earth. The bed of a lake is created by a 'dent' in Earth's surface that allows water to collect (just as it does in a puddle). All kinds of events can create a suitable 'dent'. The deepest lake in the world is Lake Baikal in Siberia. It was formed when a movement of Earth's crust created a huge, deep gully. Other lakes form in the craters of volcanoes that are no longer active, or where a glacier has carved a hollow in the landscape. Unlike mountains and oceans, lakes usually have short lives. The rivers that feed them carry sediment – small particles of soil – which in time fill up and clog the lake. As the lake fills with sediment, it turns into a marsh, which eventually dries out to become grassland. Rivers also carry sediment to the oceans.

▲ *Waterfalls, such as the Iguazu Falls in South America, form when a river flows over hard rocks onto softer rocks beneath. The softer rocks are worn away more quickly, and this creates a steep drop for the water to fall down.*

Photographs taken from space show how the Amazon River in South America turns the Atlantic Ocean brown and green over a huge area near its mouth, as freshwater and sediment from the river pour into the ocean. The Amazon contains more water than any other river.

OCEANS AND ISLANDS

THE oceans, with their salty water, cover 71 percent of Earth's surface. The Pacific is bigger than all the other oceans put together. It has an area of 166 million square kilometres. Smallest and shallowest is the frozen Arctic Ocean at 13 million square kilometres in area. It has an average depth of 1,040 metres.

▲ *An atoll is a circular or C-shaped island. It is all that remains of a volcano after it has broken the surface and, over time, slowly sunk back below the waves.*

OCEAN WATERS

The oceans are very deep. On average, the ocean floor is more than 3,500 metres below the surface of the water. The huge amount of water on the globe plays a vital part in creating Earth's weather. Water takes much longer than land to cool down or heat up, so the oceans help to prevent Earth's temperature from getting too hot in the summer or too cold in the winter.

Ocean currents are movements of warm or cold sea water through water of another temperature. The Gulf Stream in the North Atlantic Ocean, for example, is a warm current – it carries warm water northeast across the Atlantic to Europe. Ocean water also moves with the tides. As Earth spins, a mass of water is thrown to the side of Earth away from the Moon, but it is pulled back by the Moon's gravity (and to a lesser extent the Sun's gravity). This creates high and low tides twice a day.

▼ *Many changes to Earth's surface take place on the ocean floor. Magma (melted rock) seeps up through mid-ocean cracks and forces the ocean plates to move away from each other. As they collide with the thicker continental plates on each side of the ocean, the oceanic plates are forced downwards into the mantle.*

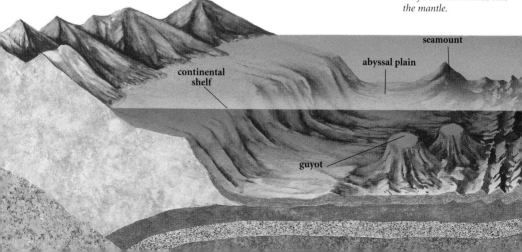

continental shelf

abyssal plain

seamount

guyot

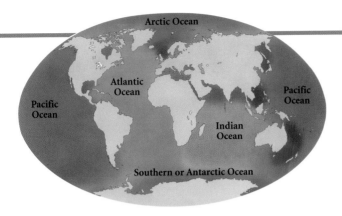

◀ The Pacific is the largest ocean. It is more than twice the size of the next largest, the Atlantic. Much of the surface of the Arctic Ocean remains permanently frozen. The deepest ocean water is the Marianas Trench in the northwest Pacific, near Japan, at 10,925 m.

▼ These arrows show the path of the South Equatorial Current across the Pacific Ocean. Surface currents are made by the prevailing (constantly blowing) wind blowing water ahead of it. Deep ocean currents are different from those on the surface.

ISLANDS

Many islands are dotted across the oceans. Most are created by the forces at work below Earth's crust. Hot magma (melted rock) from Earth's mantle oozes through cracks in the ocean floor and hardens. Sometimes it builds up slowly until it rises above the ocean's surface, creating chains and arcs of islands. Some islands form more quickly. When one of Earth's plates slides across a place where there is a powerful flow of magma, the molten rock erupts, creating a tall volcano. As the plate continues to slide, another volcano bursts upwards, and then another, creating a chain of volcanic islands. The Hawaiian islands far out in the Pacific Ocean were created in this way.

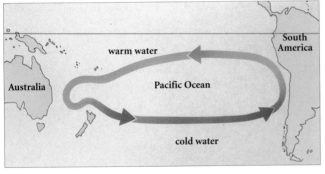

mid-ocean ridges

deep-sea trench

continental slope

WEATHER AND CLIMATE

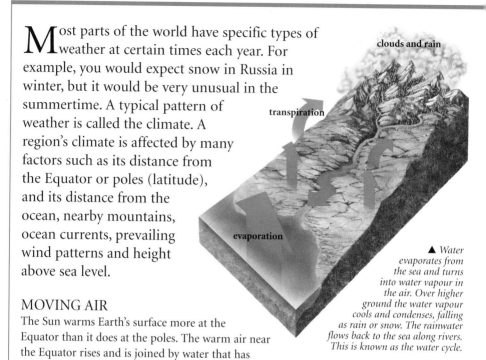

Most parts of the world have specific types of weather at certain times each year. For example, you would expect snow in Russia in winter, but it would be very unusual in the summertime. A typical pattern of weather is called the climate. A region's climate is affected by many factors such as its distance from the Equator or poles (latitude), and its distance from the ocean, nearby mountains, ocean currents, prevailing wind patterns and height above sea level.

▲ *Water evaporates from the sea and turns into water vapour in the air. Over higher ground the water vapour cools and condenses, falling as rain or snow. The rainwater flows back to the sea along rivers. This is known as the water cycle.*

clouds and rain

transpiration

evaporation

MOVING AIR

The Sun warms Earth's surface more at the Equator than it does at the poles. The warm air near the Equator rises and is joined by water that has evaporated from the oceans. Tiny droplets of water form and gather together as clouds. As the warm air rises, cooler air from other parts of the planet move in to take its place. The arrival of cold air causes the rising moist clouds to release their water. Near the Equator this falls as rain all year round.

Because Earth spins, the air moves in spirals, making its movements harder to predict. Winds are always blowing towards the Equator – these are called trade winds. Those that blow away from the tropics are called Westerlies. When a warm, damp air mass that formed over the ocean meets a cool, drier air mass that formed over land, the damp mass usually loses its moisture as rain. This collision between air masses is called a front. A front often brings wet weather that can last for days.

cold front

warm front

◀ *Funnel-shaped tornadoes are the world's most powerful storms. They cause severe damage along their path.*

DESERTS

The driest places on Earth are deserts. They form for several reasons. Most large deserts such as the Sahara in Africa lie on a band just outside the tropical zone on either side of the Equator. Air that has been warmed over the Equator and then lost its moisture descends here. Some deserts, including the Atacama in South America, lie alongside the ocean where cold currents flow. Air passing over the cold water picks up very little water vapour.

▲ *Cirrus clouds are evidence of the jet stream, a fast-moving 'river' of cold air high in the atmosphere.*

STORMY WEATHER

Storms occur when air masses with very different temperatures collide. The most severe storms are hurricanes (or typhoons) and tornadoes. Hurricanes are huge tropical storms covering areas up to about 650 kilometres across. Their winds reach speeds of more than 200 kilometres per hour. Tornadoes are much smaller but more extreme, with spiralling winds that travel at speeds of up to 350 kilometres per hour.

Many storms produce bright flashes of lightning. This happens when warm and cold air masses meet. The water droplets in the clouds are tossed up and down, causing them to become electrically charged. The electricity builds up until it releases a giant spark through the air – a bolt of lightning.

MAJOR CLIMATE REGIONS

Earth has several major climate regions. Tropical areas around the Equator generally have a hot, rainy climate throughout the year. The lands around the poles are cold for most of the year, with a brief warm summer. The large band of land between the tropical and polar regions has a temperate climate, with warm summers and cold winters.

Within these main bands, a climate can be affected by specific local conditions. Places that are high up, for example, are always cooler. 'Monsoon' regions, which include much of India and West Africa, have mostly dry weather for nine months of the year, followed by three months of very heavy rain.

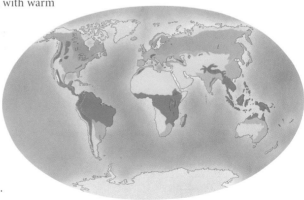

▶ *The world can be divided into a number of major climate zones.*

mountainous
polar
cool temperate

tropical
temperate
desert

WEARING IT DOWN

▲ *The steep sides of some narrow sea inlets, called fjords, have been worn away by glaciers, waves, rain and wind.*

Many forces have shaped the landscape around us. Some are dramatic, such as the movement of Earth's plates under the oceans. When these collide with continental plates, they can throw up vast mountain ranges, while plates that move apart can create giant valleys. But major features of the landscape do not remain the same once they have been created. Over time they are worn down by various processes, and the landscape changes. Most of Earth's natural features are made of rock. In order for them to change, something must happen to the rock to break it down and take it away. Two terms used to describe this are erosion and weathering.

EROSION AND WEATHERING

Many different forces can weather, or break down, rock. The word 'weather' is used because wind, rain and changes of temperature are involved. Wind, for example, can fling bits of sand onto standing rock and gradually wear it into a new shape – rather like sandpaper being rubbed over a surface. If water picks up stones and sediment and carries them along, these may slowly wear down the rock over which the water flows. The effects of this type of weathering are seen in some mountain valleys. A dramatic example is the Grand Canyon in the United States. The flowing water of the Colorado

▼ *A typical mixed landscape shows the levelling process. The peaks are weathered by natural forces, with softer rocks being eroded more quickly than harder ones. The particles or sediments are transported by wind and water, and collect in the valleys.*

River has worn its way through many layers of rock to produce a magnificent, steep-sided valley.

Water may also contain chemicals that dissolve rocks. Underground streams can eat through limestone, for example, creating huge caves. Ice is another powerful weathering agent. When water freezes it expands, so water in cracks between rocks can break them apart when it freezes. The roots of plants growing into cracks can also slowly push huge rocks apart.

TAKING IT AWAY

Erosion includes both weathering and the removal of bits of rock that have been eroded. The natural forces involved in weathering, such as wind and water, also carry away the debris. Wind and running water, as well as frozen water in the form of glaciers, can pick up bits of rock and carry them far from where they started. The same water that weathered the Grand Canyon also took away the pieces of rock that it eroded.

The effects of erosion are usually more dramatic in landscapes where there are few plants to protect the surface and hold the soil together. In deserts, sand is often blown along for great distances and piled into dunes. In many areas, people have removed plants and trees from the land, for firewood or timber. Much of the unprotected soil is then simply blown or washed away. If it clogs up rivers, major floods can result.

▼ *Uluru (Ayers Rock) in central Australia is a giant block of eroded sandstone. It rises 348 m above the plain.*

CAUSES OF EROSION

Sand-carrying wind can carve away or sand-blast weaker parts of rock to leave tall towers, or stacks.

Hot days and cold nights cause rock to expand and shrink. Outer layers can weaken and flake off.

The constant flow of the ocean's waves can eat away at rock and create caves and arches.

Plant roots can make their way into thin cracks in the rock, widening them and causing the rock to split.

Water seeps into cracks, then freezes and expands, forcing the rock apart. This is called frost-wedging.

Plant roots hold soil in place. After forests have been cut down, the loose soil is often washed or blown away.

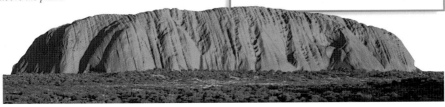

SUPPORTING LIFE

All forms of life on Earth survive in a narrow layer that includes the surface of our planet, the seas and oceans and the lower part of the atmosphere. Scientists call this layer the biosphere. The biosphere ranges from a height of about 10,000 metres above sea level, to the depths of the ocean, and also a few hundred metres below the surface of the soil. Any region outside this layer is either too hot, too cold, under too much pressure or lacking in the right gases to support life. Although the biosphere is only a very thin 'skin' of planet Earth, it contains an incredible variety of animals, plants, microbes and other life-forms. Even harsh conditions in deserts, Arctic ice and the deepest sea provide homes for life.

▶ Joshua trees have tough, twisted branches and thorny leaves – adaptations for the deserts of North America.

▲ With their thick layers of fat and white fur, polar bears are well adapted to Arctic life.

◀ The endangered giant panda lives only in a small region of western China. It eats bamboo, which grows at high altitudes.

▲ The thorny devil's spines and prickles are defences against attackers in the Australian desert. This lizard eats mainly ants and termites.

▲ The Amazon rainforest of South America has the richest variety of life in the world.

- tropical
- monsoon forest
- desert
- polar
- semidesert
- grasslands
- broad-leaved forest
- coniferous forest
- evergreen
- temperate rain forest

A PROCESS OF GIVE AND TAKE

All life on Earth makes up a complex web of plants and animals that rely on each other for survival. Plants, for example, take energy from the Sun and carbon dioxide from the air, and in return give off oxygen. Both animals and plants need oxygen to break down food for energy. Plants provide food for many animals. In return, animals help plants to exist by spreading their pollen and seeds. Animal dung, which contains some of these seeds, also has minerals that help more plants to grow.

LIFE IN THE AIR

Scientists estimate that there are some 8,700 species of birds, many of which spend much of their time in the air. The swift eats and even sleeps in the air, and is barely able to walk. Some birds hunt other birds, 'stooping', or diving, to catch their prey from a great height. Others extract grubs from the ground.

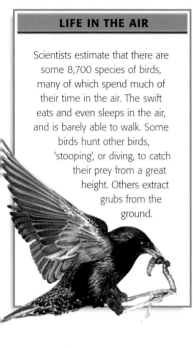

WHAT IS A BIOME?

Webs of interdependent life forms also exist within large regions that have a particular climate and landscape. These regions are known as biomes. A biome is usually described by the main types of plants that grow there, such as grassland, scrubland or forest. Some of the main biomes include tropical rainforests (which have a wider range of plant life than anywhere else on Earth), deserts, grasslands such as the African savannah, temperate forest, and tundra – the harsh, treeless, boggy Arctic landscape.

ECOLOGY

Within a biome, smaller webs of life are created by specific combinations of weather conditions, soil type, plants and animals. These areas are known as local ecosystems. Examples include a large area of woodland, a small pond or a cave. Some animals, especially larger creatures, move between ecosystems. The scientific study of the way living things interact with each other, and how they survive in their surroundings, is called ecology.

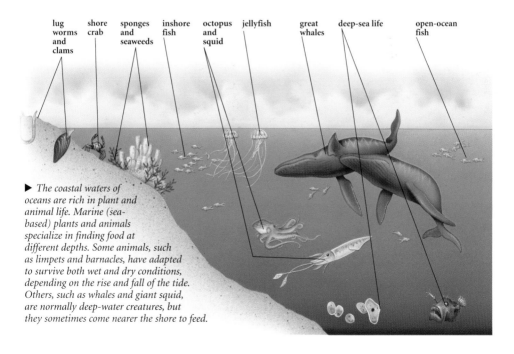

lug worms and clams · shore crab · sponges and seaweeds · inshore fish · octopus and squid · jellyfish · great whales · deep-sea life · open-ocean fish

▶ *The coastal waters of oceans are rich in plant and animal life. Marine (sea-based) plants and animals specialize in finding food at different depths. Some animals, such as limpets and barnacles, have adapted to survive both wet and dry conditions, depending on the rise and fall of the tide. Others, such as whales and giant squid, are normally deep-water creatures, but they sometimes come nearer the shore to feed.*

THREATS TO EARTH

PLANET Earth has been developing for nearly five billion years. Over that time, natural forces have shaped Earth and provided a range of homes for all types of life.

Humans have only been around for a short time in Earth's history, and in the last few hundred years have caused some of the most serious problems facing Earth. The human population has been rising throughout its history. Today's figure of more than six billion

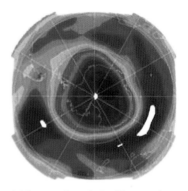

▲ *The ozone layer in Earth's atmosphere protects us from the Sun's harmful radiation. Human activities have caused a hole to appear in the ozone layer, shown here.*

people is likely to double every 40 years. All these people need somewhere to live, and more and more forests are being cut down so the land can be built on. Many varieties of wildlife lose their homes as a result. The rising population also puts a strain on food and energy supplies. Fuels such as oil and coal are running out. The land has been damaged by the effects of mining, and the seas by oil spills from wrecked tankers. Waste from nuclear power stations contains dangerous radiation and takes hundreds of years to disappear.

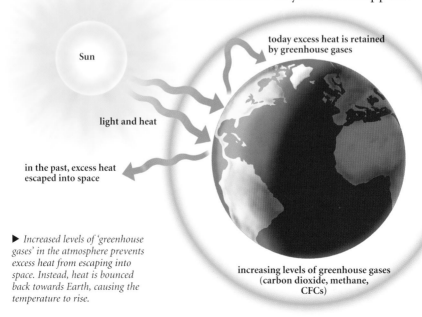

Sun

light and heat

in the past, excess heat escaped into space

today excess heat is retained by greenhouse gases

increasing levels of greenhouse gases (carbon dioxide, methane, CFCs)

▶ *Increased levels of 'greenhouse gases' in the atmosphere prevents excess heat from escaping into space. Instead, heat is bounced back towards Earth, causing the temperature to rise.*

EFFECTS ON THE ATMOSPHERE

Some of the most serious problems facing Earth are caused by humans burning fossil fuels such as oil, coal, natural gas and wood. When fossil fuels are burned, they release a gas called carbon dioxide into the atmosphere. The carbon dioxide collects in the atmosphere and traps some of the Sun's heat energy. Scientists call this the 'greenhouse effect'. The trapped heat causes Earth's temperature to rise by small amounts each year – a process called 'global warming'. Warmer temperatures will eventually melt some of the polar ice, causing ocean levels to rise. Many islands and coastal areas may be destroyed as a result.

▶ *Chemicals and other polluting materials dumped into the sea destroy the natural wildlife of coastal areas.*

Many of our industrial processes and manufactured products release other gases into the atmosphere. Some of these gases eat into Earth's protective layer of ozone, a gas in the atmosphere that filters out some of the Sun's dangerous UV (ultra-violet) radiation. Plants as well as animals are affected by this radiation. In humans it can cause serious skin diseases such as cancer.

POLLUTION

Waste products from fuel and materials that we use every day contain chemicals that seep into water supplies or into the air around us. Some of these chemicals – from factory chimneys and vehicle exhausts – mix with chemicals in rainwater to become acids. 'Acid rain' destroys whole forests. To save our Earth for future generations, it is essential that people act today to prevent such threats to the environment.

▲ *Dangerous radiation leaked into Earth's atmosphere when the Chernobyl nuclear reactor in Ukraine exploded in 1986.*

LOSING THE BALANCE

Trees, shrubs and other plants play an important role in protecting the natural balance of the landscape. Apart from providing food, shelter and shade for animals, they act as 'anchors', holding the soil firm with their deep roots. Widespread cutting of forests, known as deforestation, can be disastrous. It allows soil to wash away, creating deserts.

QUIZ

1. What is a modem?
2. What type of tiny particle inside an atom has a negative electric charge?
3. Which four things did the ancient Greeks believe were the four basic elements?
4. What is the name of the force that keeps an aircraft from falling?
5. A seesaw is an example of which type of simple tool?
6. Electricity produced from wind, sunshine and tides is called what type of energy?
7. What does a CD player use to 'read' the information on the surface of a disc?
8. In which part of a car's engine do pistons move up and down?
9. What colour do we see when all the colours of the spectrum are mixed together?
10. What do the initials WWW stand for at the beginning of an Internet address?
11. Air resistance, which acts to slow the movement of an aircraft, is an example of which type of force?
12. How does a MagLev train travel without any wheels?
13. How many of the elements are found in nature?
14. What type of transport did the Montgolfier brothers pioneer in 1783?
15. What were the earliest type of boats?
16. What term is used to describe a unit of force (it takes its name from a great English scientist)?
17. How many kilometres does light travel in a second: 3,000 km, 30,000 km or 300,000 km?
18. What do the letters DVD stand for?
19. What term describes how 'high' or 'low' a sound seems to us?
20. What type of energy is released when someone or something moves?

ANSWERS

1. It is a device to link a computer with a telephone line in order to send and receive information.
2. An electron
3. Earth, Wind, Fire and Water
4. Lift
5. A lever
6. Renewable energy (because we will never run out of the source of energy).
7. A laser
8. The cylinders
9. White
10. World Wide Web
11. Friction
12. It uses the force of magnetic levitation to keep the train from touching the track.
13. 92 (the rest need to be found using special equipment in labs).
14. Air transport (in a hot-air balloon)
15. Ancient Egyptian reed boats
16. A newton (from Sir Isaac Newton).
17. 300,000 kilometres
18. Digital Versatile Disc
19. Pitch
20. Kinetic energy

SECTION 3

SCIENCE AND TECHNOLOGY

THERE are many ways of describing science. One is the search for knowledge – about what things are made of, what they do and how they work. Science aims to uncover the processes and principles that underlie events in the Universe. Scientists develop ideas or theories, carry out experiments to test them, study the results, and gradually come closer to explanations of the truth. This applies not only to machines and inventions, but to animals, plants, rocks, oceans, Earth and space. Technology is different. It is the use of tools, machines, energy and power for all kinds of purposes. These include travel and transport, growing food, putting up buildings, healing diseases, and making equipment such as cameras and computers. Science and technology have never been so important, or advanced so fast, as they are today.

WHAT ARE ATOMS?

A car, a horse, an oak tree, a computer and a plastic ruler all have one thing in common – 'matter'. This is the material that makes up everything in the Universe, even the distant stars. The difference between each thing, or object, is the way in which its matter is arranged. The ancient Greeks believed everything was made from a combination of four substances, or elements – Earth, Wind, Fire and Water.

▲ *Scientists use electron microscopes to magnify objects up to one million times their actual size.*

MODERN ELEMENTS

Scientists today know that the ancient Greek theory which said that everything was made up of four substances, or elements, was not entirely correct. But they do agree that elements exist, and that they are the simplest chemical building blocks. Things that cannot be separated further are called elements. For example, water (a substance) can be separated into two elements, hydrogen and oxygen, but these cannot be separated further. There are 92 natural elements and at least another 25 that are artificial (made by humans).

▶ *An electron microscope uses particles called electrons, rather than light rays, to magnify objects. The electrons are shot down from an electron gun onto the specimen, and examined through a flash detector.*

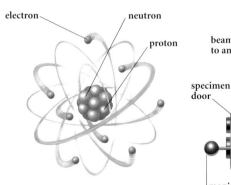

electron

neutron

proton

▲ *An atom is made up of tiny particles called protons and neutrons. These are found in the nucleus (centre) of the atom. Electrons move at great speed around the nucleus.*

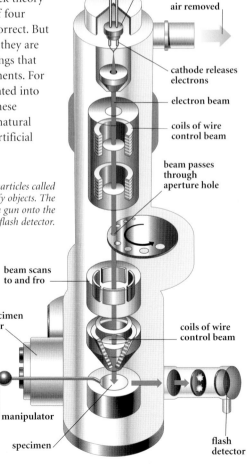

electricity supply

electron gun

air removed

cathode releases electrons

electron beam

coils of wire control beam

beam passes through aperture hole

beam scans to and fro

specimen door

coils of wire control beam

manipulator

specimen

flash detector

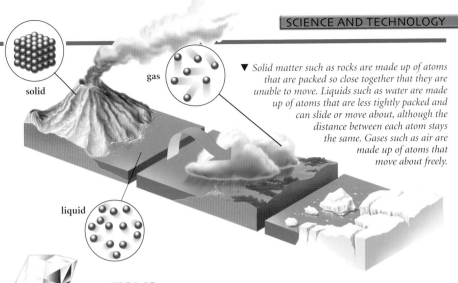

solid

gas

▼ Solid matter such as rocks are made up of atoms that are packed so close together that they are unable to move. Liquids such as water are made up of atoms that are less tightly packed and can slide or move about, although the distance between each atom stays the same. Gases such as air are made up of atoms that move about freely.

liquid

▲ Diamond is the hardest natural material. It is made of carbon atoms linked together in a rigid, repeated pattern.

ATOMS

Elements are made up of atoms. Atoms are minute, and cannot be seen without a microscope. They also cannot be broken down into anything smaller by ordinary chemical means. Atoms are so small that about nine million million of them could fit into the space of a full stop. When joined with other atoms, they make different substances, called compounds. Oxygen (O) is an element made up only of oxygen atoms. Hydrogen (H) is a gas that has only hydrogen atoms. If one measure of oxygen is combined with two measures of hydrogen, the result is water (H_2O) – a compound.

INSIDE ATOMS

Each atom is made up of even smaller parts, or sub-atomic particles. These parts are electrons, neutrons and protons. The exact number of particles in each atom determines which element it is. All atoms of a particular element have the same combination of particles. Neutrons and protons are found in the nucleus (the centre) of the atom. The electrons are much smaller and whizz around the nucleus.

▲ Soft graphite is used in pencils. It is made up of carbon atoms that are held together loosely in groups of six.

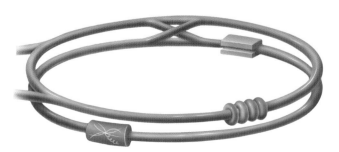

◀ A particle accelerator is a giant machine used to make tiny particles travel at very high speeds. The particles collide with each other and split open, revealing their content.

71

HOW MATTER REACTS

ATOMS are constantly colliding with other atoms. This can either bond them together or break them apart. Either way, the atoms, or the groups of atoms that have bonded together as molecules, are rearranged and new substances, called products, are created. This process is called a reaction. The substances that meet and begin the reaction are called reactants. While some reactions need energy to happen, others give off energy of their own.

Hydrogen and oxygen are the reactants that make water, which is one of the most common substances on Earth. When two hydrogen atoms and one oxygen atom join together, water is formed. By using a different reaction to reverse the process, scientists can separate water back into its two main ingredients, hydrogen and oxygen.

BASIC CHEMISTRY

A process that combines elements such as hydrogen and oxygen to create water is called a chemical reaction. The elements involved in the reaction are known as chemical elements. Chemistry is the name given to the study of the reactions of elements. A popular image of a chemist's

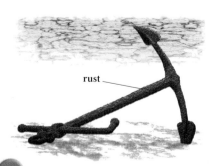

rust

▶ When atoms are split apart, they release enormous amounts of energy. Atomic weapons use this technology to produce gigantic explosions that are thousands of times more powerful than gunpowder.

◀ When water and oxygen combine together with iron, they form a hydrated iron oxide, commonly known as rust. This usually appears as a reddish-brown colour, and in time produces a flaky covering on the surface of the metal.

laboratory is of test tubes, pipes and steaming flasks of brightly coloured boiling liquids. Although chemists still use these tools today, modern laboratories are equipped with powerful computers that enable scientists to study the behaviours and reactions of the smallest particles.

NATURAL REACTIONS

Reactions are constantly taking place, as a normal part of nature. If a shiny iron object is left outside, after a week or so it begins to turn slightly reddish-brown in colour. This reaction takes place slowly as oxygen and water (both present in the air) combine with the iron to form a compound – a mixture of different elements. Scientists call this reddish-brown compound hydrated iron oxide (commonly known as rust). A compound's name tells us which elements were involved in the reaction process.

▲ *Fire is a chemical process in which oxygen combines with other substances to give off heat and light.*

▲ *When we make a cup of instant coffee, the solid coffee granules mix with, or dissolve in, liquids and form a solution.*

INSTANT REACTIONS

Rusting is a relatively slow process. Other reactions are much faster and can take place in an instant. If hydrogen gas is exposed to air, for example, there is a loud 'crack', or explosion. The sound is made as the reaction takes place. Water is the product of the reaction between hydrogen atoms and oxygen atoms in the air. When substances are combined with oxygen and they produce heat and light, this process is called combustion, or burning.

▶ *All metals have a boiling point, the temperature at which they turn from solid into liquid. Metalworkers heat iron to a boiling point of 1,535°C, at which point the metal becomes liquid. It can then be poured into a mould. When it cools it becomes solid again and can be removed from the mould. This process is used to make many things.*

TYPES OF ENERGY

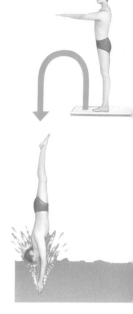

ELECTRICITY takes its name from electrons, which are some of the tiny particles inside every atom. During some chemical reactions, the electrons from one atom are exchanged with those of another. An electrical current, which supplies power, is a constant flow of electrons (in solutions electrons become ions). Scientists can use electric currents to create other reactions. For example, a metal object can be coated with silver if it is placed in a solution that contains silver, and an electrical current is passed through the solution. This makes some of the silver form a very thin layer on the metal object. The process is called silver plating.

MAKING THINGS HAPPEN

Electricity is one of the most useful forms of energy. Scientists describe energy as having 'the ability to do work' or to 'cause things to happen'. One important feature of energy is that it cannot be created or destroyed. It can only be changed from one form to another. There is a fixed amount of energy in the whole Universe, and that amount never changes. Energy can be moved and passed on, being changed and taking on new forms along the way, but it always adds up to the same amount.

▲ *A diver has 'potential' energy when standing on the board – it is stored or waiting to be released. It becomes another type of energy, called 'kinetic' energy (the energy of movement or motion), during the dive.*

CHANGING FORMS

Although the total amount of energy in the Universe never changes, energy itself can take on many forms, such as electricity, heat, light, sound, chemicals or movement. Most of the energy we use on Earth is released in vast amounts from the Sun. We receive this energy in the form of heat, light and other waves and rays. Plants absorb the light to create chemical energy – food. Plant-eating animals such as sheep take in this energy from the plants they eat. We also take in energy in our food, and convert it into different forms inside our bodies. The chemical energy in our muscles changes to kinetic energy (moving energy) when we walk or ride a bike. When we pedal a bike we use potential energy (waiting or stored energy), which is released as more kinetic energy when we go downhill. By using our bicycle brakes, kinetic energy is changed into heat energy, which comes from the friction between the brake and the wheel.

▲ *The kinetic energy of a swinging golf club is passed on to the ball, making it move.*

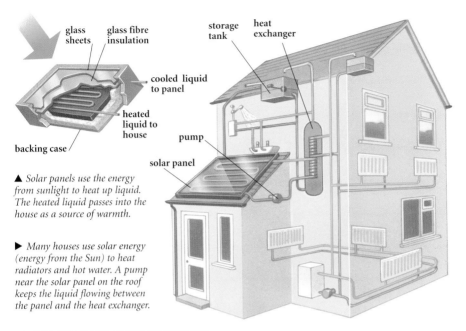

glass sheets · glass fibre insulation · storage tank · heat exchanger

cooled liquid to panel

heated liquid to house

backing case

pump

solar panel

▲ *Solar panels use the energy from sunlight to heat up liquid. The heated liquid passes into the house as a source of warmth.*

▶ *Many houses use solar energy (energy from the Sun) to heat radiators and hot water. A pump near the solar panel on the roof keeps the liquid flowing between the panel and the heat exchanger.*

ENERGY FOR THE FUTURE

People often use the word 'energy' to mean the energy we need to heat our homes or to power our cars. Such energy is usually a form of 'chemical' energy. It comes from burning 'fossil fuels' such as oil and coal in power stations to make electricity, or petrol in cars. Fossil fuels are made from plants and animals that died and rotted millions of years ago. After millions of years of being under pressure, their remains turned into oil, coal and gas. Humans are rapidly using up the world's fossil fuels, and so we need to find other renewable, or sustainable, forms of energy that can be used over and over again. So far, renewable sources of energy such as the energy harnessed from the wind, running water, sunshine or even tides has proved more expensive than burning fossil fuels.

◀ *A car engine uses the chemical energy in fuel to make heat energy in the engine. This produces kinetic (moving) energy.*

75

HOW THINGS MOVE

MOVEMENT is the force of many basic processes and reactions, both large and small. Physicists are able to predict the motion of comets in space, jet planes in the sky, balls rolling down slopes, and the tiny movements in a wristwatch by using their knowledge about one type of motion to predict how other objects will move. To do this, they must first understand something called 'force'.

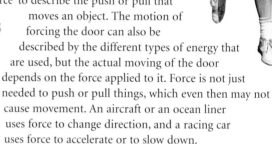

▶ *By hitting the ball with a fast-moving racket, a tennis player transfers the force from the racket to the ball.*

USING FORCE

If you try to force a jammed door open, you have to push it hard. A scientist uses the word 'force' to describe the push or pull that

moves an object. The motion of forcing the door can also be described by the different types of energy that are used, but the actual moving of the door depends on the force applied to it. Force is not just needed to push or pull things, which even then may not cause movement. An aircraft or an ocean liner uses force to change direction, and a racing car uses force to accelerate or to slow down.

LAWS OF MOTION

English scientist Sir Isaac Newton (1643–1727) was one of the first people to study the effects of force. He described these effects as the Laws of Motion. The first law says that unless a force is applied to it, an object will keep staying as it is, either moving if it is in motion or still if it is not moving. The second law says that the change in movement of an object depends on the size or amount of the force. The third law explains how each force, or action, causes an equal or opposing force or reaction. Together, these laws deal with how objects behave if force is applied to them. Scientists measure force in units called newtons.

MEASURING MOTION AND FORCE

◀ *A skateboarder judges when the force of his upward motion is balanced by the force of gravity pulling him back as he rides up the slope.*

We can measure, and often predict, how far and how fast something will move if we have enough information about it. We need to know the object's 'mass' – the amount of

▲ *Animals such as dolphins use the force from their swishing tails to propel them through the water.*

MOMENTUM

Momentum is the force of a moving object. Scientists measure momentum by multiplying the mass of an object (its weight) by its velocity (speed). A snooker ball passes its momentum on to another ball when the two balls hit each other.

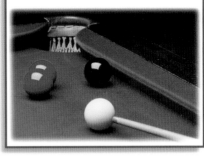

matter it contains. If we increase the force applied to an object, its speed will increase. If we apply the same force to a second object with less mass (less weight), it will go faster than the first one. For example, if you apply a kicking force to a ball, it will move at a certain speed. If you kick a ball

▲ *Sailing ships catch the wind (a type of force) in their sails and use it to move them along.*

that has half the mass (half the weight) of the first one, it will travel twice as fast. Everyday actions can be measured in the same way. The kick is a force that sets the ball moving and passes energy to the ball. The ball slows down or loses energy because of air resistance (friction from the still air against the moving ball). Finally, the force of gravity (downward pull) brings the ball back to the ground. These same principles apply to all kinds of movements.

◀ *The design of a racing car is streamlined and this helps to reduce the force of air resistance that slows the car down.*

ELECTROMAGNETIC FORCES

ELECTROMAGNETIC radiation is a form of energy. The Sun and other stars send out electromagnetic radiation all the time. Its waves fan out, or radiate, from their source like the ripples in a pond after a stone has been thrown in. The term 'electromagnetic radiation' covers many different types of radiation. Scientists can tell them apart by measuring the distance (or length) of their waves. Daylight, or white light, which contains all the colours of the spectrum, is one form of electromagnetic radiation. Beyond the violet end of the light spectrum are shorter wavelengths – such as ultraviolet, X-rays and gamma rays. Beyond the red end of the spectrum are longer wavelengths – such as infra red, microwaves and radio waves.

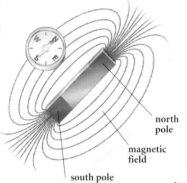

north pole

magnetic field

south pole

▲ *A magnet's force is strongest at its two ends, the north and south poles.*

magnetic field

wire coil

soft iron core

▼ *Using various types of electromagnetic energy doctors are able to scan the inside of the human body. This can help them to discover problems that are not visible externally.*

▲ *An electromagnet is made by coiling wire around an iron core. When current flows through the wire, the iron core becomes magnetized. In a simple device like an electric bell, when current passes through the coil, the magnetized iron core attracts another piece of iron, which is attached to the clapper of the bell, making it ring.*

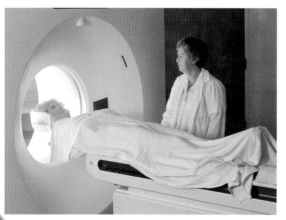

INTO OUTER SPACE

For centuries, optical telescopes, which detect light, were the only way of learning about our Universe. But for the last 50 years, scientists have been able to use radio telescopes to 'listen' for the radio waves coming from space. These telescopes look like huge satellite dishes. They examine not only

ELECTRIC CURRENT

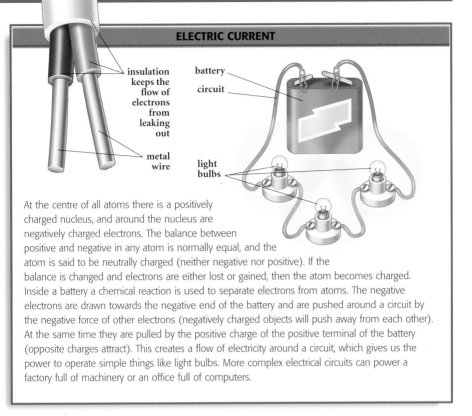

insulation keeps the flow of electrons from leaking out

metal wire

battery

circuit

light bulbs

At the centre of all atoms there is a positively charged nucleus, and around the nucleus are negatively charged electrons. The balance between positive and negative in any atom is normally equal, and the atom is said to be neutrally charged (neither negative nor positive). If the balance is changed and electrons are either lost or gained, then the atom becomes charged. Inside a battery a chemical reaction is used to separate electrons from atoms. The negative electrons are drawn towards the negative end of the battery and are pushed around a circuit by the negative force of other electrons (negatively charged objects will push away from each other). At the same time they are pulled by the positive charge of the positive terminal of the battery (opposite charges attract). This creates a flow of electricity around a circuit, which gives us the power to operate simple things like light bulbs. More complex electrical circuits can power a factory full of machinery or an office full of computers.

radio waves, but also other types of electromagnetic radiation with different wavelengths, such as microwaves, gamma rays and X-rays. Radio telescopes have given us an entirely new view of space and the Universe. Many stars, galaxies and other deep-space objects that cannot be seen by visible light can be detected by radio waves or X-rays.

▲ Microwaves are a form of electromagnetic radiation. Microwave ovens pass microwaves through food, causing the molecules of water in the food to heat up.

▶ Electric cars use powerful batteries to supply energy in the form of electric current to their motors. This fuel source may become commonplace in years to come.

LIGHT AND COLOUR

Electromagnetic radiation is a type of energy known as light. Light is only a tiny part of the total amount of electromagnetic radiation that is around us. Our eyes are adapted to absorb light, this we cannot do with most other types of electromagnetic radiation. An electromagnetic radiation wave is measured by its wavelength. A differnt wave length is seen as a different colour and the differences between the wavelengths of each colour is only billionths of a metre.

▲ A concave lens uses refraction to bend the direction of light rays passing through it. Light fans outwards on the other side.

▲ Normal 'white' light from the Sun or from a light bulb is made up of many different colours. A glass prism separates out the colours when white light is passed through it.

COLOURS OF THE SPECTRUM

The range of different colours we can see are called the colours of the 'spectrum'. Violet is at one end of the spectrum and has the shortest wavelength, and red is at the other end and has the longest wavelength. 'White' light consists of all the colours of the spectrum mixed together. Sometimes we can see the

▲ A convex lens does the opposite to a concave lens. It bends light rays towards each other as they pass through.

◄ Mirrors can bend reflected light in the same way that lenses bend light passing through them. Fairground mirrors have concave and convex curves, which distort the reflection. The reflected image can appear squashed or stretched.

▼ Laser light is a type of light in which all the waves are exactly the same length.

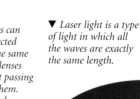

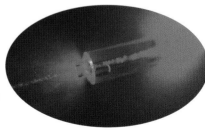

full spectrum of colours (violet, indigo, blue, green, yellow, orange and red). If you hold a triangular piece of glass or plastic (called a prism) up to the light, you will see it separate the colours of the spectrum. A rainbow also separates the colours. As sunlight passes through raindrops, they act like tiny prisms and an arc of separate colours appears in the sky.

REFLECTION AND REFRACTION

Light normally travels in straight lines. It passes through some materials such as glass, clear plastic and ice, but is reflected off objects such as mirrors. In many other cases, light is absorbed. A red apple appears to be red because it absorbs all the wavelengths of light except red, which it reflects back into our eyes.

Light can sometimes refract (bend) as it passes from one substance to another. You can see this if you place a spoon into a glass of water. The part of the handle that is out of the water seems to be at a different angle, and be a different size to, the part of the handle that is underwater. Lenses for eyeglasses, microscopes and telescopes are made from curved glass or plastic. By refracting light, the lenses magnify (make bigger) the objects we see through them.

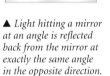
visible light

▲ *Electromagnetic radiation is a huge range of differing wave lengths. Visible light (shown in the middle) forms only a tiny part of this overall range.*

▲ *Light hitting a mirror at an angle is reflected back from the mirror at exactly the same angle in the opposite direction.*

THE SPEED OF LIGHT

Light travels at about 300,000 kilometres a second. Nothing in the Universe that we know travels faster than light. Light from the Sun takes about eight minutes to reach Earth. Scientists use the term light-year (the distance that light travels in one year) to measure distances in our Universe. The nearest star is more than four light-years away.

▼ *Light passing from one clear substance to another, such as from air to glass, becomes refracted, or bent as it travels.*

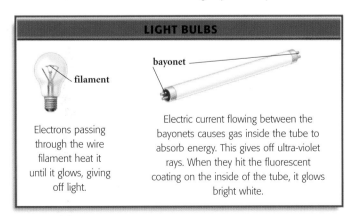
LIGHT BULBS

filament

bayonet

Electrons passing through the wire filament heat it until it glows, giving off light.

Electric current flowing between the bayonets causes gas inside the tube to absorb energy. This gives off ultra-violet rays. When they hit the fluorescent coating on the inside of the tube, it glows bright white.

SOUND WAVES

S OUND is the vibration of air that we detect with our sense of hearing. Air is caused to vibrate (move back and forth) when any object in it moves or vibrates. For example, when a drumstick hits a drum, the skin of the drum moves back and forth. This movement sets up similar vibrations in the air around it, which travel out from the drum in the form of sound waves. Sound waves can be measured, and scientists have shown that the bigger the sound wave (made by a large force), the louder the sound that we hear. Sound waves lose their energy as they travel, which is why sounds from distant objects are harder to hear.

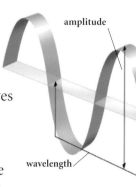

▲ Amplitude is the measure of the force of a sound wave – its volume. Wavelength describes its pitch – high or low.

HIGH AND LOW

We can hear differences in how high or low a sound is (its 'pitch'). The pitch of a sound depends on the lengths of the sound wave. Low-frequency sound waves are long waves that produce low-pitched noises. Thunder, a bass drum, a foghorn or a deep-voiced singer are all low-pitched sounds. Higher-frequency sound waves are short waves, and they produce high-pitched sounds – such as cymbals, birdsong, police sirens or young children.

▲ Sound waves travel out from the source of the sound in the same way that ripples in water travel outwards from the splash of a drip.

HOW WE HEAR

Scientists measure the frequency of sound waves in Hertz (Hz). One Hz equals one wave per second. People with good hearing can hear a range of sounds from 25 Hz (a very low noise) to about 20,000 Hz. Bats and dogs can hear sounds well above 50,000 Hz. Our ears act as funnels that collect sound waves,

▲ An ultrasound scanner bounces very high-frequency sound waves off a pregnant woman's stomach. The echoes it records give a picture of the unborn baby.

◄ *When a jet travels faster than the speed of sound, it causes a sonic boom to be heard.*

which then pass along a canal in the ear to reach the eardrum. When the sounds reach the eardrum they cause it to vibrate. These vibrations then travel to three tiny bones inside the ear, which in turn send the vibrations further into the inner ear. At this point a sensitive organ called the cochlea receives the vibrations and changes them into electrical nerve signals, which are carried to the brain where they are interpreted as sounds.

▲ *The walls of an anechoic chamber absorb all sounds, so that there are no echoes at all.*

SPEED AND VOLUME

During a thunderstorm, we hear the sound of thunder a few seconds after seeing the flash of lightning. This is because sound waves travel a million times more slowly than light waves. Sound not only travels through air. It can also travel through glass and water. In fact it travels almost five times faster through water than it does through air.

The volume of sound is measured in decibels (dB). A person can just about hear a sound of 10 dB. Sound levels of about 30 to 60 dB are comfortable, but levels above 85 to 90 dB can damage our ears, especially if they continue for a long period of time. Some musicians, and people who are exposed to loud machinery for a long period of time, can risk damage to their hearing.

▼ *Different animals make and hear sounds of differing frequencies. Humans make a fairly limited range of sounds.*

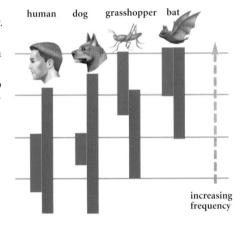

human   dog   grasshopper   bat

increasing frequency

■ **sounds heard**   ■ **sounds made**

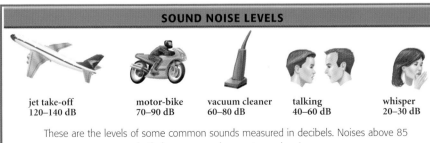

SOUND NOISE LEVELS

jet take-off	motor-bike	vacuum cleaner	talking	whisper
120–140 dB	70–90 dB	60–80 dB	40–60 dB	20–30 dB

These are the levels of some common sounds measured in decibels. Noises above 85 decibels can cause damage to our hearing.

THE POWER OF SCIENCE

Over many centuries, people have come to understand more and more about all kinds of things on our planet and in the Universe. They know what the Sun and planets are made of, how plants grow, why certain animals survive in particular places, and even what the basic building blocks of all matter (atoms) are made of. All of this knowledge is part of science. Sometimes scientists discover new knowledge very quickly, but more often than not, they must work for a long time testing and experimenting, and then repeating the processes over and over again to test their ideas to the full. Working to understand our world has brought us all kinds of things that help us in our daily lives, from medicines to electric light.

positioning gears

wind sensors

gearbox

electrical generator

pylon

rotor blade

▲ A wind turbine produces electrical energy. Wind turns the blades that drive a system of gears and power a generator.

TECHNOLOGY

Technology is one way in which scientific ideas are used and applied. Technology has led to the development of many everyday things that we take for granted, including cars, computers, refrigerators and televisions. The invention of the wheel many thousands of years ago was one of the first advances in technology.

▼ Before electricity was discovered, windmills were used to grind corn into flour. The blades of the windmill turned grinding stones inside the mill.

THE POWER AROUND US

Until the 1700s, people relied on their own strength or the strength of animals to move heavy ploughs across fields or coal barges along canals. Flowing water was employed to power waterwheels, which were attached to grindstones in mills. As the water turned the waterwheel, the grindstones rotated and ground wheat grain into flour. During the 1700s, new inventions made use of forces in nature not previously used. The pressure of steam was used to power pumps, trains, boats, weaving looms and many other kinds of new machines – it was the driving force behind the Industrial Revolution. Steam engines were able to generate more power than had been known before. In a short time, scientists learned more about energy itself. They invented engines that were powered by electricity, and before long all homes were supplied with electricity.

POWER STATIONS

Today, huge power stations supply the ever-growing demand for electricity. These are powered by water or high-pressure steam, which turns a turbine (a large wheel). This in turn makes coils of wire spin inside a magnetic field, and the spinning generates a large flow of electrons, which produce an electric current. The current that leaves the power station is too strong for use in the home, so substations in cities reduce the power of the current and feed it on to homes for domestic use.

▲ *Hydroelectric dams use the force of flowing water to power generators, which provide electricity.*

◀ *Energy can be harnessed from natural sources such as geysers. A geyser is an outpouring of hot water and steam that rises up from deep under Earth's surface. They are particularly common in New Zealand.*

POWER FROM FOSSIL FUELS

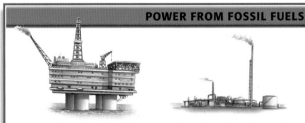

Large rigs are used to drill deep into Earth for crude oil, which provides petrol, diesel and kerosene fuels.

Natural gas is a mixture of gases that can be burned for fuel. The gas is drilled and piped to processing plants.

Coal is a rock that can be burned. It is made up mainly of carbon, formed from plants that died long ago.

MACHINES

THE word 'machine' suggests a large engine with lots of moving parts such as gears, belts and pistons – like a car engine.

But the term covers far more than just complex engines. A huge range of 'machines' help us to perform simple tasks and activities, some of which we would not otherwise be able to do. Many of the things we use or play with every day, such as bicycles and seesaws, are machines.

SIMPLE MACHINES

Basic machines are called 'simple' machines. They include the lever, the pulley, the wheel and axle, and the inclined plane (a sloping track or ramp). A screw and a wedge are also simple machines, although an inclined plane can perform the same functions.

Simple machines work by changing the strength or direction of a force. The wheel allows loads to be moved more easily because it reduces friction (resistance force) between the load and the ground. For example, it is not easy to push a pile of bricks along the ground, but it is fairly easy to push the same pile in a wheelbarrow. The wheel reduces the friction of the bricks against the ground. You may not be able to lift your best friend off the ground, but you could if they were on a seesaw (which is a type of lever). The seesaw uses your weight as a downward force and changes it to a more powerful upward force at the other end.

▲ A set of pulleys, or block and tackle, allows a person to lift a very heavy weight, although it can be slow.

◀ A shaduf was a tool used in ancient Egypt to raise water from the River Nile (the water was used to irrigate crops). It is a basic lever with a weight at one end.

▶ *Many machines use cogs (wheels with teeth) in gear systems. The cogs transfer the force from one part of the machine to another.*

HOW DOES IT WORK?

A simple machine works because of the link between force and distance. If you sit near the centre of a seesaw, it is unlikely that you would ever be able to lift a friend heavier than yourself at the other end of the seesaw. But if you move farther away from the centre pivot, lifting becomes easier. The extra distance provides the force needed to lift.

A pulley is another simple machine that uses distance to provide force. Most adults would not be able to lift another adult two metres into the air. But using a combination of pulleys, known as a 'compound pulley', the task becomes possible. Because the rope is wound round each of the pulleys, the distance has been increased, providing the force needed to lift the object.

SIMPLE MACHINES

A slide is an example of an inclined plane.

A nutcracker is a type of lever.

A wheelbarrow uses a wheel and axle.

An axe is a simple wedge.

A screw is a special (turning) type of wedge.

BUILDING BLOCKS

Simple machines are the 'building blocks' of technology. A car engine is basically a combination of many simple machines – as are lifts, submarines, aircrafts and rockets. With the right mix of machines, we can do things faster, longer, higher and with a lot less effort.

▲ *A seesaw is an example of a lever. It allows a lighter person to lift a heavier one.*

▲ *A canoeist uses a paddle as a type of lever to move forward and to stay upright in the strong current. By pressing down into the water with the paddle, the canoeist can move the boat either forwards or upwards, depending on the direction of the push.*

CARS AND TRUCKS

MOST people ride in cars, vans, buses or trucks every day without ever thinking about how the vehicle works. All of these vehicles use a combination of simple machines to make them go. They rely on fuel to power their engines. In most cars and trucks the fuel is petrol, made from crude oil.

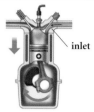

▲ *The piston is drawn down to suck fuel and air into the cylinder.*

INSIDE AN ENGINE

The petrol we put into cars is stored in a tank, which is connected by a tube to the engine at a point where spark plugs give off tiny sparks inside cylinders. The sparks make the petrol inside the cylinders burn, and the air in the cylinders expand (get bigger). The expanded air forces a piston down inside each cylinder. The pistons are linked to a crankshaft. The push from the piston causes the crankshaft to rotate. On its upward turn, the crankshaft forces the piston back up into the cylinder ready for another spark to push it back down again. The spark plugs create hundreds of tiny explosions every second, so the crankshaft is constantly rotating. The crankshaft is connected to a series of gears, which can be used to change the speed of rotation of the wheels on the road.

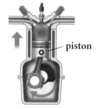

▲ *The piston rises to squeeze or compress the fuel-air mixture.*

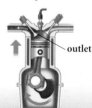

▲ *The spark plug ignites the mixture. The blast pushes the piston down.*

TRUCK TYPES

Some trucks are one-piece – the cab where the driver sits, the engine and the load are not detachable from each other. Other trucks have a joint, or articulation, between the tractor unit (the cab and engine) and the trailer unit (the load). These trucks are called 'artics'.

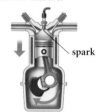

▲ *The piston rises to push out waste gases through the valve.*

▶ *Huge trucks pulling two or three large trailers are called 'road trains'. They carry freight long distances across flat, rural areas such as central Australia.*

▼ *Modern cars often have a curved 'aerodynamic' shape that reduces the force of air pushing against them.*

OTHER TYPES OF ENGINE

Petrol-powered cars use an internal combustion engine. Combustion means 'catching fire'. A rotary engine is also a combustion engine, but instead of having tube-shaped cylinders, it burns petrol in spinning rotors. Diesel engines are similar to petrol engines, but they do not have spark plugs. Petrol and diesel engines not only cause pollution with their exhaust (waste). They are also helping to use up Earth's limited resources of crude oil. For these reasons, experts are looking for other ways to power cars. Burning sugar products and hydrogen instead of oil-based fuels is one option. But more successful is using electricity, stored in batteries.

▲ *This experimental car uses solar panels to provide energy. It has a fine aerodynamic shape that cuts through wind resistance.*

▼ *The fastest cars use rocket engines to reach speeds of more than 1,000 km/h. The massive force pushing them forward is called thrust.*

POWER OF TRUCKS

A truck is built to carry or pull heavy loads, so it needs a powerful engine. The engine is the same basic type as in cars, but a truck engine usually has at least twelve cylinders, compared to four or six in most cars. Trucks also need a series of gears to allow them to climb steep hills and prevent them going too fast downhill. Cars have four or five gears for moving forward, while trucks may have as many as sixteen.

BOATS AND TRAINS

THE earliest boats were probably Egyptian reed boats, made about 3000 BC. These were powered by oarsmen. But for most of their 5,000-year history, boats were made of wood and were powered by the wind. Then in the early AD 1800s, the steam engine changed shipping forever. Steam power was used to drive engines that turned mighty propellers at the stern, or rear, of the ship. The earliest steam vessels were made of wood, but by the late 1800s large ships were made of metal to cope with the weight of the steam engines. They carried both passengers and cargo. Today, ships carry heavier cargoes than any other means of transport.

▲ Some of the earliest sailing ships had only a single square sail. Later ships, like this Roman merchant ship, had a stern sail used to help with steering.

UNDERWATER, OVERWATER

Submarines were first used as underwater warships during World War I (1914–18). They are able to dive by flooding ballast tanks that surround the main body of the boat. To rise again, compressed air is used to force the water out of the ballast tanks. Hovercrafts and hydrofoils, in contrast, barely touch the water at all. Hovercrafts travel on a cushion of air, while hydrofoils are lifted just off the water on wing-like structures called foils.

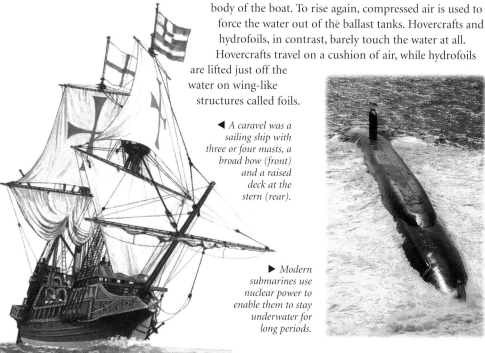

◄ A caravel was a sailing ship with three or four masts, a broad bow (front) and a raised deck at the stern (rear).

▶ Modern submarines use nuclear power to enable them to stay underwater for long periods.

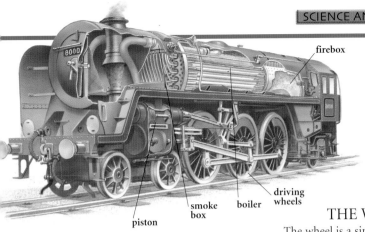

firebox

◀ A steam locomotive operates using a simple method. Coal or wood is burned, causing water to expand as steam. The expanding steam moves pistons, which transfer the energy into the motion of the turning wheels.

smoke box

boiler

driving wheels

piston

THE WHEEL

The wheel is a simple machine that allows heavy loads to be rolled along easily, rather than pulled or dragged. As early as the 1500s, people in Europe were transporting heavy goods on wagons that had metal wheels, and which ran on metal or wooden rails. Men or horses pulled the wagons. This system of early rail transport was limited in how far and how fast it could go, and in the size of the loads that could be carried.

STEAM POWER

In the early 1800s, British inventors developed steam-powered locomotives. Coal was burned to heat water in the boiler, which produced steam. As the steam expanded, it powered pistons. These turned the wheels. As engines became more powerful, longer and heavier trains were built. Locomotives were able to pull dozens of carriages containing passengers or freight.

In the 1940's, the less-polluting diesel-electric locomotives were developed, and these are still used in many countries today. Other modern trains run on electricity, supplied either by cables running above the tracks or by an extra power rail running alongside the track. The French high-speed TGV train can travel at speeds of 300 kilometres per hour.

▲ Trains known as monorails travel on one rail instead of two.

A new type of train runs on a monorail, or single track. Another kind uses powerful magnets to lift the train off the rails. Magnetic levitation (MagLev) trains do not have wheels at all – they float on a magnetic cushion.

▲ Modern trains travelling at up to 225 km/h can compete with air travel, connecting cities up to 800 km apart.

AIRCRAFT

IN 1783, the Montgolfier brothers sent a hot-air balloon 900 metres into the skies above France. It carried two volunteer travellers for ten minutes. An astonished crowd watched the balloon land. They had witnessed a remarkable event – the first manned flight through the air. Some 120 years passed before the first powered flight took place, in America. On December 17, 1903, Orville and Wilbur Wright made a number of flights in the first aeroplane. The longest flight covered a distance of just 260 metres and lasted under a minute. But a new type of transport had been born.

lift

thrust

drag

gravity

▲ *Planes fly by balancing opposite forces. The upward force of lift works against gravity, and the forward thrust offsets drag caused by air resistance.*

RAPID ADVANCES

By the time World War I broke out in 1914, fighter planes such as the Sopwith Pup were being built. The Sopwith Camel, built during the war, was faster and more easily steered, or manoeuvred.

upper deck and lounge

windshield

porthole

galley

landing gear

flight deck

jet engine

▲ *In a hot-air balloon, a burner heats the air inside the balloon until it becomes lighter than the air outside. This makes the balloon rise.*

WRIGHT BROTHERS

Orville and Wilbur Wright used their experience as bicycle mechanics to construct the first successful powered aircraft, which they called *Flyer 1*.

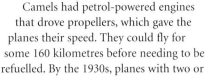

▶ *A microlight aircraft is powered by an engine not much larger than that of a lawnmower.*

▲ *Air rushing faster over the curved top of a wing has less pressure than slower air beneath the wing. The higher pressure of the air below pushes the wing up, causing the force known as lift.*

rudder

tail fin

fuselage

tailplane

elevator

baggage hold   washrooms

flap

fuel tanks within wing

aileron

▲ *A Jumbo Jet uses the same techniques as the Wright brothers' plane to fly. Its wide wings provide enormous lift, and its four powerful jet engines propel the plane forwards at cruising speeds of nearly 1,000 km/h.*

Camels had petrol-powered engines that drove propellers, which gave the planes their speed. They could fly for some 160 kilometres before needing to be refuelled. By the 1930s, planes with two or four propellers were carrying passengers over long distances, and by World War II (1939–45) formidable fighter planes like the British Spitfire and the German Messerschmitt Bf109 had been developed.

THE BIRTH OF THE JET

Jet engines began to replace propeller-driven planes in the 1940s and 1950s. The jet engine sucks air into a chamber from the front, where it mixes with fuel and burns. Exhaust, the waste from the burning fuel, rushes out of the back of the engine at high speed, pushing the plane forwards. Jet-engined planes can go much faster and farther than propeller-driven planes. Nearly all large passenger planes today use jet engines. Boeing 747s, or Jumbo Jets, for example, are powerful enough to carry over five hundred passengers. Some jets can travel faster than the speed of sound.

HOW PLANES FLY

All aircraft are affected by four forces: thrust, gravity, drag and lift. Thrust comes from the engine and sends the plane moving forwards, overcoming drag (the friction or resistance caused by air rubbing against the plane). Lift comes from the wings and is the force that keeps planes in the air. It counteracts the downwards pull of gravity. The top of a plane's wing is curved, so air passing over it moves faster than air rushing below, as it has a little farther to travel. The faster-moving air has less pressure, so the wing is pushed up from the pressure of the air on the undersurface of the wing, creating the lift needed to fly.

▶ *The US Space Shuttle has to be launched into space from a rocket, but when it returns to Earth it lands like a huge glider.*

COMMUNICATIONS

PEOPLE enjoy watching 'live' performances and broadcasts, whether by musicians, actors, sports players, politicians or media reporters. With the aid of modern communications, we can watch live coverage of events taking place thousands of kilometres away, or we can choose to see things that were recorded many years ago. We can chat via the Internet with celebrities, and can keep in touch with people over long distances. Perhaps most importantly, for the first time in modern history we can access information from experts on every topic, almost immediately.

▶ *Communications satellites (comsats) receive and send on signals for radio, TV, computers and phones.*

THE FIRST PHONE CALL

Alexander Graham Bell developed the first telephone in Boston, USA, about 1876. He found that sounds entering a telephone affected the electric current leaving it, and that these changes could be passed along a wire to another phone, where they were changed back into sounds that could be understood. Thomas Edison, made improvements to the telephone, and soon messages were being sent hundreds of kilometres. In 1877, Edison produced the first phonograph, a machine that recorded and played back sounds. People were able to listen to all kinds of music in their own homes.

▲ *Mobile phones, or cell phones, beam low-power signals to local relay towers, which send them on to the next one.*

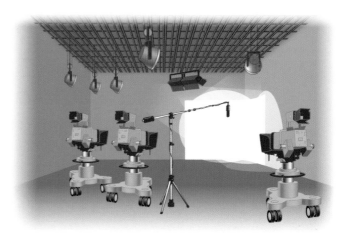

▲ *In a TV studio, a microphone on a long arm, or boom, extends towards the action area. Lights shine down from different angles, and cameras are on rollers.*

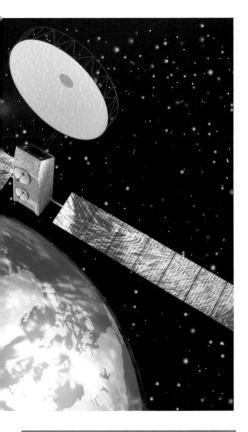

The first phonographs were clockwork, but by the 1920s they used electricity.

In the 1950s, cassette players recorded sounds onto magnetic tape. Today the most popular types of recording are the compact disc (CD) and digital versatile disc (DVD). These machines use laser light to 'read' tiny pits on the surface of the aluminium discs. The discs can store sounds, pictures, computer programs or other kinds of information, such as films.

RADIO AND TELEVISION

Radios were developed in the late 1800s for sending and receiving important messages. Today, it is a form of entertainment, but it still works in the same way. Radio waves (a type of electromagnetic radiation) are sent into the air, where they bounce off Earth's atmosphere and are picked up by a receiver thousands of kilometres away. Mobile phones also send and receive low-power radio waves.

Sending and receiving signals is called broadcasting. Radio and television are both forms of broadcasting. Television broadcasts send out radio waves that vary in pattern, representing both sounds and pictures. A TV set turns the radio signals back into pictures and sounds.

CABLE AND SATELLITE TV

Cable and satellite TV give people a greater variety of channels to watch. With cable TV, signals travel not as radio waves, but as flashes of laser light along special cables into people's houses. With satellite TV, signals are sent up to a satellite high above Earth. The signals are received and strengthened before they are beamed back down over a wide area of Earth. The signals are received by satellite dishes (aerials) attached to homes.

RECORDING

A recording studio has special tiles on the walls, ceiling and floor to reduce echoes. Microphones pick up sounds from every corner of the studio. Mixing consoles combine the different sounds and produce the finished recording.

THE GLOBAL VILLAGE

THE 20th-century revolution in communications has made the world very small. A person logging on to the Internet from a school in Finland, for example, can communicate with people anywhere in the world in an instant. People can send e-mails from hand-held computers while climbing mountains, lying on a beach, or just about anywhere. Whole books can be 'downloaded' onto a computer from a source thousands of kilometres away. These and many other developments have led the world to be described as a 'global village'.

▲ *ENIAC was one of the world's first computers. It was built in the 1940s and was used for calculating rocket flights.*

INSTANT COMMUNICATIONS

Most of the advances that have led to the global village have been in communications. Modern technology has helped us to develop the science of electronics rapidly. Electronics uses a wide range of tiny devices to change the flow of electrons in electrical currents. Inside a TV or computer, for example, there are hundreds of small, coloured parts. These are the electronic components (building blocks) of the equipment. The integrated circuits or microchips are especially powerful. Reducing the size of these component parts, or making them from different materials, has enabled smaller, more powerful computers to be built. Laptop and palmtop computers are small enough to be carried in a case or even a pocket.

◀ *Computers of the 1950s and 1960s stored their data on huge reels of magnetic tape.*

▼ *Fibre-optic cables carry information that has been coded as flashes of laser light. They can carry millions of flashes per second.*

▶ *The modern telecom network uses standard phones and phone cables on poles, as well as computers, fibre-optics, microwaves, radio and satellites.*

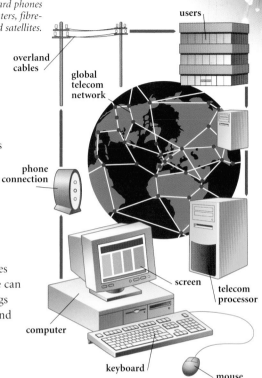

users

overland cables

global telecom network

phone connection

screen

telecom processor

computer

keyboard

mouse

A WORLD WIDE WEB

By the end of the 20th century, people had discovered how to link computers and communications. The Internet was first developed as a way of connecting military staff and scientists at different universities. Computers were linked through a telephone connection called a modem, which transferred computer messages into a form that could be sent through the telephone system.

The World Wide Web uses similar methods to send web sites or web pages from one computer to another. People can use the Web to do a multitude of things from shopping, finding information and making new friends to transferring money from one bank account to another or paying bills.

FUTURE SCIENCE

There are concerns that we are creating a world in which only a few people can afford the latest up-to-date gadgets, computers, mobile phones and portable sound systems, and that those people less able to afford them will be left struggling. But technological advances are also helping the world's less advanced nations, and on a global scale can help all nations, both rich and poor, to communicate better and move forward together.

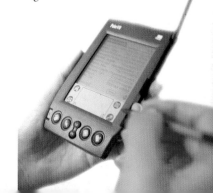

▲ *A lightweight laptop computer folds out to reveal screen and keyboard. It is powered by built-in batteries.*

▶ *Palmtop computers are smaller than a notebook and have write-on screens.*

QUIZ

1. What type of trees lose their leaves each year?

2. What is the main difference between fungi (ie mushrooms) and plants?

3. What term describes the constantly frozen soil that lies deeper than 30 cm below Arctic lands?

4. What type of plant is bamboo?

5. What is the scientific name for flowering plants?

6. The word photosynthesis, which describes how plants make food, comes from two other words. What do they mean?

7. How many food stores do dicotyledons have?

8. Plants release which gas, helping animals to survive?

9. What do pine cones contain?

10. What is the most rain that you would expect a desert to receive in a year?

11. What is the name of the tubes that take water to all parts of a plant?

12. Why must liverworts grow low and close to water?

13. Why do trees in some parts of the world, such as New England and eastern Canada, become very colourful each autumn?

14. Redwoods are examples of which type of tree?

15. Lichens, which grow on rocks or on tree bark, are a combination of which two types of living organism?

16. Which is the highest layer of a rainforest?

17. How often do biennial plants reproduce?

18. Why does a cactus have spiky leaves?

19. What are the names of the male and female parts of a plant?

20. Pampas, prairies, savannah and steppe are examples of what type of landscape?

ANSWERS

1. Deciduous trees
2. Fungi cannot produce their own food, but plants can.
3. Permafrost
4. It is a type of grass.
5. Angiosperms
6. Photo (meaning 'light') and synthesis (meaning 'making')
7. Two
8. Oxygen
9. Seeds
10. 25 cm
11. Xylem
12. All parts of the plant must absorb water directly because liverworts have no xylem to transport water inside them.
13. Because they lose their chlorophyll (green colouring), which allows the other colours to come through before the leaves drop off the trees.
14. Sequoias
15. Fungi and algae
16. The canopy (or roof)
17. Every two years
18. To reduce evaporation. Broad leaves would dry up in the desert heat.
19. The anther is the male part of the plant and the stigma is the female part.
20. Grasslands

PLANTS

WHEN seen from space, planet Earth has only a few main colours. The sea is blue, clouds and ice are white, bare rocks are brown and plants are green. Vast regions of the land are covered by the greenery of natural woods, forests, scrub and grassland, as well as farmland, with its fields of crops, orchards of fruit and timber plantations.

The smallest plants can be seen only under a microscope. The biggest plants are the greatest living things ever to have lived on the planet. What they all share is the ability to capture the energy in sunlight and convert it into energy. Plants use this for their own life processes, such as growth and reproduction. Animals, in turn, derive energy from plants by eating them. In this way plants power all life on Earth.

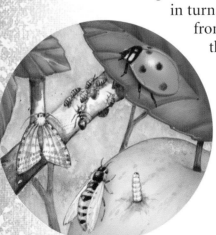

WHAT ARE PLANTS?

COVERING Earth, from the tops of mountains to the bottom of the oceans, are more than 260,000 species (individual types) of plants. They range from tiny mosses that absorb water from damp air to giant trees that draw water and other foods from the ground and pump it up more than 100 metres to their topmost leaves. Between these extremes are plant species suited to nearly every landscape and weather type on Earth.

▼ Apples, like other fruits, contain seeds that are released when the fruit dries up, rots or is opened.

FROM SEA TO FOREST

Like animals, plants have adapted (changed over time) to suit the many different environments where they grow. Some of the simplest plants do not need soil – they grow in water or in damp places where there is enough water for their needs. At the other extreme are cacti, which grow in dry deserts and have developed ways of storing water for long periods. In the dense rainforests, different plants grow at different heights, and are specially adapted to survive in the varying amounts of light available to them.

WHY WE NEED PLANTS

Plants form a basic link in the 'food chain'. This term describes the way in which all living things in a particular place rely on other living things for energy and nutrients. Many animals depend on plants for food, so plants form the first link in the chain. Meat-eating animals eat the plant-eaters, making more links. Waste matter from animals, plus their dead bodies, form food for smaller animals and microbes that break down the remains, enriching the soil. This helps more plants to grow, and the cycle of life continues.

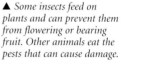

▲ Some insects feed on plants and can prevent them from flowering or bearing fruit. Other animals eat the pests that can cause damage.

▼ Many plant flowers, or blossoms, are large and colourful. This attracts bees and other insects, which feed on their pollen.

▲ Tiny hairs grow along the outside of a plant's root. The hairs help the plant absorb water and minerals from the soil.

▲ *Blossoms are the first stage in producing apples. The blossoms must be pollinated before they can develop into fruit.*

▲ *Mangrove trees grow in the damp soil of tropical seashores. Their roots are exposed at low tide.*

Plants contribute to the well-being of our world in all kinds of ways – not least because they give off oxygen, which both plants and animals need to survive. We also rely heavily on plants for food, use them to make medicines, and from plant products such as wood we build houses and make furniture. Plants also provide valuable fuels, such as coal and oil. These are made from the layers of dead plant material that build up over time on the ground, become flattened under pressure, and slowly turn into oil and coal. The roots of plants anchor the soil, making it less likely to get washed or blown away.

▶ *Leaves allow plants to 'breathe'. They absorb sunlight, which combines with substances to create the plant's food.*

▶ *Some plants eat animals. The pitcher plant, for example, attracts insects to its sticky, pitcher-shaped cups, where they get stuck and die.*

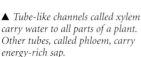

▲ *Tube-like channels called xylem carry water to all parts of a plant. Other tubes, called phloem, carry energy-rich sap.*

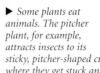

TYPES OF PLANTS

TOGETHER, all the plant species on Earth make up the plant kingdom. The other main kingdom, or large group of living things, is the animal kingdom. These two kingdoms have certain important differences. Unlike animals, plants can make their own food from non-living things – such as sunlight, water and carbon dioxide, a gas found in the air. Also unlike animals, most plants cannot move from one place to another. Their movement is concentrated in growing towards the Sun to get light. Plants also have no real senses, such as sight and hearing, with which to detect things in the way that animals do.

▲ *Dead wood can remain exposed, without rotting, for many years in dry, desert conditions.*

▶ *There are many different kinds, or groups, of plants and other plant-based living things. The main groups are shown here.*

GROUPING PLANTS

Within the plant kingdom, scientists have organized, or 'classified', all the different plant types into major groups, called divisions. Plants within each division share some basic similarities that make them unlike other plants. One of the big differences between plants of different divisions is how they obtain water. A division called the bryophytes is made up of plants that need to absorb water over most parts of their bodies. They have no tubes to carry and spread water around inside themselves. The small, simple plants known as mosses are good examples of bryophytes. They gain water by growing on damp surfaces. More complex plants have special tubes – like our blood vessels – that send water and food to all parts of the plant.

For many years, organisms called fungi, which include mushrooms and toadstools, were considered part of the plant kingdom. But scientists have now classified them as a separate kingdom. Unlike plants, fungi cannot make their own food. Instead, they rely on living or once-living things (like rotting tree trunks) to

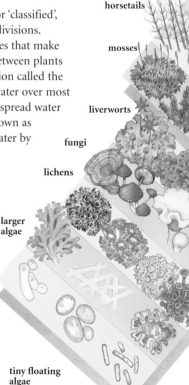

horsetails

mosses

liverworts

fungi

lichens

larger algae

tiny floating algae

◀ *Many types of plants, including seaweeds like kelp, grow on the surface of water.*

▶ *Fungi like this fly agaric toadstool look like plants, but are classified as a different kingdom because they cannot make their own food.*

trees and flowers

grasses, lilies and palms

ginkgo

conifers

cycads

ferns

club mosses

give them the food they need. Microscopic, single-celled living things are also not grouped as plants.

IDENTIFYING PLANTS

The features of a plant determine which group it belongs to. Features include its height, whether it grows on its own or near many more of its kind, and what kind of soil it prefers. Another important clue as to which group a plant belongs to is its leaves. For example, you could probably tell that a maple tree is a close relative of the sycamore tree simply by comparing the shape of the leaves. We can also tell a great deal by the way in which a plant's leaves are arranged. Do they grow on their own? Are they arranged in groups, and if so, how many are in each group?

SMALLER FEATURES

Some important features of plants are more difficult to see. The way that they reproduce to make more of their kind is extremely significant when grouping and identifying plants. But a microscope is often needed to see the tiny parts involved. Plant science is progressing rapidly, and there is much still to discover.

▶ *Gardeners can design their flower beds to blossom for months on end. A good gardener knows when each type of flower will come into bloom, and can arrange the plants so that one group begins to flower just as another starts to fade.*

103

HOW PLANTS FEED

IMAGINE being able to feed yourself just by standing in a field in all types of weather. Most plants are able to do this, using a process called photosynthesis. 'Photo' means 'light' and 'synthesis' means 'making', which is exactly what plants are able to do – they make food using light. Photosynthesis takes place in special parts of a plant's leaves. These parts are called chloroplasts, because they contain chlorophyll, a green colouring that takes energy directly from sunlight.

INGREDIENTS OF PLANT FOOD

While chloroplasts trap energy from the Sun, other parts of the leaf take in carbon dioxide gas from the air. These are two of the three ingredients needed for photosynthesis. The third, water, comes from other parts of the plant, such as the roots. Water is drawn up through a series of tubes, known as xylem, to all the other parts of the plant, including the leaves.

Once the three ingredients are together in the leaf, the plant can get to work making its food. The end result of photosynthesis is a type of sugar known as glucose. The glucose is absorbed into another system of tubes, known as phloem, which transports it to all the other parts of the plant. One of the waste products in the process, oxygen gas, is released back into the air through the leaves. Animals, including humans, and also plants, all need oxygen to live. This release of oxygen from photosynthesis helps all living things on Earth.

▲ Roots extend far out beneath a plant. They act as anchors and also gather water and minerals from the soil.

veins (bundles of phloem and xylem tubes)

energy-rich glucose sugar is taken to other parts of the plant as sap

▲ The Amazon region of South America has a warm climate and constant rain, supporting a vast expanse of rainforest. This produces the widest variety of plants in any one area of the world.

water is drawn from the soil via roots

blade (lamina) of leaf

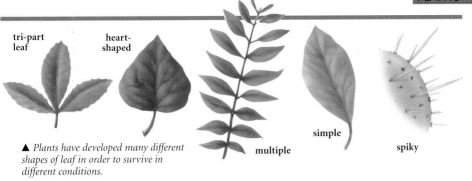

tri-part leaf

heart-shaped

simple

multiple

spiky

▲ *Plants have developed many different shapes of leaf in order to survive in different conditions.*

ADAPTING TO SURROUNDINGS

Plants use their leaves to make food in different ways, depending on where they grow. Maple trees, which grow in places where it is not always sunny, have broad leaves that are adapted to taking in as much light as possible. Such leaves would shrivel and die in very hot, dry places. Cactus plants, in contrast, have narrow, spiky leaves that can survive the great heat of the desert. The small surface area of the spikes reduces water loss through evaporation. Spikes also protect the plant from hungry plant-eating animals.

Some plants, such as the venus fly trap, use their leaves to catch live prey. Such plants are called insectivorous, or insect-eating, plants. Their leaves are specially designed to trap insects that crawl or fly into them. Once inside, the insects are digested (broken down) by the plant for food. Insect-eating plants use photosynthesis to obtain some of their food, but insects provide them with valuable minerals.

light energy from the Sun

◄ *Each plant leaf acts as a factory for producing food. The main ingredients are water (which arrives through the stem), carbon dioxide (from the air) and sunlight, which the leaf absorbs directly. The leaf cells turn these ingredients into the glucose sugar that the plant uses as energy-packed food.*

carbon dioxide gas is taken in from the air

oxygen gas is given off to the air

LIGHT IS VITAL

A simple experiment shows how plants need sunlight to survive. Cut a hole in a square piece of tape and stick it to the leaf of a plant. After a day or two, remove the tape. The covered area will have lost its green colour, because the chlorophyll in the leaf cells will have been unable to absorb sunlight.

REPRODUCTION

THE basic principle behind the way that plants reproduce (make offspring) is the same as it is for animals. To create a new life, a sex cell from a male part must combine with a sex cell from a female part. Most animals are either male or female, whereas most plants contain both male and female parts.

BRINGING MALE AND FEMALE TOGETHER

Flowering plants (flowers, trees or shrubs) make up the majority of plants. In most flowering plants, the male sex cells are contained in tiny grains called pollen, found in a male part called the anther. The female cells are found in a female part called the carpel. A male cell from one flower needs to be introduced to a female cell in another flower of the same type. This flower may be on the same plant, or it may be on another plant of the same type. The transfer of male cells to female parts is called pollination.

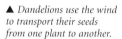

▲ *Dandelions use the wind to transport their seeds from one plant to another.*

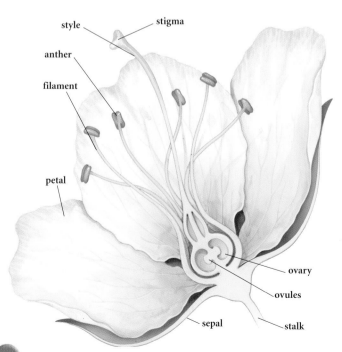

style — stigma

anther

filament

petal

ovary

ovules

sepal

stalk

NATURE'S HELPERS

As plants cannot move around, the transfer of sex cells from one flower to another needs outside help. Insects or the wind are the main helpers. Insects eat nectar, a sugary substance found at the base of many flower petals. As they feed they brush against pollen-covered anthers, collecting a dusting of pollen on their bodies. When they fly to another flower to feed, the

◀ *Pollination takes place when male cells from the anther of one plant meet the female part called the stigma in another flower of the same type.*

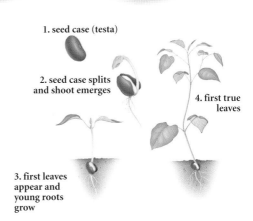

▶ *Insects such as bees go from one flower to another in search of food. As they go, pollen from one flower sticks to their legs and is rubbed off in another flower, allowing pollination to take place.*

pollen brushes against the female parts of that flower and the reproductive process begins. Flowers that are pollinated in this way generally have brightly coloured petals to attract insects.

Some plants have flowers with very little colour. They produce pollen, but no nectar, and are not attractive to insects. Catkins – the long, dangling flowers of birch trees – are a good example. Pollen is blown by the wind from the birch's male catkins to separate female flowers. After reaching the female part of a flower, a pollen grain sends out a tube that grows down through the style of the female part to the female sex cell – the egg or ovum. The male and female cells then combine in a process called fertilization, and a new life begins.

1. seed case (testa)

2. seed case splits and shoot emerges

3. first leaves appear and young roots grow

4. first true leaves

▲ *A seed breaks through its outer case, or testa, and the radicle (first root) begins to grow.*

NEW LIFE

A tiny new plant is called an embryo. Small and delicate, the embryo is surrounded by a protective case, and usually a food store, too, called a seed. Even with its casing, a new plant would have a hard time surviving if it simply fell to the ground near its parent. It would have to compete with the parent for water, minerals and light. So seeds use different methods to be transported away from the parent plant. Some stick to the fur of passing animals, some are eaten by them and are deposited in their dung, and some are carried by the wind or by water.

SEED DISPERSAL

Plants use different methods to send their seeds to places where they can grow – a process known as seed dispersal. Some seeds are carried through the air inside small fruits. Maple and sycamore trees produce 'helicopters' like this one, which carry the seeds on the wind to new places. Dandelion seeds are also blown by the wind.

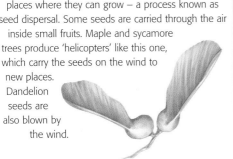

FUNGI AND LICHENS

WHEN scientists first began to group living things, they divided everything into just two kingdoms – animals and plants. This neat division no longer seems correct. Many living things that were once considered to be plants are now grouped in other kingdoms. Some are familiar to us, such as fungi – mushrooms, toadstools, moulds, mildews, rusts and their relatives. Lichens, which grow on rocks and tree bark, are a combination of fungi and simple plants called algae, which lack proper stems, roots, leaves and flowers.

▲ *Diatoms are tiny single-celled organisms that resemble plants and live in the sea. They are usually included in a kingdom of living things called protists (single-celled organisms).*

fruiting body sheds spores

spores germinate and grow into mycelium

fruiting body forms

▲ *Mushrooms reproduce by releasing millions of tiny spores. The mycelium is the first stage of a new mushroom. This develops a fruiting body, which is able to produce more spores.*

VITAL DIFFERENCES

Fungi were once thought to be simple plants with no leaves. We now know that there are many differences between fungi and true plants. Some of these differences are linked to the types of chemicals that make up fungi, which are different from those of even the simplest true plants. More importantly, fungi cannot make their own food in the way that most plants do (by the process called photosynthesis). Instead, fungi absorb food from living or dead organisms. Many mushroom species, for example, feed on the rotting wood and manure on which they grow.

▼ *Many different species of fungi grow in dark, damp places such as forest floors. They feed on rotting wood and other plant material.*

inkcap

slimy skull cap

parasol

puffball

field mushroom

fairy ring mushroom

▲ *Most algae live in the sea or along its shores, and are familiar to us as seaweeds.*

SIMPLEST PLANTS

Most types of algae live in or on water. They are described as simple plants. Most are able to produce food from sunlight and water in the process called photosynthesis, and the way they reproduce is very basic. They have no flowers or blossoms, and simply release their sex cells into the water. Collections of tiny algae form as 'scum' on a pond's surface. On the seashore, algae grow much larger, as a huge variety of bladderwracks, kelps, oarweeds, carragheen and other seaweeds. The leaf-like part of a seaweed is called the frond. It is carried on a stalk-like stipe. Some seaweeds may seem to have roots, but these do not absorb water and minerals, like true roots. Instead they are sucker-like 'holdfasts' that simply anchor the seaweed to rocks.

▲ *Lichens are a partnership between algae, which produce food, and fungi, which absorb water.*

▲ *Kelp, or seaweed, is a type of alga that can grow up to 65 m long.*

WORKING TOGETHER

Lichens are able to survive in some of the most difficult conditions on Earth – in poor soils, on rocks and in some of the coldest regions near the Arctic. Most lichens grow very slowly. They can survive in such harsh conditions because they are made up of both fungi and algae – neither of which would survive on their own. Usually, a layer of algae forms the middle of a 'sandwich' of two layers of fungi. The fungi layers of a lichen protect and absorb water for the algae, while the algae produce food both for themselves and for the fungi, through the process of photosynthesis.

dryad's saddle

wood blewit

fly agaric

death cap

many-zoned bracket fungus

devil's boletus

mealy tubaria

PRIMITIVE PLANTS

THE first plants appeared in the water many hundreds of millions of years ago. Then, about 435 million years ago, they adapted to live on land. The earliest land plants developed from algae that had lived in the sea. On land they found no soil, only rocks and stones. But at first their survival was helped by the fact that there were no animals to eat them. Some of the most familiar plants around us, such as mosses and ferns, have changed little since that time.

▼ *Horsetails are tall, fern-shaped plants. They have leaf-like parts that resemble the spokes of a wheel, and cone-shaped reproductive parts. Horsetails often grow as weeds on disturbed ground.*

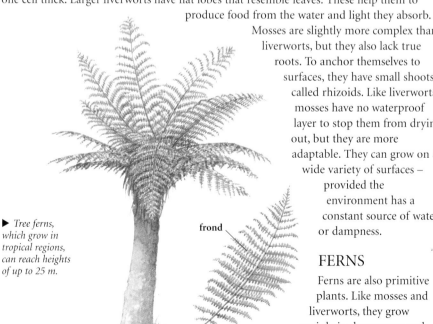

BARE ESSENTIALS

Mosses and their relatives, the liverworts, are low-growing plants found mostly in moist areas. They have no waterproof outer layer to protect them from drying out. They also lack a system of vessels to carry water and other materials to different parts of the plant. Instead, they must remain low-growing and close to their supply of water, which they absorb directly rather than through roots. Liverworts are very basic, with flat bodies that are sometimes just one cell thick. Larger liverworts have flat lobes that resemble leaves. These help them to produce food from the water and light they absorb.

Mosses are slightly more complex than liverworts, but they also lack true roots. To anchor themselves to surfaces, they have small shoots called rhizoids. Like liverworts, mosses have no waterproof layer to stop them from drying out, but they are more adaptable. They can grow on a wide variety of surfaces – provided the environment has a constant source of water or dampness.

▶ *Tree ferns, which grow in tropical regions, can reach heights of up to 25 m.*

frond

FERNS

Ferns are also primitive plants. Like mosses and liverworts, they grow mainly in damp areas and

▲ *A liverwort has a two-stage life-cycle, with sex cells developing from a part called the prothallus.*

button-like structures containing spores

▲ *Ferns reproduce by releasing spores from button-like structures on the undersides of their leaves.*

need to have a ready supply of water or moisture. But ferns also have some of the features of more advanced plants, including proper roots, stems and leaves, and systems of tubes called vascular bundles that carry water and sap. These adaptations mean that ferns can grow much larger than mosses or liverworts. Most ferns have no trunks. Their feathery leaves, called fronds, grow directly from a short, underground stem called a rhizome. But in tropical regions, where there is plentiful sunlight and lots of rain, tall tree-ferns with woody trunks can grow as high as 25 metres. Their branchless trunks are topped with clusters of fronds.

USING SPORES

One of the main differences between primitive plants – including ferns – and more advanced plants is the way they reproduce. Primitive plants produce spores instead of seeds. A fern, for example, produces thousands of tiny spores that are blown to a new place by the wind. These grow into small, inconspicuous plants that then make male and female sex cells. A new fern can only grow if these male and female cells join together on the small plant produced by the spore. This two-part life cycle is called 'alternation of generation'.

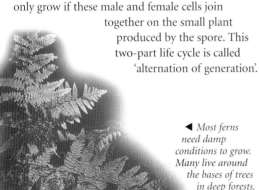

◀ *Most ferns need damp conditions to grow. Many live around the bases of trees in deep forests.*

▲ *Liverworts are flat and spongy, and thrive along streams and rivers.*

CONIFERS

I T IS hard to imagine just what tiny mosses and ferns could have in common with giant conifer trees such as the redwoods of North America. But there is one main similarity. Neither the primitive plants nor the redwoods reproduce from flowers. Redwoods are just one of 500-plus species of conifers. Other conifers include spruces, firs, larches, cypresses, junipers, hemlocks, podocarps and pine trees. Like all more advanced plants, conifers use seeds (rather than the spores of primitive plants) to reproduce. Unlike flowering plants, which carry their seeds inside fruits or nuts, conifers carry them in woody cones. The word 'conifer' comes from this structure – the cone. One tree may produce thousands of cones in a year.

▲ *The monkey puzzle tree is a distinctive conifer from the Andes mountains of South America.*

▼ *Conifers come in many shapes and sizes and grow in most parts of the world. The tallest conifers, such as Douglas firs, can grow to more than 100 m in height.*

WHAT IS A CONE?

Conifers have separate male and female cones made up of a series of scales. Pollen (containing male sex cells) is produced on male cones, which are generally smaller and more ball-shaped or button-like. The female sex cells usually lie on the scales of the female cones. Wind carries pollen grains to the female sex cells and fertilization takes place.

| Italian cypress | Stone pine | Phoenician juniper | Cedar of Lebanon | Coast redwood | Norway spruce | Silver fir |

▶ *This shows a cross-section of a ginkgo, or maidenhair tree, a close relative of conifers.*

The male and female cells fuse to form a seed (a new life). Female cones start out soft, but after fertilization they harden with woody tissue, which protects the seeds until they are ripe. Once the seeds are ripe, the cone either opens slightly or falls apart to let them fall to the ground.

WINTER GREENERY

A conifer's overall shape makes it easy to identify. It has a straight trunk with horizontal branches that are progressively shorter nearer the top of the tree, and its outline resembles a tall, pointed cone. Typical conifers prefer cooler climates, and most are 'evergreen' – their needle-shaped leaves stay on the tree all year round.

GIANTS OF THE PLANT KINGDOM

The largest of all conifers are the sequoias of western North America. One type is the redwood, which can be up to 112 metres in height and very bulky. Other sequoias are shorter and even more massive, such as the tree named the General Sherman, in Sequoia National Park, USA. It measures 84 metres tall and 25.3 metres wide at a point 1.4 metres above the ground. Scientists estimate that it weighs about 2,500 tonnes.

▲ *Dark conifers stand out among the new green leaves of deciduous trees.*

▲ *Some redwoods are more than 7 m across – wide enough for a car to drive through a hole in the trunk.*

FLOWERING PLANTS

THE largest of all groups in the plant kingdom, containing more than 250,000 different species, is the group of flowering plants. This huge group contains not only the plants we call blooms, or 'flowers', such as daffodils, roses and tulips, but also grasses, herbs, vegetables and all the trees, shrubs and bushes that are not conifers. A typical flowering plant produces flowers of some kind, fruits and seeds. The plant's female sex cell is found inside a part called the ovary. When this cell is fertilized by a male sex cell, the male and female cells fuse and a seed is formed within the ovary. Seeds may be surrounded by fleshy fruits or berries, such as plums and raspberries, or by hard cases, as in nuts.

▲ *Squirrels enjoy eating the seeds inside nuts, which they store for the winter.*

▲ *Most grass-like flowers, such as these rushes (reedmace or bulrush), cast their pollen into the wind from fluffy flower parts.*

THE ANGIOSPERMS

Flowering plants make up the great majority of the greenery on Earth. The scientific name for flowering plants is angiosperms, from the Greek words *angio*, meaning 'enclosed', and *sperma*, meaning 'seed'. Their stems, leaves, shoots, buds, seeds and fruits are important food for all kinds of herbivorous animals. Some animals are particularly attracted to juicy, fleshy fruits. When they eat the fruits, the seeds pass through the animals' digestive systems and emerge in their droppings, ready to grow.

▶ *Hundreds of flowers blossom each spring on trees such as the horse chestnut, popularly called a conker tree.*

MONOCOTS AND DICOTS

Flowering plants are divided into two main groups, depending on the number of food stores inside their seeds. Monocotyledons have only one

cotyledon, or food store. They include grasses, rushes, sedges, flowers such as orchids and lilies, and palm trees. Most of these plants have leaves with thickenings, or veins, that lie in rows parallel to each other. They also have flower parts arranged in threes or multiples of three. Dicotyledons have two cotyledons. They include the great majority of flowers, herbs and trees not mentioned above. Most of them have leaf veins that form a branching pattern, like a tree itself.

ANNUALS AND PERENNIALS

Different species adopt a life-cycle that will ensure their survival. Some plants, known as annuals, grow from seeds, produce flowers and seeds, and die within a single year. Others, known as biennials, work on a two-year schedule. In their first year they grow and then die back. The following year, they grow further and reproduce. Plants called perennials live for many years. They continue to produce flowers and seeds each spring, allowing new plants to grow. Most bushes and trees are perennials.

PLANT EXTREME

The rafflesia flower grows up to 90 cm across and is the world's largest bloom. It smells like rotting meat!

▼ *Bamboos are types of grasses with tall, stiff, woody stems.*

▼ *Chestnut trees produce many tall clusters of flowers in spring.*

▶ *The saguaro cactus blooms only at night. It produces white flowers.*

▼ *The flowers of the prickly pear cactus appear only rarely.*

GRASSLAND PLANTS

EACH of the world's continents, except Antarctica, has large areas of wide plains covered with grass. These mainly flat, rolling regions have different names depending on where they are in the world: in North America they are called prairies, in South America they are pampas, in Africa they are savannah, and in Europe and Asia they are called steppes.

WHERE AND WHY

Grasslands usually form in areas where water evaporates faster than it falls as rain. These areas would become deserts if they did not receive just enough rain in one season to support flowering herbs and different types of grasses. The rainy season is summertime in grasslands near the Equator and winter in grasslands farther from the Equator. Grasslands lie mainly in the centre of continents, away from coastal areas where rainfall is more constant (from clouds that form over the oceans). The limited amount of rain that falls on grasslands is not enough to support large trees with shallow roots. Grasses have adapted to long, dry periods by having deep root systems that are protected from the heat of the Sun. Some species of grass send roots down more than five metres to find water.

▲ *At the start of the rainy season, huge storms drench the parched grassland plains.*

acacia tree

▼ *For most of the year, the African plains are covered with grasses that gradually turn from green to brown in the fierce Sun and drying winds.*

giraffes

zebra herd

marabou stork

drying waterhole

lion

▶ *Elephants eat mainly grass stems and shoots, but also browse on the trees dotting the African savannah.*

RHYTHM OF THE SEASONS

During the brief rainy season, grasses and herbs grow quickly. The land becomes green with new growth, and brightly coloured flowers blanket the ground. The flowers create seeds rapidly, but dry out and die once the rains stop. Fires often start naturally on grasslands, usually from lightning strikes. The ash from burning plants nourishes the soil further, allowing new plants to grow quickly when the rains fall again. Naturally occurring fires also prevent forests from spreading across the edges of grassland areas, and stop desert shrubs from gradually taking over.

Africa's grasslands are home to huge herds of grazing animals. They arrive as soon as the rains have turned the grasslands green. The plants and the animals help to feed each other. The huge amount of droppings that the animals leave enriches the soil with nutrients.

GRASSLANDS CREATED BY HUMANS

Although most large grasslands have developed naturally over many thousands of years, others have been created by humans. The grassland farming regions of Europe and parts of other continents were once covered in forest. People cleared the forest to create farmland, using the wood for building and fuel. If left undisturbed, such land would gradually revert to forest, because it receives enough rain to support large trees.

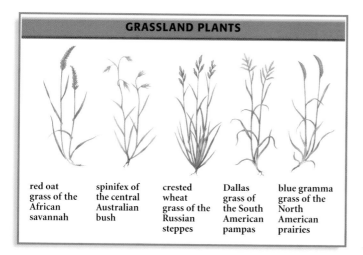

GRASSLAND PLANTS

red oat grass of the African savannah

spinifex of the central Australian bush

crested wheat grass of the Russian steppes

Dallas grass of the South American pampas

blue gramma grass of the North American prairies

▶ *The kangaroo is well adapted to life on the Australian grasslands. It feeds on small plants and grasses and its teeth are similar to those of sheep – perfect for grazing and browsing.*

IN THE FOREST

MUCH of the landscape of Canada and the vast area of northern Asia known as Siberia is covered in huge tracts of trees extending as far as the eye can see. These forests are the remains of great woodlands that once covered most of the cooler parts of the world. In most of Europe and the USA, this woodland has been cleared to make way for towns and cities, and to give farmers more land for growing crops.

COOL-CLIMATE CONIFERS

The great forests of Canada and Siberia are made up of conifer trees. Conifers in these regions have adapted to survive extremely cold winter weather – temperatures can remain below -30°C for months at a time. In such cold temperatures, water – which all plants need for survival – is locked away as ice all winter long. Conifers have adapted by having thin leaves like needles. The narrow shape of the needles allows little water to evaporate, so the tree is able to conserve its water supplies for the dry winter period. The conifers are also evergreen, which means their leaves do not fall to the ground each year.

In most of eastern North America and western Europe, where winter temperatures drop below freezing, but not so severely or for as long as in northern regions, forests contain both conifers and deciduous trees – oak, elm, beech and maple, for example. Deciduous trees lose their leaves in autumn. Shedding

UNDERGROUND

rhizomes

bulbs

tubers

In winter, some plants store food in rhizomes, bulbs or tubers. Rhizomes are stems under the surface, bulbs are balls of fleshy leaves, and tubers are parts of stems or roots swollen with extra food.

bracket fungus

birch sapling

ferns

mushrooms

leaves is another adaptation that allows trees to conserve water until milder temperatures and more rain arrive in spring.

AUTUMN COLOUR

The leaves of some trees become more colourful just before they fall, turning to shades of yellow, gold, orange and red. The colours change as the leaves lose their chlorophyll (green colouring), allowing other colours to become visible. Each year, millions of visitors travel to New England and eastern Canada in North America to see the autumn colours.

Forest trees in warmer areas, such as the Mediterranean, are both evergreen – like most conifers – and also broadleaved, like deciduous trees. The leaves are broad in order to capture enough light to create food through photosynthesis. They remain on the trees all year because the milder winters mean there is a constant supply of water, so evaporation does not have to be as severely restricted as in colder regions.

▲ *Forest fires, caused by lightning or by humans, usually develop after a long, dry period.*

▲ *Wildflowers grow well in forests and other areas where humans have not added chemicals to the soil.*

THE FOREST COMMUNITY

A forest contains much more than just its trees. Small flowers grow on the forest floor and in grassy openings called glades, especially in early spring. Shrubs and small trees spend their lives in the shadow of taller trees. Mosses, ferns and other smaller plants also grow in the shade. Forests support a wide variety of animal life, too. Birds, insects and mammals rely on forest plants for food and protection. In return, these animals supply plants with nutrients (from their droppings) and spread seeds and pollen through their feeding and movements.

▼ *Many different types of plants and fungi live together in the forest. Fungi break down rotting wood, helping to clear the forest floor for other plants.*

fly agarics

bluebells

cuckoo pint

foxglove

acorn

THE RAINFORESTS

▲ *The world's largest rainforest lies in the valley of the Amazon River in South America.*

D ENSE, tropical forests known as rainforests are found in areas near the Equator, where it is wet and warm all year round. Equatorial regions have never had very cold weather (unlike regions that were affected by the ice ages). A history of constant sunshine and rain has allowed some rainforests to survive for millions of years, whereas forests in areas that were affected by climate changes are relatively 'young'.

PROTECT THE RAINFOREST

Over such a long period of time, and with such ideal growing conditions, many different types of plants have had a chance to develop in the rainforests. Today, these forests contain a wider variety of living things – both plants and animals – than any other part of the world. For this reason, conservationists are very concerned to protect areas of rainforest that are being cut down by people wanting to grow crops or build settlements.

THE ROLE OF RAIN

Most rainforests receive between 150 and 400 centimetres of rain each year. Unlike grassland areas, they do not have a dry season, so the plants do not dry out and die or become dormant (inactive). Plants grow quickly in the warm, wet conditions. In order to expose their leaves to sunlight (to make food by photosynthesis), some rainforest trees grow up to 50 metres tall.

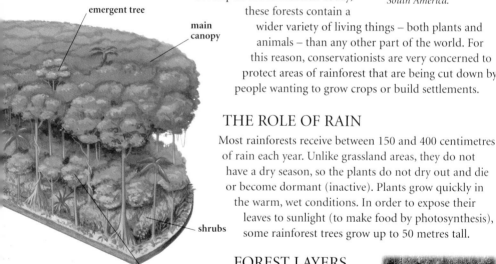

emergent tree

main canopy

shrubs

understorey

▲ *The layers of the rainforest include emergent tall trees, the canopy, the understorey and the shrubby layer near the ground.*

FOREST LAYERS

The leaves of the tallest trees form a scattered top level of the rainforest. Sunlight passing between these trees allows a second, lower, more even layer to grow – the main canopy, and the densest part of the rainforest. The canopy is tangled with vines and epiphytes. Epiphytes have no roots and grow on tree branches, absorbing water from rain or damp air. Because the middle layer blocks out

▶ *Ferns cover the forest floor in the temperate rainforest around Fox Glacier in New Zealand.*

most of the remaining sunlight, the forest's lower layers – on or near the ground – have few plants. Some seedlings grow there, as well as fungi and other organisms that do not need much light.

▲ These Amazon orchids are epiphytes – plants that grow on other plants.

MOUNTAIN RAINFORESTS

The largest rainforests, such as those beside the Amazon River in South America and the Congo River in Africa, are flat and low-lying. But some tropical forests blanket the sides of mountains. The trees here are shorter, and more plants grow on or near the ground. The highest mountain rainforests are called 'cloud' forests, because much of the forest is covered in low clouds, providing moisture for all kinds of mosses, ferns and herbs.

harpy eagle

spider monkey

anaconda

WATER CYCLE

Earth's water is constantly moving in a process called the water cycle. Seas, lakes and rivers store water, which evaporates into the air. Precipitation (rain) falls when the air cools. The rainwater is taken up by trees and other plants, which act like sponges. Cutting down forests removes the 'sponge' and greatly disrupts the cycle.

prevailing wind

excess runoff

blue-grey tanager

bromeliad

flaming poison arrow frog

▶ Covering much of northern South America, the Amazon rainforest is home to more species of plants and animals than any other place on Earth. Some colourful species are shown here.

DESERT PLANTS

A TYPICAL plant has four main needs, two of which are abundant in most deserts – sunshine and warmth. But the other two, mineral-rich soil and water, are not. Yet even in the world's driest places, a variety of plants find a way to thrive.

WHAT ARE DESERTS?

Rain falls nearly everywhere on Earth, returning to the air through evaporation. Deserts form where the rate of evaporation is greater than the rainfall (less than 25 centimetres a year). Many deserts are extremely hot during the day, others are warm. But at night temperatures generally fall to well below freezing. These huge temperature swings are typical, because deserts lack cloud cover to hold the daytime warmth through the night. All deserts – hot or cold – are usually windy, with poor soils.

The very driest places in most deserts have no plants, because the soil is too rocky or sandy to support them. But in most areas there are usually plants with special adaptations to cope with daytime heat and lack of water. Adaptations

▲ *Joshua trees, native to the deserts of North America, grow to a height of about 9 m. They provide food and shelter for many desert animals.*

▼ *The largest plants in most deserts are called succulents. Their thick, fleshy stems or leaves keep water inside the plant by reducing evaporation.*

include deep roots, able to reach water far underground, or wide-spreading roots that spread themselves close to the surface. Shallow roots are able to take up surface moisture quickly from heavy dews and occasional rains.

Some flowering desert plants are visible for only a few days. Their seeds lie dormant (inactive) in the soil, perhaps for years, until a good shower enables them to germinate and bloom quickly. These quick-growing flowers are called ephemerals. Their whole life-cycle – from one generation of seeds to the next – can last just two or three weeks.

SPINY DEFENCES

Desert plants have special adaptations to stop water evaporating from their leaves. Most have small, hard, tough-coated leaves. The reduced surface area means there is less

▲ *Even though the Namib desert lies on the southwest coast of Africa, near the Atlantic Ocean, it has very few desert plants.*

leaf exposed to the hot sunlight that makes the plant's water evaporate. Other desert plants, such as cacti, have no leaves at all. The process of photosynthesis, by which plants convert sunlight into energy, is done in their stems. Cacti and other desert plants, such as acacias and tamarisks, store precious water in their stems and roots. Sharp thorns, which are actually modified leaves, guard their water from animal invaders. These plants may take in and store valuable carbon dioxide only at night. During the day, their pores are closed to prevent evaporation.

▶ *Palm trees grow in the poor soil of oases – areas of desert that have a regular supply of fresh water.*

▲ *Dates are the fruit of the date palm, which thrives in the oases of the Sahara desert in northern Africa. Dates are grown as a crop in many other regions.*

CACTI

Cacti are a particular type of succulent. The 1,650 different species of cactus are nearly all native to the Americas. A typical cactus has a fleshy stem and narrow, needle-like leaves.

POLAR PLANT LIFE

JUST as desert plants are adapted to make the most of brief periods of rain, plants in the northern polar region must await brief periods of warmth. For the rest of the year (up to ten months) they may lie buried beneath snow and ice in temperatures of -40°C or colder. In the southern polar region, most of the land of Antarctica is covered with ice all year round. Only a few small patches of thin soil thaw briefly in the southern summer. These areas support about 300 species of algae, mosses, lichens and other simple plants, and a handful of small flowering herbs.

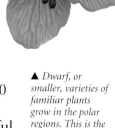

▲ *Dwarf, or smaller, varieties of familiar plants grow in the polar regions. This is the flower from an Arctic dwarf willow.*

THE VAST TUNDRA

The area immediately around the North Pole is a frozen ocean, so no plants grow there. But around the shores of the ocean, within the Arctic Circle, are vast regions of boggy, marshy land called tundra. The Arctic tundra supports more than 400 species of flowering plants, including heathers or lings, crowberry, bilberry, anemones, stonecrops and saxifrages. Other plants include mosses, lichens, grasses (three to five centimetres high), sedges (grasslike plants) and heather (up to 20 centimetres high). Only a few trees can grow on the tundra, because even in summer the soil – known as permafrost – is frozen below the top 30 centimetres.

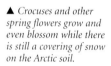

▲ *Crocuses and other spring flowers grow and even blossom while there is still a covering of snow on the Arctic soil.*

BRIEF SUMMER

Colourful flowers blossom on the tundra during the brief summer weeks, when the Sun never sets. Short, stunted, twisted willow and birch trees cling to the ground in more protected hollows, spreading their roots wide in the shallow areas of thawed soil. Caribou, or

▼ *Grazing animals such as caribou (reindeer) and moose (elk) find food on the tundra floor in the short spring and summer months. Many wildflowers seem to blossom overnight.*

PERMAFROST

Most plants in polar regions must grow in the top 30 cm or so of soil. Below that depth, the soil remains constantly frozen – even during the summer. This is called the permafrost region.

reindeer, scrape away the snow to feed on reindeer moss – a type of lichen.

The only part of Antarctica with a real variety of plants is the Antarctic Peninsula, which juts northwards and extends just beyond the Antarctic Circle. About 350 plant species – mostly lichens, mosses and algae – grow there, along with three species of flowering plant.

OTHER COLD REGIONS

The polar regions are not the only places on Earth where plants have adjusted to bitterly cold temperatures. The weather is extremely cold at the tops of mountains in the Alps, Himalayas, Rockies, Andes and other snow-capped ranges. High on these peaks are small plants – often called arctic or alpine species – normally found in the polar regions. Like polar plants, these mountain species show various adaptations to cold. Their leaves are hairy, to withstand cold and frost. The plants grow low down out of the wind. They often form small mounds, or cushions, in which the leaves and shoots in the centre are protected from the cold by those around the outside.

▼ *Because polar lands are so far from the Equator, the length of daylight changes greatly over the course of a year. The Sun never rises above the horizon during winter, but it never sets for a few weeks around midsummer. People call this the Midnight Sun.*

PUTTING PLANTS TO USE

W E all depend on plants every day in order to survive. Our planet needs plants for many reasons. Plants form the basis of the food chain – the cycle of life that keeps a region, and the whole planet, in balance. Animals, including human beings, eat either plants or other animals that rely on plants for their own food.
Although we eat only a tiny proportion of all the many plant species, plants as a whole continue to keep the world healthy by producing oxygen as they feed themselves by photosynthesis.

WIDER NEEDS

▲ *Every spring, pipes in sugar maple trees tap the sap into buckets. The liquid sap is heated until the water boils away, leaving maple syrup.*

Many of the world's largest nations, such as China and India, rely on just a few types of plants, such as rice, for most of their food. Countries also make money by selling plant products to other countries – coffee, cocoa, cotton and cereals, for example.

Timber from forest trees provides us with building materials and furniture. Other plants are grown to produce fibres for fabrics and clothing.

A MATTER OF LIFE AND DEATH

Our need for plants does not end with food, shelter and clothing. About one-half of

▲ *Biosphere 2 was an enclosed living space where people stayed for months on end. They conducted experiments to grow many types of plants in conditions similar to those on a space station.*

▼ *These six products are a few of the hundreds of natural medicines that can be extracted directly from herbs and other plants.*

golden seal

echinacea

bee pollen

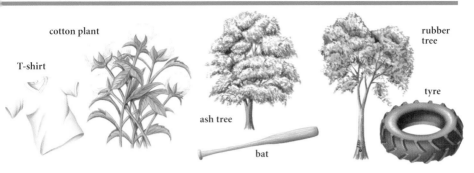

cotton plant

T-shirt

ash tree

bat

rubber tree

tyre

▲ *Three of the most widely used plant products are cotton, wood and rubber. They are shown here with the plants from which they are derived.*

STAPLE FOODS

Each region around the world has its major food crops. Many are types of grasses called cereals. Rice (shown here) – the world's major staple crop – is a cereal. It is grown in most warm regions, especially Asia. Other cereals include wheat, corn (maize), barley, oats, rye, sorghum and millet. Root or underground crops include potatoes, sweet potatoes, turnips, carrots and swedes. Fruit trees and bushes such as apple, pear and orange yield a further range of foods.

the medicines we use to heal sickness and cure disease come from plants. Their leaves, stems, flowers and sap have been used since earliest times for medicinal purposes. Today many medical drugs are tailor-made in the laboratory, but scientists often use plant substances as their starting points. Scientists can now alter the genes (the growing and living instructions) in plants such as soybean to make them grow faster or better able to resist drought and pests. Some people believe that these genetically modified plants could help to feed the world. Others fear the consequences of tampering with nature.

Korean ginseng

Saint John's wort

ginkgo biloba

QUIZ

1. What percent of all animal species have backbones?
2. What is an exoskeleton?
3. How does a boa constrictor snake kill its prey?
4. What type of mammal gives birth to tiny offspring, which then crawl into a pouch on their mother to continue growing?
5. What do we call an animal's ability to blend into background colour or patterns, in order to be almost 'invisible' to attackers?
6. *Archaeopteryx* was an ancestor of what sort of animal?
7. What is the name of the large group of animals that have no backbones?
8. How long does an adult mayfly live?
9. What is gestation?
10. What type of animal has 'warts', which are sometimes poisonous, on the surface of its skin?
11. How does a bat find its food?
12. What type of animal can detach its tail to distract an attacker?
13. Fossils are usually found in what type of rock?
14. What do we call the sensitive sheets near a fish's mouth that filter oxygen from the water that passes through them?
15. Where do Barbary apes, Europe's only primates, live?
16. What does the mammary gland of an adult female mammal produce?
17. For how many years does a baby elephant rely on its mother's milk?
18. How many legs does an insect have?
19. What is unusual about rheas, cassowaries and kiwis?
20. What is the main food of a carnivore?

ANSWERS

1. One percent
2. The tough outer layer of arthropods and some other animals.
3. It wraps itself around another animal and slowly crushes it to death.
4. A marsupial
5. Camouflage
6. Birds
7. Invertebrates
8. One day
9. The time that it takes for a mammal to develop inside its mother before it is ready to be born.
10. A toad
11. It sends out high-pitched squeaks and then listens for the echoes that bounce back off insects and other objects.
12. A lizard
13. Sedimentary rock (made from layers of once-living things)
14. Gills
15. Gibraltar
16. Milk to nourish her young.
17. Nearly 5
18. Six (three pairs)
19. They are all birds that cannot fly.
20. Meat

ANIMALS

CREATURES have colonized all parts of our planet – they can be found flying high in the sky, crawling in dark caves deep underground, clambering on icy mountain peaks and creeping on the bottom of the sea. The animals most familiar to us live around towns, on farmland and in woods and meadows. They include butterflies, bees and other insects, spiders, worms, birds and furry mammals such as cats, dogs, deer and squirrels.

Habitats that are less familiar to people, such as deserts, marshes, mudflats and deep lakes, also teem with weird and wonderful creatures. Tropical rainforests and coral reefs are especially rich in animal life. Fossil remains show that many other kinds of creatures – long since extinct – once lived on our planet. These ranged from small marine animals such as trilobites to the mighty dinosaurs.

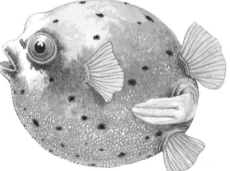

WHAT ARE ANIMALS?

THERE are five kingdoms, or major groups, of living things, the largest being animals. Scientists have described and named more than one million species, or kinds, of animals. All animals share certain features. They are all multicellular, which means they are made up of many cells – the tiny 'building blocks' of living things. They also all need to take in ready-made food, which is one of the main things that makes them different from plants. Plants make their own food from non-living things.

▲ On a tropical coral reef, animals such as sponges and anemones are often difficult to distinguish from the varied plant life.

SEARCHING FOR FOOD

Animals have developed almost as many ways of finding food as there are items to eat. Herbivorous creatures, as diverse as antelopes and parrot-fish, consume only plant foods: leaves, grass, fruits or seaweed. Carnivorous animals are meat-eaters, specially adapted to killing and eating other animals. Omnivores, such as bears and monkeys, can eat both meat and plants.

▼ An animal's colours and patterns serve many purposes. They attract mates, allow the animal to blend in with the surroundings, and even serve to scare away attackers.

Special features, or adaptations, help each type of animal to perform food-related jobs suited to its habitat and diet. A giraffe's incredibly long neck, for example, is ideal for reaching leaves and twigs near the tops of tall trees, while a bat's keen hearing allows it to detect insect prey as it hunts at night.

Not all animals are able to move from one place to another. Simple sea animals called polyps, which form coral reefs, catch tiny pieces of food as they flow past in the water.

◀ The male narwhal, a type of whale, has a 3-m tusk that it uses in battles with rival males. The tusk is an elongated upper tooth.

KEEPING ENEMIES AWAY

Some animals are armed with weapons such as tusks, antlers or horns. A male deer displays its antlers to intimidate other males, to attract females and to ward off predators. A skunk's defence is a foul-smelling liquid that it ejects at its predators. Other animals, such as tortoises, have a hard, armour-like shell for protection. Many creatures avoid being seen by predators by being camouflaged – their colours and patterns allow them to blend into the background.

▼ Animals with backbones (vertebrates) make up only 1 percent of the million or more animal species. There are more arthropods (including insects and spiders) than all other species combined.

THE SIMPLE ANIMALS

▲ *Most of the 1,500 species of starfish have five arms. If one gets broken off, another will grow in its place.*

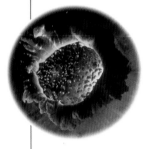

▲ *Tiny, soft-bodied polyps make stony, cup-shaped cases for themselves, which form the rock of a coral reef.*

▼ *Brittlestars, relatives of starfish, feed on decaying matter on the muddy sea bed.*

ANIMALS that lack a backbone – a spinal or vertebral column – are known as invertebrates. Some, such as insects and mussels, have a firm outer covering to support their bodies. Others, such as worms and squid, lack a hard body casing. Although invertebrates are mostly smaller than vertebrates, in many ways they are just as complex. They have specialized body parts such as wings, legs and eyes, and they display a wide variety of intricate and fascinating behaviour.

▲ *The nudibranch is a sea slug. Its 'branches' are gills, which it uses for breathing.*

FILTERING FOR FOOD

The simplest invertebrates, such as sponges, are made up of two layers of cells. A sponge cannot move about, and it has no arms or legs with which to catch prey. Instead, it obtains food from the surrounding sea water. Tiny, whip-like hairs, called cilia, direct water through the sponge's body cells, allowing it to filter out minute food particles from the water.

Many ocean-dwelling invertebrates are predators. The anemone has a stalk-like body with a mouth at the upper end, surrounded by waving tentacles that resemble flower petals. The anemone uses its tentacles to

▼ *Anemones usually remain attached to rocks or coral, but they can shuffle slowly along on the base of their stalk to find a better site with more passing prey.*

catch and sting small fish and shrimps that pass by, and draw them into its mouth.

Another simple type of animal is the jellyfish. It drifts through the sea, largely at the mercy of winds and currents. But, like the anemone, it is an efficient predator. Its trailing tentacles trap small creatures and guide them towards its mouth, on the lower side of its body.

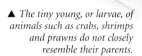

▲ The tiny young, or larvae, of animals such as crabs, shrimps and prawns do not closely resemble their parents.

WORMS AND SNAILS

There are more than 11,000 species of 'true' worms, such as earthworms, which have bodies made up of segments. Earthworms help keep soil fertile by turning it over and trapping air as they move through it. There are also many thousands of non-segmented worms, such as nematodes (roundworms). Some live inside other creatures, surviving by eating food inside the digestive system of the 'host' animal.

▲ Sponges are simple sea animals. They lack a brain or nerve system, and feed by filtering seawater.

Snails are members of the invertebrate group known as molluscs. Most are herbivores, but some attack other creatures. Molluscs also include slugs, sea slugs, shellfish, octopus, and the largest of all invertebrates – the giant squid, which can measure more than 10 metres long and weigh one tonne.

▲ Earthworms breathe through their skin, absorbing the air that gets trapped between tiny particles of soil.

TYPES OF CORAL

Living coral polyps build on the cup-like cases left behind by polyps that have died. As the polyps grow, spread and accumulate, they form the distinctive rocky shapes of a coral reef.

soft coral

mushroom coral

gorgonian coral

▲ The sea wasp is a type of jellyfish with a powerful sting – it can kill a person in less than four minutes.

INSECTS AND SPIDERS

INSECTS and spiders, along with scorpions, centipedes and crustaceans (such as woodlice, lobsters and crabs), all belong to a large group of invertebrates called arthropods. The word arthropod means 'jointed leg'. As well as having jointed legs, arthropods have segmented bodies and a hard skeleton on the outside, called an exoskeleton (as opposed to a skeleton on the inside, like humans have). Insects have three pairs of legs. Other arthropods usually have more – some millipedes have more than 100 pairs.

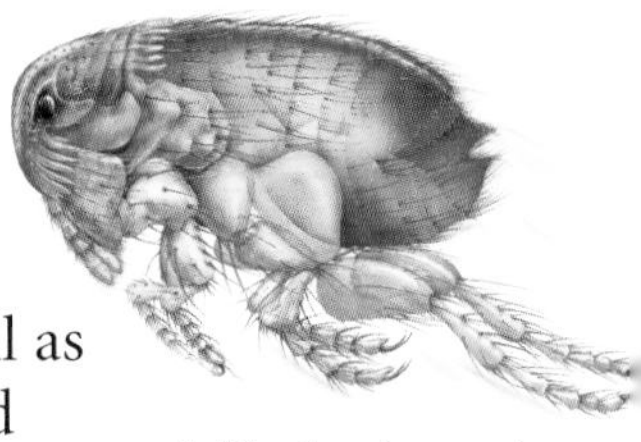

▲ *The tiny claws and hairs on the legs of a flea help it to anchor onto the skin of a host animal. It feeds by sucking the host's blood.*

INSECTS – A SUCCESS STORY

Insects are by far the most common types of animals. More than nine out of ten living species are insects. They flourish in nearly every part of the world, except under the sea and in the very coldest places.

Social insects – termites, ants, bees and wasps, for example – live together with their own kind in large, complex groups called colonies. Within a colony, the insects work together as a team to find food and shelter. Usually only one female in the colony, the queen, lays eggs. Many insects have effective defences against other animals. Bees and wasps, for example, can sting, while ants have a strong bite.

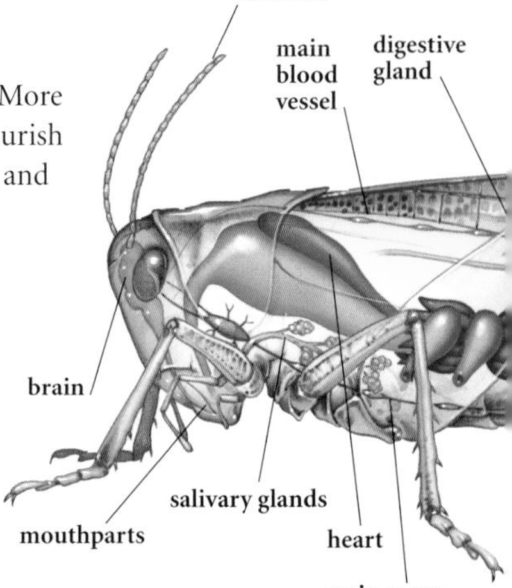

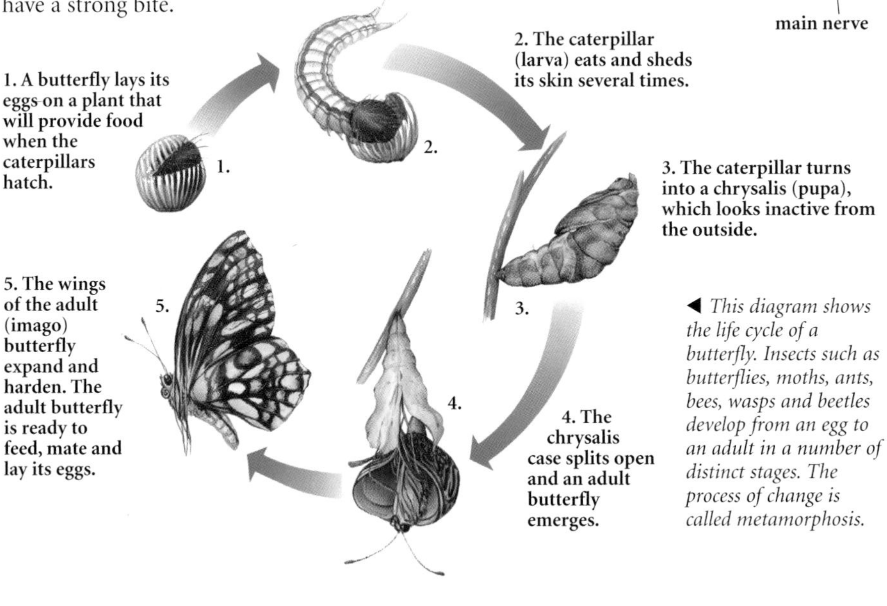

antenna

main blood vessel

digestive gland

brain

mouthparts

salivary glands

heart

main nerve

1. A butterfly lays its eggs on a plant that will provide food when the caterpillars hatch.

2. The caterpillar (larva) eats and sheds its skin several times.

3. The caterpillar turns into a chrysalis (pupa), which looks inactive from the outside.

5. The wings of the adult (imago) butterfly expand and harden. The adult butterfly is ready to feed, mate and lay its eggs.

4. The chrysalis case splits open and an adult butterfly emerges.

◄ *This diagram shows the life cycle of a butterfly. Insects such as butterflies, moths, ants, bees, wasps and beetles develop from an egg to an adult in a number of distinct stages. The process of change is called metamorphosis.*

▲ *Many spiders weave sticky webs to trap insects and other small animals for food.*

wing

hind gut

breathing tubes (trachea)

▲ *A grasshopper has the body parts of a typical insect. Insects breathe through a network of tubes (trachea) that lead from small holes (spiracles) along the body.*

THREE-PART BODIES

Insect bodies are made up of three separate sections. The front section is the head, which has eyes, a mouth and 'feelers', called antennae, used for sensing the environment. The middle section is the thorax, with legs and wings attached (although wings are missing on some species). The last section is the abdomen, which contains the body parts used for digesting food and reproducing. Insect offspring that resemble the adults are called nymphs. Other insect young change their appearance at least twice before they become adults, in a process called metamorphosis.

SPIDERS AND SCORPIONS

Spiders and scorpions form a group of arthropods called arachnids. Like insects, spiders and scorpions have a tough exoskeleton, but they have four pairs of legs instead of an insect's three. A spider has two main body parts – the one-piece cephalothorax, with the head and legs attached, and the abdomen. Unlike insects, spiders and scorpions lack antennae and wings. Instead, they have specialized mouths with pincer-like fangs called chelicerae, which they use to catch their food. All spiders and scorpions are predators, and nearly all are poisonous – the spider with its bite and the scorpion with its tail sting. A few spiders are venomous enough to harm people.

CRUSTACEANS

Most crustaceans live in water. Their bodies are divided into two sections, and they have at least ten pairs of legs. Lobsters, the largest crustaceans, have some of the toughest of all exoskeletons. They also have two pairs of long, sensitive antennae.

▲ *Lobsters have strong pincers, used to crush and tear food. They also have complicated eyes that jut out from the body.*

FISH

FISH were the first vertebrates (animals with backbones) to appear on Earth, about 500 million years ago. They remain the most numerous of all vertebrates – today there are more than 23,000 fish species around the world. Most fish have a number of fins to help them move about. The side-to-side movements of a fish's body and caudal fin, or tail, help to propel it forwards. The pairs of fins on the sides of the body help it to steer and slow down, and the fins on the upper and lower body provide stability.

▲ *Puffer fish, sometimes called blowfish, can inflate themselves to several times their normal size in order to scare off attackers.*

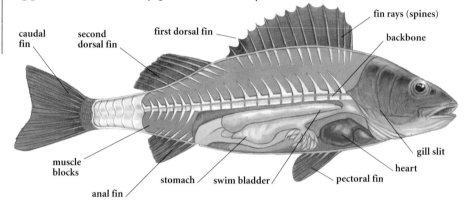

caudal fin

second dorsal fin

first dorsal fin

fin rays (spines)

backbone

muscle blocks

stomach

anal fin

swim bladder

pectoral fin

heart

gill slit

▲ *All fish are aquatic – they live in water. Most have a streamlined shape that enables them to swim quickly. They use their fins to move forwards and to steer themselves.*

BREATHING UNDER WATER

Like all animals, fish need oxygen to survive. They take in dissolved oxygen from the water through specialized organs called gills. Fish gills are thin, sensitive, feathery sheets, located inside chambers at either side of the back

DEEPWATER FISH

The silver-coloured hatchet fish lives deep in tropical waters.

The angler fish has a spine with a bulb of glowing flesh on the end that it uses to lure prey.

The lantern fish has a row of spots along its body that light up to attract a mate.

of the head. As water flows over the gills, oxygen dissolved in the water passes into the fish's bloodstream via blood vessels in the gills, and waste products from the fish's blood pass out into the water. The fish expels the water from its gill chambers through narrow gaps just behind its head, called gill slits.

Most fish die if they are out of water for more than a few minutes. However, a few fish, like the lungfish, have a lung that allows them to breathe air in much the same way as humans. Mudskippers and some eels can also survive out of water by carrying pools of water in their extra-large gill chambers.

UP AND DOWN

Most fish have a special organ called a swim bladder that enables them to move up and down. The swim bladder takes gases from the fish's blood and either fills up or deflates like a spongy balloon, according to whether the fish needs to rise or sink. It makes constant small adjustments to keep the fish at the same level in the water. The bladder also helps fish to withstand the pressure of the water at great depths.

Sharks, skates and rays do not have a swim bladder. They also lack a bony skeleton, and are known as cartilaginous fish.

▲ *Rays are related to sharks and live in nearly all waters around the world. Their pectoral (side) fins are greatly enlarged and resemble wings.*

▶ *Most of the 370 or more species of sharks are hunters. They use their keen sense of smell to locate prey.*

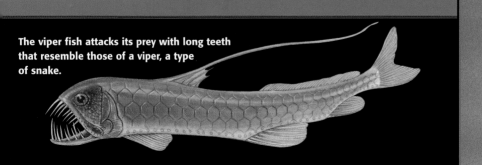

The viper fish attacks its prey with long teeth that resemble those of a viper, a type of snake.

AMPHIBIANS

THERE are more than 4,500 species of amphibians, the most familiar of which are frogs and toads. Others include newts, salamanders and caecilians. All amphibians are cold-blooded, which means that they cannot control their body temperature internally. Amphibians were the first vertebrates to move from the sea onto land, almost 400 million years ago. They developed from a group of air-breathing fish, whose fins, over time, became more and more powerful and finally evolved into legs. These early amphibians had to return to water to breed, as do most species today. The word amphibian means 'double life', reflecting this two stage lifestyle of breeding in water and living on land.

▲ *Most newts, like this rough-skinned newt, spend their lives near water, eating small snails and insects.*

FROM TADPOLE TO FROG

Like both fish and insects, amphibians lay many eggs – the more they lay, the greater the chance that some will survive. The soft, jelly-covered eggs, known as spawn, hatch into young, which must fend for themselves with no parental protection. A newly hatched frog, called a tadpole, looks quite different from its parent. It has fins, a tail, no legs, and breathes through gills like a fish. Gradually the tadpole develops legs and forms lungs, and it loses its tail. By now a young frog, it moves onto land, where it spends

eggs (spawn)

tadpole hatching from egg

adult frog

older tadpoles

froglet

▶ *Frogs pass through several stages as they develop. Fish-like tadpoles, with gills, hatch from eggs in the water and feed on tiny plants. As they develop into frogs, they begin to hunt for insects and spiders.*

most of its life. Frogs only return to water when it is time to breed, usually in spring. Many frogs have webbed feet that help propel them through the water. Using their strong back legs, they can leap from the water to grab low-flying insects with their long, sticky-tipped tongues.

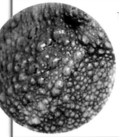

FROG OR TOAD?

Toads usually walk or waddle, whereas frogs hop or leap. Toads also have drier, rougher, more lumpy skin than frogs. The bumps or 'warts' on a toad's skin (shown here) release a fluid that can be poisonous, providing effective protection against predators such as otters and herons.

TREE FROGS

Hundreds of species of frogs live in damp, tropical forests such as the Amazon rainforest of South America. Some have sticky pads on their fingers and toes that enable them to grip the slippery leaves and branches. Many tree frogs spend all their lives high above the ground, laying their eggs in small pools of water that collect in leaves or branch forks.

▲ *This view of a frog's skeleton shows its highly developed rear legs and short backbone. The powerful rear legs enable frogs to make great leaps and to swim quickly in search of prey.*

toad

newt

SALAMANDERS, NEWTS AND CAECILIANS

Salamanders and newts both keep their long tails and resemble slippery lizards. They are commonly found scrambling through reeds and grass near the water's edge. Some salamanders can produce a dangerous poison. Caecilians resemble worms or snakes and have only the tiniest of feet, or none at all.

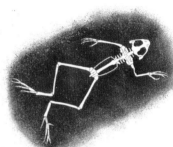

▲ *Axolotls, found only in Mexico, are unusual salamanders in that they never grow up. As adults, able to breed, they still resemble tadpoles.*

139

REPTILES

REPTILES include lizards, snakes, crocodiles, alligators, tortoises and turtles. The first reptiles appeared more than 300 million years ago. They were probably descended from a type of amphibian that had evolved a scaly, waterproof skin and eggs that did not shrivel up on dry land. Reptiles are cold-blooded. They rely on basking in sunshine to warm up their bodies. Most reptile eggs are tough, leathery and waterproof. In some species the eggs hatch inside the female's body, and she gives birth to live young. Newly hatched reptiles look like small versions of the adults.

▲ *A rattlesnake shakes the loose, horny scales at the end of its tail when it feels threatened.*

▼ *The narrow-jawed gharial of India (A) and the South American caiman (B) are two members of the crocodile family.*

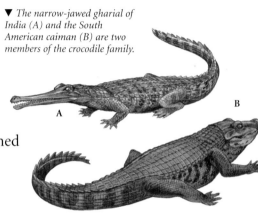

A

B

DINOSAUR RELATIVES

Reptiles range in size from lizards just a few centimetres long to the huge, seven-metre-long saltwater (estuarine) crocodile. But even this giant is small compared to the biggest reptiles that once stalked the Earth – the dinosaurs. Of the 7,000-plus reptile species alive today, nearly half are lizards and more than 2,400 are snakes.

vertebrae (backbones)

spinal cord

kidney

liver

lung

brain

gullet

eye socket

ovary

intestine

stomach

heart

clawed toes

windpipe

◀ *A crocodile swishes its powerful tail to launch itself at its prey, which it grabs with its sharp teeth.*

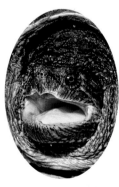

▲ *A snapping turtle can grab prey as large as an adult frog in its wide jaws.*

HUNTING FOR PREY

Most reptiles are predators, seeking out prey to kill or scavenging for food scraps left by other animals. They have developed many methods of hunting. Some snakes, such as the boa constrictors and pythons, wind themselves around an animal and slowly crush it to death. Others, such as rattlesnakes and vipers, inject a deadly venom from their fangs into their prey. By dislocating, or pulling apart, their jaw bones, they can open their mouths wide enough to swallow animals that are much bigger than their mouths. Most reptiles use stealth when hunting, waiting quietly in hiding before launching a sudden attack. Huge crocodiles and alligators, for example, float low in the water, resembling harmless logs, then suddenly spring into action. Lizards are generally more active hunters, chasing quickly after their prey.

◄ *Iguanas are large lizards that live in the trees of Central and South America. They have a crest of spines running from neck to tail.*

C

D

▲ *Alligators (C) and crocodiles (D) resemble each other, but alligators have wider, shorter bodies and a different arrangement of teeth.*

▲ *The Komodo dragon of Indonesia is the largest lizard in the world, measuring up to 3 m long. It eats monkeys and other large animals.*

AVOIDING ATTACK

Many reptiles have hard, scaly skin that helps to protect them if they are attacked. Turtles and tortoises are protected by shells, formed from curved slabs of bone and horn. Other reptile species have different defence tactics. Some lizards let their tail drop off, so the attacking animal becomes confused and strikes for the tail, allowing the lizard to escape. The lizard then grows a new tail. The generally slow lifestyles of many larger reptiles helps them to survive for a long time. The giant tortoises of the Pacific can live for more than 100 years.

HOW ANIMALS FEED

ALL animals need food in order to live. Food produces energy, which is needed to help cells grow and repair themselves, and to give an animal strength to move around, seek out more food and protect itself from other animals.

▲ *Bats find their night-flying insect prey by sending out a series of high-pitched squeaks. The bat detects the echoes from these squeaks as they bounce off insects in its path. This method of hunting is called echo-location.*

TYPES OF FEEDING

Nearly every animal has special adaptations that allow it to feed on plants, other animals, or both (in the case of omnivores). Size is not the determining factor – a bumble bee and an elephant are both plant-eaters, for example. Adaptations relate to how an animal finds its food and turns it into energy. Some tree-dwelling creatures, such as the Australian marsupial possum and the Madagascan aye-aye, have evolved a highly specialized fourth 'finger', or digit, used for extracting wood-boring insect grubs from their holes in trees. Although the two animals are unrelated, they have evolved the same adaptation in response to their feeding habits. Anteaters have also evolved remarkable adaptations for their specialized diet. They have a keen sense of smell for detecting their prey, toughened claws for digging into rock-hard termite mounds, and a long, sticky, worm-shaped

▲ *House flies use chemicals to break down food into liquid, which they suck into their bodies. Their hairy legs can pass on harmful diseases when they come into contact with human food.*

▼ *Female lions creep up on their prey until they have it almost surrounded. Then they attack immediately, killing the victim by crushing its windpipe in their jaws.*

▶ *The long neck of a giraffe gives it an advantage over other African animals, enabling it to feed on the tallest branches of trees and shrubs.*

tongue used for extracting the ants and termites. Plant-eaters have their own special adaptations. Digesting plant material can be difficult, so many animals have several chambers in their stomachs where food is digested over and over again until it is broken down. Bees have a very unusual adaptation. When they have found a good food source, they return to their hive and do a complicated dance that tells the other bees exactly where to find the food plants.

THE FOOD CHAIN

The food chain is the process whereby energy is passed from plants to herbivores to carnivores and back to the soil. There may be many links in the chain – if, for example, large predators feed on smaller ones – but the overall effect is the same. If one of the three main links is missing, the habitat must support fewer animals. Without predators, plant-eaters would soon eat all of the plants. The plants would not be able to reproduce, so there would be less food for animals.

▶ *This example of a food chain is typical of the savannah grasslands of Africa. The rich soil and sunlight allows plants to grow and make their own food. Herbivores such as gazelles eat the leaves and branches of the plants, which give them energy. The gazelles in turn are eaten by predators such as lions. When any animal – herbivore or predator – dies, insects break down the body and enrich the soil, allowing more plants to grow. And so the cycle continues.*

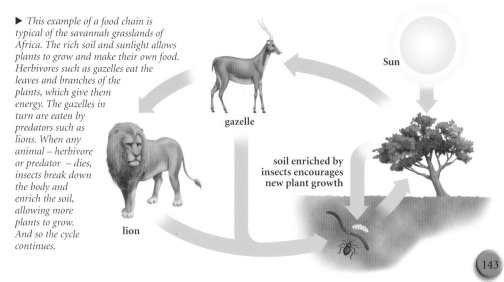

Sun

gazelle

soil enriched by insects encourages new plant growth

lion

FOSSIL RECORDS

WHEN plants and marine animals die, their remains settle in the sand and mud on the sea bed. Over time, this layer of sand and mud is covered by more layers of sand, mud and remains. After thousands of years, the sediments harden into rock, the oldest layers at the bottom, the newest ones at the top. Millions of years later, such rock may become exposed, forming part of a landmass. The hardened remains of the animals and plants preserved in the layers of sedimentary rock are called fossils. Scientists can tell how old fossils are by testing the rock and comparing the different levels. Fossils tell us a great deal about the animals that once lived on Earth and are now extinct.

▲ *Until 1938, when several were caught off the southeast coast of Africa, scientists believed that coelacanths had died out 70 million years ago.*

EXAMINING THE EVIDENCE

From fossil evidence, scientists know that giant dinosaurs lived on Earth from about 225 to 65 million years ago. They also know that woolly mammoths survived until just a few thousand years ago. Fossils of mammoths – and even their frozen bodies, with the hair still intact – have been found preserved in the ice of Siberia, Russia.

◀ *Experts can reconstruct fossil teeth, bones and scales to show what dinosaurs such as* Tyrannosaurus *may have looked like.*

▲ *Fossils of huge shellfish called ammonites have been found measuring 2 m or more across.*

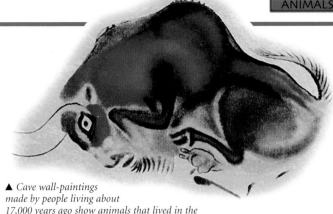

▲ *Cave wall-paintings made by people living about 17,000 years ago show animals that lived in the region at the time. This bull is from a cave at Lascaux in France.*

EVOLUTION

Scientists who study nature, plants and animals are called naturalists. They believe in 'evolution', a set of ideas that were first developed in the mid 1800s. The theory of evolution deals with how living things change over long periods of time. It suggests that animals alter or adapt to suit the conditions of their environment. According to evolution, if an animal develops some special adaptation for survival – for example, greater speed or sharper teeth – it has a better chance of reproducing than a similar animal that lacks the adaptation. Over time, more and more individuals with the adaptation occur, while those without it die out.

By examining fossils, scientists are able to see just how living things evolved into new species. The first animals were small, simple and lived in the seas. After a time fish appeared, then some fish made their way onto land and developed into amphibians. Some early amphibians, in turn, developed into reptiles, which were able to survive on land without needing to go back into the water to breed. Mammals first appeared more than 200 million years ago, followed by the first birds, about 150 million years ago.

▲ *It takes great care and patience to uncover the fossilized remains of animals. Scientists mark the position of each fossil before they begin the long task of brushing away dirt and chipping away stone.*

▲ *The hoatzin, a South American bird, is described as a 'living fossil'. When it is young, it has claws on its wings like those of bird-like animals that lived 150 million years ago.*

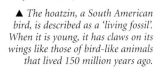

145

WILDLIFE IN DANGER

THE delicate balance of nature means that plants and animals rely on each other in order to survive. Disrupting the balance can have wide-reaching effects. Often an animal species becomes rare because it has been hunted by humans, or because its habitat – a rainforest, marsh or pond, for example – has been destroyed. But sometimes the animal is wiped out altogether – it becomes extinct – and this affects all the plants and animals that depended on it for their own survival.

▲ In Africa, elephants are killed by illegal hunters, or 'poachers', for their tusks, which are sold to make ivory trinkets. To prevent this happening, park rangers burn the tusks.

▲ Thousands of seabirds can die when oil leaks from a tanker ship. The oil sticks to the birds' feathers, making it impossible for them to fly.

THREATS TO ANIMALS

Earth has gone through many changes in its 4,600-million-year history. Scientists know that a huge meteorite crashed into the planet about 65 million years ago, darkening the skies with a cloud of dust. This affected the plants that grew, which in turn affected the plant-eating animals and the carnivorous animals that ate the plant-eaters. The result is believed to have been the extinction of all the dinosaurs and many other types of animals. In more recent history, a number of very cold periods, called ice ages, covered much of the globe in sheets of ice. The ice ages were at their peak about 16,000 BC. Many animal species died out as their food supplies dwindled.

Today, the biggest threat to animals comes from humans. The human population is constantly growing, so more and more people need food and places to live. Huge areas

▲ Turtles and other sea creatures often become entangled in nets used for commercial fishing.

▶ Although whale hunting has now been banned by many countries, some species are extremely rare and in danger of extinction.

CONSERVATION

▲ *By 1881, hunters had reduced the buffalo population in the USA from millions to just 551 animals. But by being protected, numbers have risen again to more than 30,000.*

International organizations such as the World Wide Fund for Nature and the International Union for the Conservation of Nature monitor animals and plants that, without protection, are in danger of becoming extinct. Most threatened species are at risk from hunting, habitat destruction or pollution. Without our help, some are in danger of disappearing for ever.

▲ *Rhinos in Africa are endangered because illegal hunters kill them for their horns. A small number of people, particularly in China, are prepared to pay high prices for rhino-horn powder, which they claim has medicinal properties. Both black and white rhinos have been reduced to a few thousand in the wild.*

of natural forests and grasslands are being cleared so people can grow crops, farm livestock, and build homes, roads and factories. The human population explosion has caused a massive amount of habitat destruction, threatening the survival of many species and causing many to become extinct.

POLLUTING THE EARTH

Another major threat to the environment comes from pollution. Car fumes and chemicals that are pumped into the air from factories pollute the atmosphere, causing the Earth's climate to get warmer. This process of 'global warming' can cause great damage to plant and animal populations, which are unable to survive the changes.

FIGHTING BACK

People are increasingly aware of the damage they are causing to Earth and its wildlife. Many environmental and conservation groups, both locally and internationally, warn us of the dangers and help protect both creatures and the environment. Many of the world's governments have passed laws that force factories and cars to be cleaner. But for many people in poorer regions, starvation is a daily threat, and their own survival outweighs the needs of local animals. While some big companies continue to get rich through activities that pollute environments and destroy habitats.

▼ *The giant panda is a symbol of nature conservation. Very few survive, partly because huge areas of bamboo forests in China where they live have been cut down for farmland.*

REPRODUCTION

REPRODUCTION – the ability to produce offspring – is one of the most important features of any living thing. Differences in the method of reproduction, and the way in which the young grow and develop into adults, are among the key things that set animal species apart. For most animal species, two individuals – a female and a male – must mate in order to produce offspring. But this is not always the case. Some of the simplest animals, such as sponges, reproduce with just one parent.

ASEXUAL REPRODUCTION

Simple creatures such as some sponges and anemones are neither male nor female. A new sponge may begin as a side branch, or 'bud', on the parent. Gradually it develops into a separate individual. The offspring has exactly the same genes (instructions for growth and development) as its parent – it is a 'clone'. This form of reproduction, in which there is only one parent, is called 'asexual reproduction'. It is similar to the way many plants can be reproduced from cuttings taken from the stem.

SEXUAL REPRODUCTION

Most animals are divided into two genders, or sexes – female and male. The two sexes must come together and mate to produce offspring, a process called 'sexual reproduction'. Each individual has specialized cells for reproduction. The male sex cells are called sperm and the female sex cells are eggs. When a male and female mate, the sex cells come together and join, creating a fertilized egg.

▲ *Bird chicks use an 'egg tooth' on their beaks to break a hole in the shell from inside the egg.*

▲ *The chick pecks at the shell until a crack appears all the way round.*

▲ *The chick then hooks its feet into the crack and pushes the two halves of the shell apart. It usually takes about a minute for the chick to emerge completely from the broken shell.*

◄ *A female elephant gives birth to her first calf in her fifteenth or sixteenth year. The calf can follow the herd within days, but it relies on its mother's milk for nearly five years.*

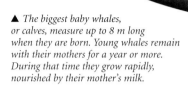

▲ *The biggest baby whales, or calves, measure up to 8 m long when they are born. Young whales remain with their mothers for a year or more. During that time they grow rapidly, nourished by their mother's milk.*

▼ *Crocodiles take more care of their offspring than most reptiles. A mother will carry her newly hatched babies to safety in her open mouth.*

The fertilized egg has a combination of genes from both parents, so the offspring that it develops into has features resembling each parent. The fertilized eggs of animals such as reptiles, birds, amphibians and insects are contained in protective cases, or shells. The mother usually lays her eggs in a sheltered place, where they will be safe when they eventually hatch. Some female animals, such as crocodiles and earwigs, care for and protect their eggs, and sometimes their offspring. Birds are much more protective of their young, feeding them for days or even weeks. But many sea creatures, such as jellyfish and worms, simply cast their eggs or sperm into the water and leave the development of the offspring to chance.

LIVE YOUNG

All mammals (except monotremes) give birth to live young rather than laying eggs. A mammal's fertilized eggs grow into babies inside the mother, until they are ready to be born. This period of growth is known as 'gestation', or pregnancy.

Mammals that are in danger of being hunted in the open, such as deer and antelopes, give birth to well-developed offspring that are able to run after just a few hours. Other mammals, such as monkeys and apes, spend months or even years with their young, caring for and protecting them.

EARLY DANGER

One of the most dangerous times of an animal's life is the time immediately after it has been born, or has hatched, when it is most vulnerable. Some species, such as insects and frogs, lay hundreds of eggs to ensure that, by chance, some of the offspring will survive. Mammals such as deer give birth to only a few young, and remain alert in order to protect their defenceless offspring.

ANIMAL EXTREMES

ANIMALS exist in a vast array of shapes and sizes. They have adapted their body shapes, diets and behaviours to survive in every kind of habitat. Even the most unpromising surroundings have been colonized by creatures of some kind.

▼ *The platypus, shown here, is one of only three mammals to lay eggs, rather than giving birth to live offspring. The other two are the short-beaked and long-beaked echidnas.*

RIGHT SIZE FOR THE JOB

A feature as basic as an animal's size is important in its struggle for survival, which depends on its ability to find food, shelter and mates. Neither flying insects nor hummingbirds (the world's tiniest birds) would be able to feed on the sweet nectar inside flower blossoms if the creatures were any bigger.

Some animals have evolved unusual characteristics for their group, such as flightlessness in birds. The kiwi, a flightless bird from New Zealand, lost the ability to fly partly because there were few predators on the islands where it lived, so it did not need to take to the air to make a rapid escape. Other flightless birds, such as rails, evolved separately on different islands. But for one bird, flightlessness was its undoing. The dodo was unable to survive when humans arrived on its remote island home in the Indian Ocean and hunted it for food. It became extinct in the 1600s.

Massive body size has evolved for various reasons. Whales are huge partly as a defence against enemies such as sharks, and partly because a large, warm-blooded body keeps in heat more effectively in cold seas than a small body.

▼ *At nearly 30 m in length, and weighing 100 tonnes, the majestic blue whale is the largest living animal on Earth. No creature in history has ever been bigger.*

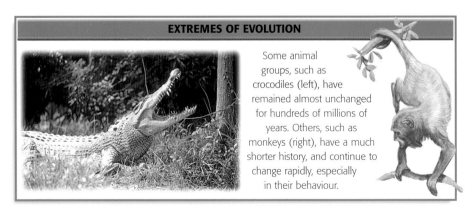

EXTREMES OF EVOLUTION

Some animal groups, such as crocodiles (left), have remained almost unchanged for hundreds of millions of years. Others, such as monkeys (right), have a much shorter history, and continue to change rapidly, especially in their behaviour.

▶ Elephants have the longest gestation period (the time it takes for the baby to develop in the womb) of any animal – more than 21 months.

▲ Bats are the only mammals that can truly fly. They navigate in the dark by making high-pitched sounds and listening to the echoes.

ALL IN A LIFETIME

In general, smaller animals have shorter lives. Some tiny flies can complete a whole generation, from egg, to larva (young), to the adult which lays eggs again, in only a few weeks. Some insects go through stages of development of very different lengths. The mayfly, for example, spends up to two years as a water-dwelling nymph at the bottom of a pond or river. Then it changes into a winged adult and survives for just one day – time enough for it to mate and lay eggs. Some adult mayflies have no working mouthparts because their adult life is so brief that they have no chance to feed.

Life-span may depend on the social way of life of an animal. A queen bee is fed and protected by other bees, and may live as long as three years. Some queen termites survive for more than ten years. The largest animals, such as elephants, whales, giant tortoises and crocodiles, may live for 50 years or more, and in rare instances, perhaps twice this long. The secretive, deep-diving beaked whale is difficult to track and monitor, but it is thought that some individuals have lived for well over 100 years.

▼ The cheetah is the fastest runner on Earth. It can reach speeds of 110 km/h as it chases its prey across the African grasslands.

BIRDS

THE first birds probably developed from reptile ancestors more than 150 million years ago. Scientists found traces of one of these early birds in layers of rock. They named it *Archaeopteryx*, meaning 'ancient wing', because although it had many reptile features such as teeth and a lizard-like tail, it also had feathers and wings. Birds continued to develop over time, losing their reptile traces and becoming specialists in flying. Wings took the place of front legs, and a strong, light beak, made of horn, replaced the heavy teeth.

▲ *Hummingbirds beat their wings so fast that they can hover as they sip nectar from flowers.*

▲ *The resplendent quetzal, one of the most brightly coloured of all birds, lives in the forests of Central America.*

ADAPTED FOR FLIGHT

There are some 9,000 species of birds in the world, most of which can fly. Several features of a bird's body make this possible. Its has thin, hollow bones, which reduce weight, and its feathers are also lightweight. Wing feathers form large, airtight surfaces that provide lift when the bird flaps its wings. Some of the feathers on the wings are used for steering. The body feathers provide protection and help keep the bird's body warm (birds and mammals are the only two warm-blooded animal groups). Extremely large, powerful pectoral muscles on a bird's chest enable it to beat its wings up and down.

FEEDING FEATURES

Birds use their beak, or bill, to perform tasks that many mammals do with their front limbs – collecting food and preparing it for eating, for example. The shape of a bird's beak is suited to the way it feeds. A bird of prey such as a hawk has a hooked beak, ideal for tearing prey apart. A parrot's curved beak is stronger, but less sharp, and is used for cracking open seeds and nuts. A kingfisher has a long, sharp beak, which it uses to

▶ *The bald eagle, the symbol of North America, feeds on fish that it snatches with its sharp talons during low swoops over the water.*

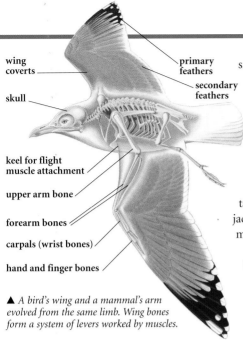

wing coverts

skull

keel for flight muscle attachment

upper arm bone

forearm bones

carpals (wrist bones)

hand and finger bones

primary feathers

secondary feathers

▲ *A bird's wing and a mammal's arm evolved from the same limb. Wing bones form a system of levers worked by muscles.*

snatch fish from the water. A woodpecker has a chisel-like beak that it uses to drill its way into trees in search of insects under the bark. Birds' feet have also adapted to suit their particular lifestyle. Ducks and swans have webbed feet, used for paddling and swimming. Eagles grasp animals as large as rabbits in their powerful, claw-like talons. And the wide-splayed toes of the jacana, or lilytrotter, allow it to walk on soft mud and floating leaves.

COLOURFUL DISPLAYS

Some birds, such as sparrows and thrushes, have dull plumage that helps them to blend in with leaves and bushes. Other birds have colourful plumage, usually for display. Male peacocks, for example, display their spectacular vivid plumage in order to attract females during the breeding season.

FLIGHTLESS BIRDS

Some birds have lost the power of flight. Among them are a number of large, long-legged land-dwellers, such as ostriches, emus and rheas. But what the ostrich has lost in flying ability, it has gained in running ability. An ostrich's legs are extremely powerful and the bird can reach speeds of up to 80 km/h when running away from predators on the African plains. The wings of a penguin have evolved into flippers that

▶ *Penguins have a thick layer of fat under their feathers and skin that keeps in body warmth in the cold polar seas.*

enable it to swim quickly through the cold Antarctic waters in search of fish prey. The flippers beat up and down like wings, allowing the bird to 'fly' through the water.

◀ *Huge flocks of geese and other birds make long journeys, called migrations, twice a year. They move away from cold regions in autumn, in search of food, and return to them again in spring.*

153

MAMMALS

bat

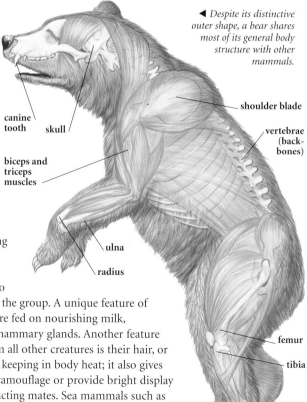

MAMMALS, like birds, are warm-blooded. This means they can keep their bodies at a steady, raised temperature without needing to bask in the heat of the Sun. Being warm-blooded allows mammals to live in most parts of the world, even icy polar seas and on frozen tundra. Some mammals, such as whales and dolphins, spend their whole lives in the ocean. Others, such as polar bears and otters, are at home on land and in the water. But most mammals live on land. Nearly every mammal has four limbs, which it uses for walking or running. In some mammals, the front legs have become wings, as in bats, or flippers, as in whales.

◀ Dolphins communicate underwater using a 'language' of clicks, whistles and other sounds.

NATURAL ADVANTAGES

Many mammals show a more complicated range of behaviour than other creatures. In particular, they have a greater ability to learn from their own experiences. Some mammals, such as monkeys and dolphins, can also understand and learn from others. Their ability to learn is one reason why some mammals have developed complex living arrangements. Herds of elephants and troops of monkeys, for example, help to protect the young or weak in the group. A unique feature of mammals is that the young are fed on nourishing milk, produced by their mother's mammary glands. Another feature that sets mammals apart from all other creatures is their hair, or fur. Not only is fur useful for keeping in body heat; it also gives protection, and it can act as camouflage or provide bright display colours and patterns for attracting mates. Sea mammals such as whales and dolphins have only a tiny amount of bristles.

◀ Despite its distinctive outer shape, a bear shares most of its general body structure with other mammals.

canine tooth

skull

biceps and triceps muscles

shoulder blade

vertebrae (back-bones)

ulna

radius

femur

tibia

tarsals

MARSUPIALS

Most of Australia's native mammals, such as koalas (below) and kangaroos (right), are marsupials. Female marsupials give birth to tiny, blind, underdeveloped young that have only partially formed limbs. These tiny offspring are able to crawl to their mother's pouch, where they continue to develop.

FOOD TYPES

Some mammals are specialized feeders. The anteater has a long, sticky tongue for probing deep into the nests of termites and ants, which it licks up. Many grazing mammals, such as deer and cattle, have multi-part stomachs for digesting grasses. Tigers and other predators have sharp teeth for tearing apart the animals they kill. More generalized feeders are called omnivores. Many members of the dog and fox group (canids) catch large prey, but can also survive on insects and berries, or by scavenging on dead bodies.

LIVING IN GROUPS

Some predatory mammals are social and live in groups. Wolves form packs in which pack-members cooperate in hunting large prey, such as deer. Most cats live and hunt alone. The only group-dwelling big cat is the lion, which lives on the African plains in extended family units, called 'prides'. Weasels, stoats and badgers live in small family groups, caring for their young as they learn to hunt. Many plant-eating mammals live in large groups for protection.

◀ *Elephants are the largest living land mammals, standing up to 4 m tall. They eat up to 200 kg of grass, twigs and other plant matter in a single day.*

▲ *Tigers are the largest members of the cat family, weighing up to 300 kg. They are solitary hunters, sometimes covering 20 km a night in search of a kill.*

155

MONKEYS AND APES

THE PRIMATE group of mammals includes
lemurs, bushbabies, monkeys and apes (as well as
humans). Most primates have a number of adaptations
suited to a life spent living in trees and leaping or
swinging through the branches. They have strong,
flexible fingers, able to grasp and manipulate food
and other items. Their eyes are on the front of
their heads, rather than at the sides, giving them
detailed vision and the ability to judge
distances accurately. And primates' limb joints
are flexible, allowing a wide range of
movements in the arms and legs. A primate's
brain is, on average, much larger in relation to
its body size than that of other mammals.

▲ The proboscis
monkey takes its name
from the male's fleshy
nose, or proboscis. The
female's nose is slightly
less elongated.

LIVING TOGETHER

Primates form some of the most complex and long-lasting social groups of all
mammals. The group members help each other to find food and shelter, and they
keep a look-out for attackers. They will also team up to help look after
younger members of the group, sometimes for as long as seven
years in the case of some apes. Primates communicate
information and moods, such as fear, pleasure or anger, using a
complex 'language' of sounds, facial expressions and body
postures. In many primate groups there is a 'pecking
order', or dominance hierarchy. Certain group
members are higher in the order and have first
choice of food, resting places and mates.
Others are lower in rank and must take
what is left, unless they can
successfully challenge a higher-
ranking member.

◀ Chimpanzees are the most
intelligent of primates after
humans. They live
in groups of up to 80
individuals, and are able to
make and use a range of
tools in their search for food.

TROPICAL HOMES

Nearly all primates, apart from humans, live in tropical forests. They can be found on every continent except Australia and Antarctica. Europe's only primate is a tail-less monkey called the Barbary ape, which lives on Gibraltar, off southwest Spain. The northernmost of all primates is the Japanese macaque, from the snowy mountains of Honshu island. Madagascar, off the east coast of Africa, is home to a unique group of primates called lemurs. Most lemur species are skillful climbers, but their eyesight is not as sharp as that of monkeys and apes. Many monkey species in Central and South America have strong, prehensile tails that can grasp objects, working as a fifth limb. Monkey troops often chatter and screech in the treetops at dusk and dawn, warning rivals to keep out of their territory. The whoops and yells of Howler monkeys are among the loudest noises produced by any animal.

▲ *Despite its size and appearance, the gorilla is a peaceful primate. Gorillas live in small family groups and eat leaves, shoots and fruits.*

▲ *The Japanese macaque survives cold winters by bathing in naturally hot springs to keep warm.*

APES

Apes resemble monkeys, but lack tails. There are about 10 species of gibbons (a smaller, or lesser, ape) in Southeast Asia. Gibbons swing through the branches using their very long, powerful arms. Common chimps, bonobos (pygmy chimps) and orang-utans are also apes. But the largest ape is the gorilla. A large male gorilla stands almost two metres tall and can weigh over 200 kilograms.

▶ *The orang-utan is a species of large ape that lives in the dense forests of Southeast Asia. Its name means 'man of the forest'.*

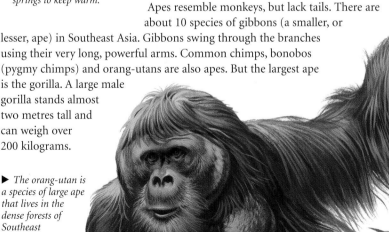

QUIZ

1. Which ancient empire built its capital, Tenochtitlan, on a series of lakes?
2. What is Egyptian picture-writing called?
3. Which major empire was divided into khanates, or little kingdoms?
4. Which warrior people based in present-day Turkey conquered Babylon in 1595 BC?
5. Most scientists agree that the first humans appeared on which continent?
6. Who was crowned as the first Holy Roman Emperor in AD 800?
7. Why is the Huang He in eastern China sometimes called the Yellow River?
8. Which great religion was developed by the Aryans?
9. Which Israelite king led a successful revolt against the Philistines in 1050 BC?
10. Which ancient people developed a type of writing known as cuneiform?
11. What do we call the series of 'holy wars' conducted by European Christians to seize the Holy Lands from the Muslims?
12. Octavian became first what in 27 BC?
13. Which famous person was the son of King Philip II of Macedonia?
14. Memphis was the capital of which ancient civilization?
15. On which Mediterranean island did the Minoan civilization develop?
16. Which animals, carried aboard trading ships, brought the Black Death to Europe in 1347?
17. The Fertile Crescent lies between which two rivers in the Middle East?
18. What great skill enabled the Phoenicians to set up a string of colonies along the Mediterranean Sea from about 1250 BC?
19. How old was Alexander the Great when he died?
20. Which sporting event first took place in Greece in 776 BC?

ANSWERS

1. The Aztec Empire
2. Hieroglyphs (or hieroglyphics)
3. The Mongol Empire
4. The Hittites
5. Africa
6. Charlemagne
7. Because of the rich, yellow-coloured soil that washes up along its banks.
8. Hinduism
9. Saul
10. The Sumerians
11. The Crusades
12. Roman emperor
13. Alexander the Great
14. Egypt
15. Crete
16. Rats
17. The Tigris and the Euphrates
18. Sailing
19. 33
20. The Olympic Games

ANCIENT HISTORY

WE can learn a great deal about
the people that came
before us by looking at
their written records. The
Sumerians, living in western
Asia, developed the first
form of writing more than
5000 years ago. At about the
same time, new cultures were
developing along rich river valleys
in India and China. Later
civilizations, such as the ancient Egyptians, Greeks
and Romans, valued knowledge and military
power in equal measure. This same combination
lay behind the rise of Christian countries in
Europe during the Middle Ages, the Islamic empire
that extended across much of Africa and Asia, and
the great Aztec and Inca
civilizations of the
Americas.

Studying history
joins up the
pieces of this
world-wide
ancient jigsaw
puzzle. It helps
tell us who we are
today – and why.

THE FIRST HUMANS

HUMAN beings are animals, and animals of all types change over long periods of time. Some types may die out, but many others evolve, or develop, into more advanced forms. Scientists describe this process of change as 'evolution'. Human beings belong to a group of mammals called primates. Our nearest relatives are the African great apes – chimpanzees and gorillas. About 5 million years ago, certain great apes developed larger brains and began to walk upright. Over the next 3 million years, some of these ancestors of human beings developed even larger brains, and their teeth adapted to become suitable for eating many types of food.

▲ Homo habilis, *which means 'handy man', lived about 2 million years ago. Evidence shows he could make stone tools.*

THE FIRST TOOLS

The big change came about two million years ago. Scientists have found stone tools from that time – evidence that ancestors of humans were able to think in a way that was like humans, and were beginning to control aspects of the world around them. Their next step was to use fire, which no other animal had ever done before. During this period of evolution, the brains of these creatures were growing bigger. About 1 million years ago, the first humans to stand and walk upright, instead of on all fours, evolved in Africa. Their remains have been found in Africa, Asia and Europe. They were the first type of human. It was some 200,000 years ago that a new type of human appeared – people who in many ways were like humans today. They were called Neanderthal, because some of these people's fossils (bones that have been preserved in rock) were found in the Neander Valley in

The map shows fossil locations:

Swanscombe
Boxgrove
Dolni Vestonice
Grimaldi
Cro-Magnon
Vindija
Dmansi
Skhul
Shanida
Tabun
Bahr el Ghazal
Omo
Hadar(Lucy)
Nariokotome
Olduvai
Laetoli
Kabwe
Sterkfontein
Taung
Swartkrans
Klasies River

● Australopith,1-4 mya
● H.hablis,2.5-1 mya
● H.ergaster,2-05 mya
● H.H'berg,500-100,000 yrs
● N'thal 250-30,000 yrs
● H.Sapiens 30,000 yrs

◀ *This map shows where many important fossils have been found, giving us clues about the origins of human beings.*

▲ *Cro-Magnon people were among the first examples of our own species of modern humans, Homo sapiens.*

◀ *British scientists Louis and Mary Leakey discovered some of the earliest tools – made about 2 million years ago – in Olduvai Gorge in Tanzania, Africa.*

Germany. The Neanderthal people were shorter and stockier than modern humans. They lived in natural shelters such as caves, and knew how to make fires for heat and cooking. They used stone knives for hunting animals and cutting meat. The Neanderthals died out about 30,000 years ago, finally overtaken by the first 'modern' humans. These modern humans, sometimes called Cro-Magnon people, looked like us and used many more tools than the Neanderthals. Perhaps – although no one can be sure – the Neanderthals died out because they were not such efficient hunters as the Cro-Magnons.

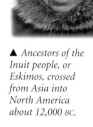

▲ Homo erectus *came after* Homo habilis. *He had greater brain power and was more skilled.*

EVERYDAY LIFE

From evidence left behind by Cro-Magnon people and those who followed them, scientists know a great deal about their everyday life. They worked together to hunt and build houses, they buried their dead, and they began to plant crops and herded goats and sheep. Vivid paintings on the walls of caves reveal that they believed in spirits – an early form of religion. They also shared the task of looking after their children.

▲ *Ancestors of the Inuit people, or Eskimos, crossed from Asia into North America about 12,000 BC.*

As human beings advanced, the need for more food and better living conditions, and maybe simple curiosity, took them on long journeys. Humans found their way into nearly every part of Africa, Europe, Asia, Australia and the Americas. About 10,000 years ago, they began to take things a stage further, developing civilizations.

▲ *Neanderthal man had a powerful, stocky build. He lived until about 30,000 years ago.*

◀ *Early humans relied on fire for warmth, cooking and protection from wild animals.*

THE SUMERIANS

THE Sumerian people created one of the first civilizations. Civilizations grow up when people have advanced enough to build up a whole way of life, based on shared language, beliefs and an agreed system of government. The Sumerians also created the one element that has allowed us to learn about their ideas – written language. The key to how people became this advanced was food.

▲ *The Fertile Crescent is the name given to the rich lands of Mesopotamia lying between the Tigris and Euphrates rivers, in present-day Iraq.*

EARLY FARMERS

The earliest humans were 'hunter-gatherers', who roamed the land hunting for animals and gathering nuts, fruit and berries to eat. But when people learned how to plant seeds and grow their food, they settled in villages. For the first time people had more food than they needed, so they were able to trade some of it for tools or clothing that other people now had time to make (because they were not always having to look for food). Small villages grew into towns, and some of these became cities.

◀ *A statue of Gilgamesh, hero of a Sumerian legend written about 4,000 years ago.*

◀ *All the major Sumerian cities were built on the Tigris and Euphrates rivers, or were linked to them by canal. Merchants plied the rivers exchanging surplus food for metals and tools. They sailed as far as the Persian Gulf and beyond.*

ÇATAL HÜYÜK

One of the earliest-known towns is Çatal Hüyük, in Turkey. It developed about 9,000 years ago as a cattle-trading centre. As protection against invaders, the houses were built up against each other, and their 'front doors' were on the roof. Ladders were pulled up in times of attack.

EARLY MESOPOTAMIA

It is not surprising that one of the first civilizations grew up in one of the best places for growing food. About 5000 BC, a group of people called the Ubaidians settled in Mesopotamia, the land between the Tigris and Euphrates rivers, in present-day Iraq. This area is sometimes called the Fertile Crescent, because the soil is so rich. The Ubaidian settlements grew into cities, which attracted many people to the area, either to live or to raid from the townsfolk. One of these groups, the Sumerians, arrived after about 3250 BC.

▶ *The people of Mesopotamia built huge temple-towers, called ziggurats. A series of steps led to the temple at the top, where many gods were worshipped.*

The Sumerians lived alongside the Ubaidians and gradually became the dominant people. They helped the area to become rich and powerful, building many large temples and monuments, and creating beautiful carvings. They learned how to make and use the wheel, and had excellent metal-working skills. They also established a rule by kings, backed up with laws, and a religion that worshipped many gods in huge temples.

▲ *The Sumerians developed the first alphabet about 5,000 years ago. Each of the 600 'letters' represented a word or part of a word.*

WRITTEN IDEAS

Most importantly, the Sumerians developed a system of writing on clay. This writing, known as cuneiform (or wedge-shaped) script, became the main type of written communication in the area for about 2,000 years. By studying clay tablets inscribed with cuneiform writing, a great deal has been learned about how the Sumerians lived. The Sumerian clay writings include medical handbooks, receipts, decisions of courts, marriage announcements and lists of items stored in warehouses. They also give a full picture of the Sumerian religion, with its four main gods and dozens of lesser gods.

THE GLORY OF EGYPT

THE civilization of ancient Egypt grew up along the banks of the longest river in the world – the Nile. The River Nile flows through the dry North African countryside, providing water for growing crops and depositing rich soil on its banks. People first began settling in villages along the Nile about 4500 BC. Like the Sumerians, they soon developed metalworking skills, making tools and ornaments from bronze and other metals. They also began organizing themselves into kingdoms. By 3500 BC there were two powerful kingdoms, Upper Egypt (to the south, further 'up' the Nile) and Lower Egypt to the north. These two kingdoms were united under Menes, the first great pharaoh, or ruler. The capital was Memphis, in the north.

A LIVING GOD

Egyptian civilization lasted for nearly 3,000 years. It was a deeply religious society. The people believed that the pharaoh was a god living on Earth. There were strict rules about how to live and how to prepare for life after death. Daily life was governed by duty to the hundreds of different gods and to the pharaoh. The civilization prospered because the Nile's waters made food

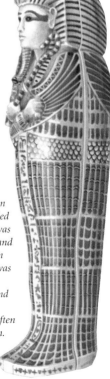

▶ *When an important Egyptian died, his mummified (preserved) body was wrapped in linen and placed in a wooden coffin. The coffin was then put inside a brightly painted and outer case. A thin layer of gold was often used for decoration.*

DESERT WONDERS

The pyramids were built as tombs for the pharaohs by the ancient Egyptians. These huge structures – rising to almost 150 m – were built beside the River Nile. The largest pyramid, at Giza, was made from more than 2 million huge blocks of stone, placed by hand without the use of machinery.

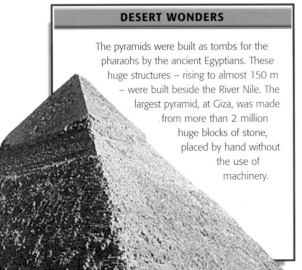

production possible. The pharaoh's men organized huge teams of workers to build canals so that farmland could be irrigated. Farmers invented ploughs, pulled by oxen, and grew many crops in the rich soil: wheat, barley, lettuces, onions, beans, melons and cucumbers. People also brewed beer and enjoyed making music on harps, flutes and other instruments.

▲ *Daily life in Egypt remained almost unchanged for thousands of years. Egyptians lived beside the Nile and its canals, farming the rich black soil. People still rely on the Nile to water their fields, and for transport.*

GREAT ACHIEVEMENTS

The Egyptians were skilled in many areas, especially science and building. Astronomers studied the heavens and plotted the course of the stars. They developed a calendar with 365 days, like our own. Egyptian doctors understood a great deal about surgery, the bloodstream and how to protect wounds against infection.

Perhaps the Egyptian's greatest achievements, however, were the great temples they built to honour their gods and pharaohs, and the pyramids, which we can still see today. These massive monuments contained the tombs of pharaohs. Their sides were triangular in shape to represent the slanting rays of the Sun. The Egyptians believed that the Sun's rays carried the pharaoh's body to the land of the dead. In preparation for the journey, the pharaoh's body was dried and wrapped in bandages. The body, known as a mummy, was placed inside a brightly painted coffin, which was put in the tomb along with many rich treasures.

◄ *Cats and dogs, preserved as mummies, were left with human mummies to keep them company after death.*

165

ANCIENT CHINA AND INDIA

TWO early civilizations developed in Asia – one in China and one in India. Like the Sumerian and Egyptian civilizations, these both grew up alongside rivers, where people were able to grow and water grains and other crops in the rich soil. In eastern China, farmers settled beside the Huang He about 7,000 years ago. Gradually settlements flourished alongside the river – sometimes called the Yellow River because of the rich yellow-coloured soil that washes up along its banks – and by about 1700 BC civilization had developed in this area. In India, another great ancient civilization grew up from about 2500 BC, when people began making settlements along the banks of the Indus River (in present-day Pakistan).

PEOPLE OF THE HUANG HE

The farmers living along the Huang He kept dogs, pigs, sheep and goats. Settlements grew up as the farmers traded their food for other goods. Over time people developed new skills such as pottery-making, weaving, making silk and carving fine jade ornaments.

Villages soon became towns and cities. The capital was at Anyang. Head of the ruling Shang dynasty was a king, who ruled with the

▲ *In ancient China, many houses were circular and had an open fire for cooking.*

▼ *Artists in ancient China were among the first in the world to carve jade, a green, precious stone.*

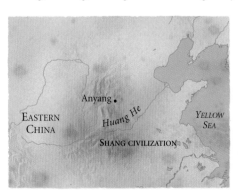

EASTERN CHINA

Anyang

Huang He

YELLOW SEA

SHANG CIVILIZATION

◀ *The fertile Huang He valley in eastern China was ideal for early farming.*

▼ Mohenjo-Daro was a brick-built city housing up to 40,000 people. Many of the buildings surrounded inner courtyards.

▲ The Indus Valley civilization is thought to have had up to 100 settlements. Two of the largest are shown here.

▲ This carved Indus Valley seal dating back more than 4,000 years may have been used on merchants' goods.

help of powerful noble families. The Shang people were excellent warriors. They also produced great works of art. Chinese writing developed at this time and written records have survived that tell us about religious practices and also about trading missions to other parts of China.

A later civilization, known as the Zhou dynasty, developed the Shang way of life and spread it across China. Large areas of the country came to be controlled by the Zhou dynasty.

THE ROOTS OF INDIA

Like other early civilizations, the Indian civilization began with farming communities, and grew as people developed new skills. The Indus people built many settlements, the two largest cities being Mohenjo-Daro and Harappa. Mohenjo-Daro is thought to have housed up to 40,000 inhabitants. Knowing that the Indus River was liable to flood, the people devised excellent drainage systems for their cities. The streets were laid out at right angles on a grid system, and the houses and grain stores were built from mud bricks. The cities thrived for about a thousand years from 2500 BC. They may eventually have been devastated by earthquakes and floods – it is not known for sure what brought about the end of the Indus Valley civilization.

About 1500 BC Aryan people from central Asia moved into India from the north, settling in the Indus and then the Ganges river valleys, enriching the culture with a new language. They merged with the original people and developed one of the world's great religions – Hinduism.

▲ This terracotta statuette was found in the ruins of Mohenjo-daro.

167

THE MEDITERRANEAN

FROM about 2000 BC a number of civilizations grew up around the eastern end of the Mediterranean Sea. Egypt, to the south, remained a powerful kingdom. To the east, the Babylonian Empire had replaced the Sumerian civilization in the Fertile Crescent. New people were entering the region, trying to find space for themselves and often fighting the powers that they found in place there.

▲ *A volcanic eruption in 1470 BC destroyed much of the Greek island of Santorini, a centre of Minoan culture.*

THE ROOTS OF GREECE

The mighty Minoan civilization developed on the island of Crete, just to the south of mainland Greece, in about 2000 BC. For six centuries the Minoans controlled the seas with their powerful navies. On Crete itself, they built large, beautiful palaces and developed a form of writing that we now know to be an early form of Greek. Many vases and palace walls have inscriptions written in this language. The Minoans were also adventurous merchants who traded with Egypt.

From about 1700 BC, a series of earthquakes destroyed many of the Minoans' grand buildings. At about this time the people came under attack from the Mycenaeans – warriors from mainland Greece who gradually took power from the Minoans. The Mycenaeans

▲ *The Minoans had many legends about great bulls, including the Minotaur (half man and half bull).*

▼ *The Phoenicians established trading and colonizing routes throughout the Mediterranean region. Many traders sailed beyond the Mediterranean as far north as the distant island of Britain.*

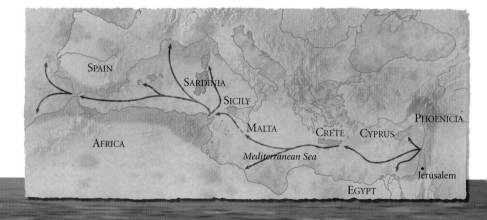

SPAIN

SARDINIA

SICILY

MALTA

CRETE   CYPRUS

PHOENICIA

AFRICA

Mediterranean Sea

Jerusalem

EGYPT

were also great traders, and made beautiful gold jewellery. They reached the peak of their power between 1600 and 1100 BC, after which their civilization began to decline. Why they lost their power remains a mystery.

EASTERN SHORES

New peoples also arose on the eastern shores of the Mediterranean. The Hittites, a warrior people based in present-day Turkey, conquered Babylon in 1595 BC. Their empire stretched into what is now Syria and also extended across the northeast coast of the Mediterranean. It became a rival of Egypt, and

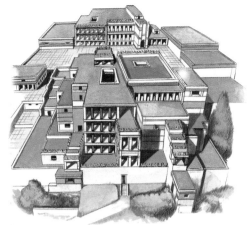

▲ *The Minoans built a huge palace at Knossos about 1700 BC. A major fire destroyed the building 300 years later, leaving only ruins.*

▲ *Decorative clay pots were used by traders to carry wine and oils across the Mediterranean.*

the two empires fought several battles. However in the end it was not Egypt but a wave of attackers known as the 'Sea People' who destroyed the Hittite Empire. At this time, a people known as the Phoenicians rose to power, mainly through trading by sea – they were expert sailors. From about 1250 BC onwards, they set up colonies all along the coast of North Africa.

BIBLICAL EVENTS

By 1250 BC, the Israelite people – whose story is told in the Bible – had long been captives in Egypt, far away from their homeland, today's Israel. Their escape, known as the Exodus, took place in about 1200 BC. Once back on the eastern shores of the Mediterranean, the Israelites still faced powerful enemies, especially the Philistines. In 1050 BC, the Israelite's King Saul defeated the Philistines. Forty years later, David became king. He captured Jerusalem and made it capital of Israel.

▼ *The Phoenicians were the most widely travelled traders of the ancient Mediterranean world. Their colonies stretched from Tyre (in modern Israel) to Gades (Cadiz, in southern Spain).*

▲ *Worship at the Western Wall in Jerusalem, the holiest place for modern Jews, who claim descent from the ancient Israelites.*

GREECE: THE GOLDEN AGE

ANCIENT civilizations have shaped the way we live in all kinds of ways. The Babylonians developed laws, for example, and the Minoans used a system of weights and measures that encouraged fair trade. But few civilizations have had such an influence on our lives as the Greeks. In just a few centuries, from about 800 BC, the people from this small country set up systems of government and developed ways of thinking that are still important today.

▲ Greek influence extended well beyond the Greek mainland, particularly into the Mediterranean islands and the west coast of Asia (present-day Turkey). They generally established colonies in places with good harbours and rich farmland.

RIVAL CITY-STATES

About 2000 BC a number of peoples settled in mainland Greece. Over the next few centuries they absorbed the language and customs of the Minoan civilization, based on the island of Crete. The Greeks spread their influence beyond the mainland, setting up small colonies on the eastern shore of the Mediterranean, on Sicily, in southern France and Italy, and north to the Black Sea. The colonies were rivals in trade, but all shared a Greek identity.

By about 800 BC, many of the cities on the Greek mainland, including Athens and Sparta, had become city-states – they were like small countries based around a single city. The city-states chose different types of government. Some were ruled by a single person,

others were governed by a group of rich men. Athens chose a system of government called 'democracy', by which the people themselves (in Athens, only males over 18) chose who ruled them.

BANDING TOGETHER

Despite their rivalries and different types of government, the Greeks had much more in common than simply their language and religion. Events such as the Olympic

▲ *The Parthenon is the magnificent temple on the Acropolis, a hill in the heart of Athens.*

Games – which first took place in 776 BC – strengthened this shared feeling. But the strongest ties developed when the Greek city-states decided to unite against an attack by the powerful Persian Empire to the east. The Persian army threatened to crush Athens, but in 490 BC it was defeated by the Greeks at the Battle of Marathon. Ten years later, the united Greeks fought off another Persian attack, both on land and at sea – they sank the Persian fleet at the Battle of Salamis.

▲ *Many modern buildings, such as the entrance to the British Museum in London, are based on designs of the ancient Greeks.*

THE RISE OF ATHENS

After the Persian Wars, Athens became the most powerful Greek city-state. Its rulers encouraged people to write poetry and plays, to make sculptures and to build beautiful temples. Scientists and mathematicians made important discoveries, and philosophers (who study ideas) discussed the best ways to allow people to live together in freedom. The Golden Age of Athens lasted from about 480 BC to 404 BC. Many of the ideas that influence our lives today can be traced to the thinkers of Athens at that time. The Golden Age ended when Sparta, a warlike city-state, defeated Athens in 404 BC. Not long after that, both of these city-states were overshadowed by the rise of a powerful neighbour to the north – Macedonia.

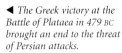

◄ *The Greek victory at the Battle of Plataea in 479 BC brought an end to the threat of Persian attacks.*

▶ *Armoured spear-carriers known as hoplites formed the backbone of the Greek army.*

ALEXANDER THE GREAT

THE Greeks were brave warriors and skillful military thinkers. But they had one main disadvantage – they were unable to remain united for long. It took someone who was not Greek himself, but who admired Greece, to achieve this. Known now as Alexander the Great, he created one of the largest empires of the ancient world.

▲ The main weapons used by Greek foot-soldiers were long spears. They carried shields for defence.

▲ Alexander the Great was one of the greatest generals in history.

MACEDONIAN CHILDHOOD

Alexander was born in Macedonia, a northern neighbour of Greece, in 356 BC. Three years later his father became King Philip II of Macedonia. Philip greatly admired the Greeks and hired Greek teachers to act as tutors to the young Alexander. One of them was Aristotle – one of the greatest philosophers ever known. Philip's ambition was to become ruler of a united Greece. After a series of battles with different city-states, he defeated the Greek opposition in 338 BC. Philip was made commander of all the Greek armies, and declared war on Persia. While preparing to attack in 336 BC, he was killed. Alexander, only 20 years old, became the new king of Macedonia, and immediately carried out his father's plan of attack.

▶ This statue of one of Alexander's soldiers is at Ephesus, a Greek city in present-day Turkey.

▼ Petra in Jordan, with its beautiful rock-cut buildings, was a great trading centre with Arabia and the Persian Empire.

THE PERSIANS

The Persians were a military people who for many centuries had ruled a powerful empire in Asia, centered around present-day Iraq. From 490 BC they had fought a series of wars with Greece – the Greek colonies on the eastern shore of the Mediterranean had refused to accept Persian rule. The Persians were defeated by Greece, Greek freedom was secured, and the Persian Empire began to weaken.

▲ *The conquests of Alexander the Great extended south as far as North Africa and east through present-day Turkey and Iraq to India. Many of the cities Alexander founded were named after him.*

By the time Alexander became king of Macedonia, the Greeks believed that they themselves could go on the attack.

ACHIEVING GREATNESS

Alexander was an excellent commander, whose troops were famously loyal to him. He defeated the armies of the Persian leader Darius III in a series of battles, and in 333 BC freed Egypt from Persian rule. There he founded a new city, named Alexandria, at the mouth of the River Nile. After further conquests in the heart of the Persian Empire, his victory was complete. By 331 BC the whole Persian Empire had been crushed.

▲ *The Greeks used their scientific knowledge to produce deadly weapons such as the catapult.*

THE LONG MARCH

The Persian Empire had once included part of western India, so Alexander marched his army eastwards into this vast, unknown region. He crossed the Indus River in 326 BC and conquered large parts of northern India. By now, though, his men were tired and homesick, and refused to go any further. Alexander turned for home. He and his men marched back across the desert to Babylon. He was still planning further conquests, but developed a fever and died suddenly in 323 BC, aged 33. Alexander's empire extended Greek influence well into Asia. He built many new cities and encouraged peaceful trade. But within a few years of his death, his vast empire began to fall apart.

▶ *Only a few carvings remain in the Persian capital of Persepolis, which Alexander destroyed in 330 BC.*

MIGHTY ROME

▲ *At its peak, Rome's empire included England, southern Europe, the North African coast, and lands east as far as the Persian Gulf.*

F ROM a small island – an ancient crossing place – in the middle of the River Tiber, Rome grew to become the powerbase of a mighty empire. Its position on the west coast of Italy, and central within the Mediterranean Sea, allowed it to trade with, and learn from, other cultures of the Mediterranean, such as the Greeks and the great North African cities of Carthage and Alexandria.

AN EXPANDING POWER

According to tradition, Rome was founded in 753 BC. It developed by either conquering or forming alliances with nearby peoples such as the Etruscans, the Sabines and the Umbrians. During its early history, Rome was ruled by kings. Then, in 509 BC, it became a republic. Decisions were no longer made by a king, but by a group of high-ranking senators. Over the next few centuries Rome expanded, and by 272 BC it controlled the whole Italian peninsula.

▼ *The Romans built elaborate temples around the warm natural springs in Aquae Sulis, their name for the English city of Bath.*

▼ *To defend themselves from enemy spears, Roman soldiers grouped into a square formation and locked shields, forming a 'testudo', meaning 'tortoise shell'.*

◀ *The Colosseum in Rome was the greatest arena built by the ancient Romans. More than 50,000 people flocked there to watch fights between gladiators and wild animals, and even battles between ships – for which the arena was flooded with water.*

CONTROL OF LAND AND SEA

From 264 BC Rome fought, and eventually won, a series of wars against Carthage. This meant that Rome not only gained control of the Mediterranean Sea, and hence all sea trade there; it also gained new territories – the strip of coast along North Africa, as well as parts of Spain and France. The highly disciplined Roman armies became feared everywhere, and Rome went on to conquer the lands once controlled by the Egyptians and Greeks.

IMPERIAL ROME

Rome's great military leaders came to have more and more power until one of them, Octavian, was made emperor in 27 BC (taking the name Augustus). This marked the beginning of Imperial Rome. During this time the city of Rome prospered. Great temples were built to honour the Roman gods. Traders and politicians met in the Forum (an assembly place and market), and

▲ *The Roman cities of Pompeii and Herculaneum were destroyed when Vesuvius erupted in AD 79.*

the people were entertained at theatres, race tracks and a vast arena called the Colosseum. The empire continued to grow for about 200 years. Emperor Constantine abandoned the Roman gods in AD 313 to become a Christian. He set up a new capital city, Constantinople, in present-day Turkey. But Rome itself began to come under attack by peoples from the north, until in AD 476 the last Roman emperor was replaced by a German king. All Rome's empire in Europe was lost; only around Constantinople did the Eastern Empire continue.

▼ *Roman cargo ships carried wine, grain, oil and many other goods to the furthest outposts of the empire.*

THE MIDDLE AGES BEGIN

FOR several centuries after the overthrow of the last western Roman emperor (in AD 476), powerful tribes from central Europe fought each other for possession of new territories in the former Roman Empire. The Angles, Jutes and Saxons swept into Britain, pushing the Roman British (whom they called Welsh) into the western mountains. Slavs, Huns and Vandals fought to control parts of what is now France, Spain and Germany. Many of the Germanic tribes had never been ruled by Rome, and they destroyed much of the Roman way of life. Historians once called these violent times the Dark Ages, because the 'light' of learning and civilization seemed to be snuffed out. Now it is generally referred to as the start of the Middle Ages ('Middle', because it falls between the time of ancient civilizations and the modern era).

▲ *Vercingetorix, a leader of Gaul (ancient France) won a series of battles against the Romans before being defeated by Julius Caesar in 52 BC.*

▼ *The Vikings arrived in northern Europe from Scandinavia in search of plunder.*

▲ *The Vikings were fierce warriors, but they were also skilled craftsmen, making intricate gold jewellery.*

PROTECTING THE PEOPLE

Over time, powerful warriors gained control of local regions and defended them against outsiders. They built castles to protect themselves and the townspeople around them. The first castles were simple mounds, which were gradually fortified. By AD 1000, castles had become the military strongholds of noblemen or lords, able to hold out against sieges, or prolonged attacks, by the enemy. During a siege, townspeople took shelter inside the castle, living off stores of food that sometimes had to last for several months.

NEW KINGDOMS

Many of the countries of Europe have their origins in the Middle Ages. They gradually formed as noblemen united under, or were conquered by, powerful rulers. Charlemagne, leader of a warlike people known as the Franks, conquered much of present-day Austria, northern Germany, Italy and France. This area became known as the Holy Roman Empire. Charlemagne was crowned as its first emperor in AD 800. His quarrelling successors broke up the empire, and by AD 987 France had become a separate kingdom.

England at that time was divided into many small kingdoms. These were rivals, but they shared various customs, including a language – English. The kingdoms came under constant attack from the Vikings. In the late 800s, one of the English kings – later known as Alfred the Great – won a series of battles against them. By the mid-900s the Viking threat had been lifted and kings ruled over a united country known as England.

▲ *The rule of Charlemagne (centre) brought a period of peace and unity to Europe after several centuries of fighting and disputes.*

CASTLES

By the late 1200s, most powerful European rulers had built castles to defend themselves. The living quarters were in the main building, or keep, which was surrounded by outer walls and a moat. In the event of attack, the draw-bridge over the moat was pulled up to keep enemies at a distance.

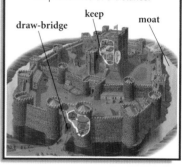

draw-bridge   keep   moat

THE ROLE OF THE CHURCH

Christianity had become the official religion of the Roman Empire in its later years, and many Europeans remained Christian after Rome fell. So although new countries were forming – and often fighting each other – many people shared the Christian religion. The Christian Church, led by the Pope, was based in Rome. Priests and bishops in different countries obeyed the Pope and often tried to resolve differences between rival kings. Many churches and great cathedrals were built throughout Europe. The Church tried to preserve much of the ancient knowledge of Greece and Rome.

Monks, living in secluded monasteries, spent their lives copying out ancient books by hand. For centuries almost the only books in Europe were those kept in monastery libraries. Other monks travelled to parts of Europe that had never been ruled by Rome, teaching the people about Christianity.

◀ *Monasteries were places where monks were able to live and worship together. These monastery ruins are in Ireland.*

177

CONFLICT WITH ISLAM

ONE of the world's great religions developed in the 600s in Arabia. This was where the prophet Muhammad began preaching the religion known as Islam – 'obedience to God'. Its message, set out in a holy book called the Koran, calls on people to live a fair, just life and to worship one God, Allah. Muhammad was forced to leave his home city of Mecca in 622, because rich merchants disagreed with his message about helping the poor. He gathered an army and later captured Mecca, which is still the most important city for Muslims (followers of Islam).

▲ *The Dome of the Rock in Jerusalem is a Muslim shrine built on the site of the first Jewish temple.*

SPREADING THE WORD

Arabia's many different peoples soon united under the new religion. After Muhammad's death in 632, Muslim armies swept out of Arabia, spreading the message of Islam and capturing large territories. Among its conquests was the city of Jerusalem and other parts of the Holy Land (at that time Palestine and Syria). The Muslims then moved eastwards into Asia and westwards

▲ *Millions of Muslim pilgrims go each year to their holiest shrine, the Ka'abah in Mecca.*

▼ *Muslim warriors (on the right) rode swift horses and wore light armour, which gave them the advantage of speed over the heavily armoured European knights (on the left) during the battles of the Crusades.*

▲ *Muslims ruled the Iberian peninsula for nearly 800 years. This Moorish (Muslim) castle is in Sesimbra, Portugal.*

across North Africa, converting people as they went and establishing Muslim governments. By the mid-700s, Muslims had spread as far as China in the east and Spain in the west. Muslim rulers allowed Christians and Jews to practice their religion, and encouraged scientists and poets.

RELIGIOUS RIVALRY

In 1020 Christians from the east were given back all their property in Jerusalem. The Holy Land was at peace until about 1050. But from 1071 the Muslims prevented Christian pilgrims from visiting Jerusalem. Pope Urban II preached a sermon calling for a 'holy war' to recover the Holy Land from the Muslims in 1095.

The response was dramatic. Thousands of Europeans, mainly from France and southern Italy, set sail for the eastern Mediterranean in 1096. This First 'Crusade' (from the Latin word for 'cross') captured many Muslim strongholds and eventually Jerusalem fell to the Christian Europeans in 1099. The Crusaders slaughtered large numbers of innocent Jewish and Muslim people in Jerusalem, and their victory left behind great bitterness.

ENGLAND
HOLY ROMAN EMPIRE
FRANCE
EUROPE
SPAIN
ITALY
Black Sea
BYZANTINE EMPIRE
Mediterranean Sea
HOLY LAND
•Jerusalem
AFRICA
ARABIA

▲ *There were eight Crusades from Europe between 1096 and 1272. Nearly all had Jerusalem as their destination.*

FIGHTING BACK

Attack by Christian invaders caused the Muslims to unite more strongly. Within 30 years they had won back much of the Holy Land, causing the Europeans to launch a Second Crusade in 1147. This effort failed, but European kings and religious leaders urged further attacks. In a tragic Children's Crusade, thousands of young volunteers died or were sold into slavery before they reached Palestine. Later Crusades saw great heroism on both sides – particularly from Richard the Lionheart (King Richard I of England) and his Muslim opponent Saladin. The last Crusade ended in 1270. By then it was clear that Muslims would retain control of the area.

MONGOL HORSEMEN

IN LESS than 50 years during the early 1200s, a group of warrior-horsemen established a huge empire that extended from China in the east to Russia in the west. These warriors were the Mongols, whose home was the vast, windswept plain of Mongolia, to the north of China. One of the harshest places on Earth, it is a near-desert with extremely hot summers and freezing winters. The Mongols lived as nomads (wanderers), moving their sheep and horses from one known grassland to another. They were superb horsemen. Skilled Mongol archers were able to fire arrows with deadly accuracy while galloping at full speed on their tough, fast little horses.

▲ *The Chinese royal family built the Forbidden City in Beijing after the Mongols finally retreated in the late 1300s.*

THE RULE OF GENGHIS KHAN

One of the reasons the Mongols kept on the move was constant rivalry between different groups. In the early 1200s, one Mongol leader, Temujin, succeeded in defeating all his rivals. In 1206 he was accepted as overall leader, and was given the title Genghis Khan, 'ruler of all'. Genghis Khan decided to go on the attack with his newly united army. He invaded China, crossing the Great Wall from the north and capturing large territories, including the capital, Beijing. Then his horsemen rode westward through the powerful kingdoms of the Turks and Arabs. In 1222 the Mongol armies crushed resistance in an area of Russia extending from the Persian Gulf in the south almost as far north as the Arctic Ocean. The Mongols set up khanates, or 'little

▼ *Mongol horsemen swept into Russia, crushing resistance and conquering a huge area that extended almost as far north as the Arctic Ocean.*

kingdoms', within the larger empire. A single ruler, the 'great khan', had overall control. Genghis Khan died in 1227 and his son Ogadai became great khan. Under Ogadai and other rulers, the Mongols continued their conquests. They captured the cities of Baghdad, Delhi and Samarkand. Mongol troops swept through Poland and Hungary, and in 1241 were preparing to take the rest of Europe, when they heard that Ogadai had died in China. The army retreated. Europe had been spared.

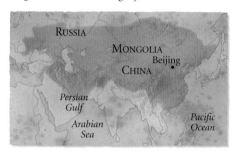

MANAGING AN EMPIRE

The Mongols were fierce fighters, but they allowed the people they conquered to practise their own religion, and Mongol khans welcomed religious leaders to discussions. The Mongols improved roads and made trading routes safe from bandits. Europe and Asia became linked as they had never been

▲ *The Mongol Empire was one of the largest land empires in history, extending from the Pacific Ocean in the east to the edge of western Europe.*

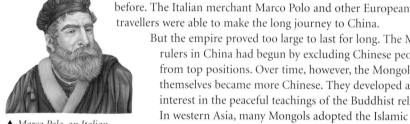

before. The Italian merchant Marco Polo and other European travellers were able to make the long journey to China.

But the empire proved too large to last for long. The Mongol rulers in China had begun by excluding Chinese people from top positions. Over time, however, the Mongols themselves became more Chinese. They developed an interest in the peaceful teachings of the Buddhist religion. In western Asia, many Mongols adopted the Islamic faith of the people they ruled. Although they continued to rule the area that is now southern Russia until the late 1400s, elsewhere their empire collapsed.

▲ *Marco Polo, an Italian trader, spent several years in the palace of the Mongol emperor Kublai Khan in the 1260s.*

▶ *Tamerlane, the Mongol conqueror, captured the Central Asian city of Isfahan in 1387. He is said to have massacred 70,000 inhabitants. This beautiful mosque was built about 200 years later.*

THE BLACK DEATH

A TERRIBLE infectious disease known as bubonic plague killed millions of people in Asia and Europe in the 1300s. At the time, no-one knew the cause of the plague, or how it was passed from one person to another. They called it the Black Death, because its victims developed bleeding spots that turned black.

In fact bubonic plague is caused by tiny organisms called bacteria. It was spread by infected fleas, which having bit (and killed) the rats that carried them, went on to bite humans. The disease affects the lungs. Humans can pass it on to other humans through the droplets they produce when coughing or sneezing.

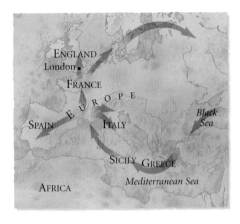

▲ *This map shows how the bubonic plague, or Black Death, entered Europe from Asia via the Black Sea and then swept across the continent.*

CROSSING CONTINENTS

The Black Death appeared in China in the 1320s. By 1400 it had killed 35 million people there – nearly a third of the population. Travelling merchants unknowingly spread the disease west through India and the Middle East. In 1347, traders from Black Sea ports brought the disease to the island of Sicily in a ship carrying infected rats. In less than three years it had swept through all of Europe and North Africa. About 25 million Europeans were killed by this first wave of the Black Death. Entire villages were wiped out. The disease returned to

▲ *Plague spread because infected fleas, having killed the rats they bit, went on to bite humans.*

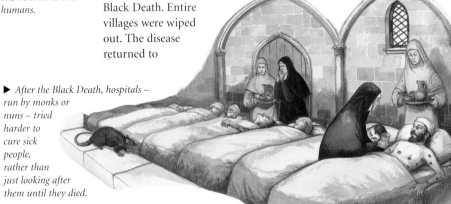

▶ *After the Black Death, hospitals – run by monks or nuns – tried harder to cure sick people, rather than just looking after them until they died.*

Europe again in 1361–63, 1369–71, 1374–75, 1390 and 1400. It killed a greater proportion of the world's people than any other disease or war in history.

FINDING REASONS

People in Europe wanted to find out what caused the terrible disease. Because fleas and rats were so common, no-one connected it to them. Some people thought that bad smells or warm air were responsible, others thought that plague could be caught just by a look from an infected person.

Some people believed that the disease was God's punishment for evil behaviour. Groups of these people, known as

▲ *Many Europeans responded to the widespread deaths by becoming more religious. Flagellants (people who deliberately whipped themselves) marched through many towns.*

'flagellants' wandered across Europe, whipping themselves, carrying religious pictures and praying aloud for God's forgiveness. Other people blamed the Jews and killed thousands of innocent Jewish people.

FAR-REACHING EFFECTS

Ships carried the disease to Greenland, where the population was completely wiped out. It is now believed that the plague was the reason why other distant Viking settlements – including those in North America – disappeared. In Europe the effects were widespread. With a third of the population dead, there was a great shortage of workers. Those who survived began to demand higher pay for their work and more freedom to travel. Some of these workers went on strike to force their masters to meet their

▲ *The nursery rhyme 'Ring-a-ring o' Roses' dates from the Great Plague of 1665. The 'roses' refer to the bleeding spots of a plague victim. "A-tishoo, a-tishoo, we all fall down," tells of people sneezing and dying from plague.*

demands. The Peasants' Revolt shook England in 1381. Poor people, led by a former soldier named Wat Tyler, marched on London to protest against a harsh tax used to pay for wars against France. King Richard II crushed the revolt, but he had learned a lesson – no similar taxes were ever seen again in England.

▶ *Those who survived the plague, like these fighters in the Peasants' Revolt in England, tried to improve living conditions for the poor.*

EMPIRES OF THE AMERICAS

CENTRAL and South America has seen the rise and fall of many great civilizations. Perhaps the three greatest were the Maya of Central America (c. 300 BC–c. AD 1500s); the Aztecs, also of Central America (c. AD 1300–1521); and the Incas of South America (AD 1100s–1532).

THE MAYA OF CENTRAL AMERICA

The Maya people of Central America began developing their civilization more than 2,500 years ago, mainly in the region of today's Guatemala and eastern Mexico. By 300 BC they

▲ *Mayan statues usually depicted gods, but sometimes showed events in ordinary life. Outside the cities, most Mayans were farmers.*

were building huge, pyramid-like temples, where human sacrifices to the gods took place. Over time their temple complexes became more elaborate, and by AD 600 they included large squares, ball courts and huge stone carvings of Mayan gods. Mayan astronomers studied the heavens and worked out a calendar that was more advanced than the pre-1700s European calendar. The people had a written language, and created colourful paintings, beautiful jewellery and precious works in jade. The Mayan civilization was probably at its peak from the 4th to the 9th centuries. But the people were not warlike, and over the next few centuries their civilization declined, possibly as they were conquered by other peoples.

▲ *The carvings on this Mayan tomb are from Palenque, a powerful city-state in southern Mexico. They tell of royal events in Mayan history.*

MEXICO AND THE AZTECS

The long central valley of Mexico was the site of several advanced civilizations. Farming settlements grew up there more than 4,000 years ago, growing fruits and

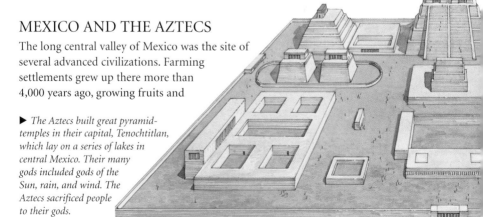

▶ *The Aztecs built great pyramid-temples in their capital, Tenochtitlan, which lay on a series of lakes in central Mexico. Their many gods included gods of the Sun, rain, and wind. The Aztecs sacrificed people to their gods.*

▲ *Serpents, sometimes covered in feathers, are common subjects for the art of the Maya, Aztec and other Central American civilizations.*

vegetables in the fertile soil. By about AD 100, one group of people, influenced by the Mayas, built a huge city called Teotihuacan, where more than 200,000 people lived. At its heart were several huge, pyramid-shaped temples. About AD 1000, the warlike Toltecs invaded the valley and established their own civilization. Some 300 years later the even more powerful Aztecs arrived. The Aztecs were fierce warriors, but they valued the skills of their predecessors, the Maya and the Teotihuacan people. They built a new capital, Tenochtitlan, on a series of lakes, and formed an empire that covered most of present-day central and southern Mexico. But in 1521 the empire was brought down by a small Spanish force, led by Hernando Cortés, and a large number of Indian allies.

THE INCA EMPIRE

The Inca civilization began to develop high up in the Andes of present-day Peru about AD 1100. Inca cities were built from massive stones carved to fit together precisely, without mortar. Unlike the civilizations of Central America, the Inca had no written language. Instead they recorded information on knotted pieces of string. In the 1400s the Inca began building an empire. They moved southward along the Andes, eventually conquering an area about 4,000 kilometres long and 800 kilometres wide. A network of roads and bridges linked places in the mountains. The Inca Empire was still growing when its people fell to the Spanish. An army led by Francisco Pizarro landed in 1532, killed the Inca emperor, and by 1537 controlled the whole Inca Empire.

▲ *Extent of the two great civilizations of Central America – the Maya and the Aztecs – and the Incas of South America.*

▶ *Inca messengers worked in relays to carry knot-messages long distances across the empire.*

STUDYING THE EVIDENCE

WHEN we talk about history, we really mean written history. Although it is possible to learn something about a lost civilization by looking at buildings, tools and pottery artifacts, we really need to have an idea of what the people thought. This usually comes from some sort of written record, such as the cuneiform writing of the Sumerians, the hieroglyphs (picture writing) of ancient Egypt, or the Latin inscriptions of the Roman Empire.

▲ These carvings decorate a wall of Angkor Wat in Cambodia, said to be the largest religious complex ever built. The temple is sometimes threatened not only by people fighting, but also by some tourists who break bits off as souvenirs.

▲ The Rosetta Stone helped historians learn to read Egyptian picture writing, or hieroglyphics. It was inscribed with the same message written in hieroglyphics, Greek and another ancient Egyptian language.

HOW ARCHAEOLOGISTS WORK

The people who study physical evidence left by past cultures are called archaeologists. They work slowly and painstakingly, digging through layers of dirt and stones to find ancient objects buried there. Sometimes an item as small as a coin can provide new information about a lost civilization. When archaeologists find an object, they treat it with great care, because items that have been buried for thousands of years can disintegrate when exposed to the air. They also make sure that they do not ignore objects that at first sight may seem unimportant, such as rubbish or broken plates. These can tell us a great deal about how people lived in ancient times.

◀ Archaeologists work slowly and carefully at one of their 'digs'. They use brushes as well as small spades to dig up objects. Sometimes they rinse away dirt with small amounts of water. They mark the exact spot where each object was found before taking it away for analysis.

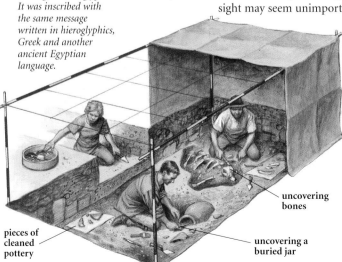

uncovering bones

pieces of cleaned pottery

uncovering a buried jar

◀ *The Dead Sea Scrolls – 2,000-year-old, hand-written copies of the Old Testament books of the Bible – were discovered by accident in 1947. They are now on display at museums in Israel and Jordan.*

NEW FOR OLD

In Rome today, many of the buildings are about 500 years old. Some lie on the foundations of even older buildings, dating from the time of the Roman Empire or even earlier. In some cases, the 'newer' buildings were made using bricks and other materials from the older ones, which makes unravelling their history a difficult puzzle.

Many other cities have similar 'layers' of history. Bath, in western England, for example, has many fine buildings dating from the 1700s and early 1800s. Below these lie traces of houses built about 500 years earlier. And below these archaeologists have found evidence of temples, markets and houses from the time when the Romans lived in the city, nearly 2,000 years ago.

KEEPING IT SAFE

Some precious historical buildings have been destroyed by war. During World War II (1939–45) many cities – including Coventry in England, Dresden in Germany and Hiroshima in Japan – were destroyed by bombs. Historical sites may also be lost when new buildings are built over the top of ancient remains. To prevent this happening, conservation groups campaign to save them.

In the 1990s, the US state of Florida purchased for $27 million a piece of land that was about to be built on. Historians and conservation groups had discovered that the land contained the remains of an ancient temple built by Native Americans. Because of this purchase, we will learn more about the earliest people who lived in that part of North America. But it is hard to raise enough money to save every site, and archaeologists often need to examine material quickly before the builders move in.

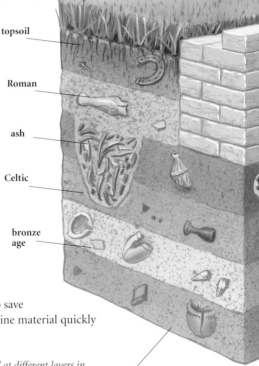

topsoil

Roman

ash

Celtic

bronze age

stone age

▶ *This cross-section of soil shows historical objects buried at different layers in the ground. Archaeologists take great care to record at which layer objects are found, because this provides information as to how old the objects are.*

QUIZ

1. Who did the United States fight for control of Puerto Rico and the Philippines in 1898?

2. What was the name of the Polish trade union that led the struggle against communism in the 1980s?

3. By what name were the Mongol horsemen known in Russia?

4. Which invention helped spread the Protestant faith in the early 1500s?

5. Which were the three main members of the Axis powers in World War II?

6. What year was the US Declaration of Independence signed?

7. Powerful city-states in which country led the way during the Renaissance?

8. At which major sea battle of 1805 was Napoleon defeated?

9. 'Black Thursday' – October 24, 1929 – was the start of what?

10. In 1488 Bartolomeu Dias of Portugal became the first European explorer to sail east past which major landmark?

11. Which war began after Archduke Franz-Ferdinand of Austria-Hungary was killed in Bosnia?

12. What do the letters NATO stand for?

13. Which islands of the New World did Columbus find first in 1492?

14. Which organisation was formed after the Allied leaders' meeting in Yalta at the end of World War II?

15. What was Grand Prince Ivan III of Muscovy known as?

16. Which great religious event took place in AD 1054?

17. The United States dropped atomic bombs on which two Japanese cities?

18. How did King Louis XVI of France die in 1793?

19. What was one of the major causes of the Thirty Years' War in Europe?

20. Which rebel leader set up a communist government in Cuba?

20. Fidel Castro
Protestants
19. Religious differences between Catholics and
French Revolution.
18. He was beheaded on the guillotine during the
17. Hiroshima and Nagasaki
branches of Christianity split.
16. The western (Catholic) and eastern (Orthodox)
15. Ivan the Great
14. The United Nations
13. The Bahamas (off Florida)
12. The North Atlantic Treaty Organisation
11. World War I
of Africa
10. The Cape of Good Hope on the southern tip
9. The Great Depression
8. Trafalgar
7. Italy
6. 1776
5. Germany, Italy and Japan
4. The printing press
3. Tatars
2. Solidarity
1. The Spanish

ANSWERS

MODERN HISTORY

WHAT we call modern history begins with a look back to the past. In the late Middle Ages, Europeans recaptured some of the skills and ideas of ancient Greece and Rome and made them the basis for new inventions and ideas. In the early 1500s, the printing press helped spread knowledge across Europe, including the new religious ideas of Protestants. Discoveries included new lands, where people settled and found previously unknown goods to trade. They established new ways to rule themselves, and in time developed new ways of making things, using machines powered by steam. Technological advances led to the creation of ever more efficient weapons. Two world wars in the twentieth century killed many millions of people. Conflicts continue, but examining the past helps us to put the present into context, and can fill us with hope for the future.

REDISCOVERING THE PAST

A FTER the break-up of the Roman Empire in the late 400s AD, Latin was still used as the international language of educated people. But from about 1200 onwards, languages such as French, English, Italian and German began to be used for songs, stories and poems. All over Europe the Church grew more powerful

▲ *The Italian city of Florence was one of the major centres of art during the Renaissance.*

and people built more elaborate cathedrals as a way of praising God. Crusaders returning from Muslim countries in the east brought back new ideas that enabled the builders to raise high, pointed arches and fill windows with stained glass. Wells Cathedral in England and Chartres in France, both built in the late 1100s to early 1200s, are just two examples.

A FRESH START

In the early 1300s a new movement of ideas began in Italy. Powerful, rich city-states such as Florence, Venice and Milan controlled much of the country. The rulers and rich merchants in these cities encouraged artists, who – along with some Italian writers – began to look again at the ideas of ancient Greece and Rome. Inspired by the ancient buildings and books around them, they realized that to the ancient Greeks, the way that humans

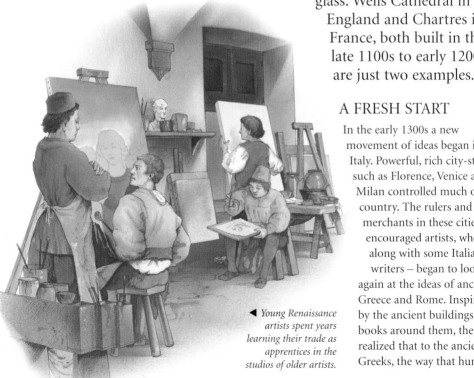

◀ *Young Renaissance artists spent years learning their trade as apprentices in the studios of older artists.*

tried to live was more important than religious teaching. The emphasis that Italian writers and artists gave to the importance of humans – 'humanism' – was at the heart of this time of discovery, which we call the Renaissance (French for 'rebirth').

NEW AND OLD

Renaissance artists used new techniques to create works that seemed more life-like than before. Architects adopted the Greek and Roman style as the basis for beautiful churches and public buildings. Some artists turned their hand to other things for inspiration. The artist and sculptor Michelangelo, for example, also wrote poems, while Leonardo da Vinci not only painted many masterpieces, but also designed weapons, pumps, bridges and even an early type of helicopter. A new artistic wave swept across Europe in the 1400s and 1500s. Even the great English playwright William Shakespeare is often described as a Renaissance writer, because his plays were the first since those of ancient Greek writers to deal with the joys and sorrows that all humans share.

▲ *Renaissance artists were inspired with new ideas by Greek and Roman art and architecture, the remains of which survive all around the Mediterranean region.*

▼ *New painting techniques gave a sense of life to familiar subjects, especially stories from the Bible. This painting, called* Il Creator, *is by Michelangelo.*

CHRISTIANITY DIVIDED

THROUGHOUT the Middle Ages, countries in Europe were often at war with each other, but one thing united them – religion. They were all Christian, converted by missionaries, who were religious people sent to convert others. Missionaries had 'spread the word' of the Christian faith to the Franks, Saxons, Danes and other peoples who had settled in many parts of the former Roman Empire.

CENTRE OF THE FAITH

Although Rome fell as a political power in the 400s, the city remained the centre of the Christian faith for people in Europe. The leader of the Church, the Pope, lived in Rome and directed the activities of the Church from his palace on the Vatican hill. Western European Christians were all Catholics, who believed – and still believe – that the Pope was the representative of Christ on Earth. They also respect the clergy – bishops, priests and monks – as representatives of the Pope and leaders of public worship. In 1054, Christians in eastern Europe and those in the western Church split. Eastern Christians became known as the Orthodox Church. They still shared most of the beliefs and practices of the Catholic Church, but rejected the power of the Pope.

▲ *Martin Luther triggered the Reformation in 1517 when he nailed his 95 theses to the door of a German church.*

▼ *The spirit of questioning spread far beyond religious disputes. European doctors used their new scientific knowledge to study the human body more closely.*

◀ *France was torn apart by religious wars in the late 1500s as Catholics and Protestants fought over their beliefs. Both wanted to put a king of their choice on the French throne.*

CRITICISM FROM WITHIN

During the Middle Ages the Catholic Church, which owned a great deal of land, became extremely wealthy and powerful – it could even force kings to obey its wishes. Many people within the Church wanted to reform it by removing some of its power. They protested that many clergy had grown dishonest, were living immoral lives, and took gifts from people in return for 'blessings' that would help them be 'saved' from going to Hell.

THE BIG BREAK

In 1517 a priest named Martin Luther nailed a list of 95 criticisms to the door of Wittenberg church in Germany. He outlined the many ways in which the Catholic Church needed reforming and questioned the power of the pope in Rome. Luther believed that religious services should be conducted in the everyday language of the people, rather than in Latin. He felt that people should be able to come to God directly through prayer, rather than relying on priests to do it for them. Other religious 'protesters' gave their support to Luther, which is why such Christians became

▲ *Printed religious books, especially the Bible, helped spread the Protestant faith quickly round Europe in the early 1500s.*

known as Protestants. The printing press, a new invention in Europe, spread Luther's message far and wide. In 1521 he made his final break with Rome. The conflict between Protestants and Catholics soon divided Europe. Thousands of people left the Catholic Church to become 'Lutherans'. Some Protestant reformers made even more extreme changes. A number of rulers joined the new faith because it criticized Rome's control over their power. Others fiercely protected the Catholic cause. The differences led to bloodshed in many countries and was one of the causes of the Thirty Years' War (1618–48).

▼ *Early printing presses were slow and clumsy, but they could produce books very much faster than it took monks to write them out by hand.*

193

NEW WORLDS TO EXPLORE

UNTIL the Middle Ages, as far as we know the peoples of Europe, Africa and Asia had no contact with the Americas. Widespread trade and stories of adventurous merchants meant that Europeans, Africans and Asians at least knew of each other's existence, but North and South America remained totally cut off from the rest of the world. The first long-distance explorers were Vikings, who sailed from Scandinavia to Iceland. From there they sailed to Greenland and established a settlement, and in the 1000s they reached the northeast coast of North America. Other Europeans learned little about these journeys, and it was not until the 1400s that they first started to explore lands beyond Europe themselves.

◀ In his first voyage across the Atlantic in 1492, Christopher Columbus took three ships with a total crew of 120 men. The ships sailed west at first, then southwest. On October 12, 1492, they sighted land – the island now known as San Salvador in the Bahamas.

▼ In 1519 the Spanish conquistador (soldier-explorer) Hernando Cortés led a group of 600 men into Mexico. The Native Americans had never seen horses or guns, and Cortés's men were able to conquer the mighty Aztec empire in less than two years.

PUSHING THE LIMITS

In the early 1400s, merchant-explorers from Portugal were eager to find a sea route to Asia, so they could bring back spices, silk and precious stones for trade in Europe. Throughout the 1400s they gradually sailed farther and farther southwards down the west coast of Africa, and in 1488 Bartolomeu Dias rounded the southern tip of Africa – the Cape of Good Hope. Ten years later Vasco da Gama, followed Dias's route and continued on to India. Exploration made Portugal rich, and European countries competed to find more direct routes to Asia for trade. Christopher Columbus obtained backing from King Ferdinand and Queen Isabella of Spain for an expedition to find a westward route around the world. He set off on his famous voyage across the Atlantic and reached the Bahamas in October 1492. Believing he had reached Asia, he made three more voyages. When he arrived at what is now Venezuela, in 1498, he realized he had 'discovered' a new land – later known as the Americas.

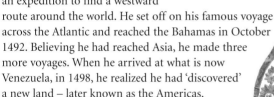

▲ *French Catholic priests used traditional Native American canoes to voyage deep into North America. They converted many Native Americans to the Christian faith.*

▼ *The Inca, a Native American peoples of the Andes of Peru, were skilled craftsmen. This elaborate headdress is made of gold and jewels.*

A NEW WORLD

Spain was quick to send armies to Central and South America. The Conquistadors (conquering soldiers) crushed the native Aztec and Inca civilizations, and set up colonies.

Meanwhile, other European nations sailed to the 'New World' – as the Americas were called – and claimed areas for themselves. Portugal took what is now Brazil, the largest country in South America. France, England, Holland and Sweden all rivalled the Spanish to set up colonies in North America. The English colonies along North America's Atlantic coast later became the United States of America.

◀ *In 1620, a group of 102 English people known as the Pilgrims settled in Massachusetts. Only half lived through the first winter.*

RUSSIA UNITES

THE country we call Russia was formed out of kingdoms based on the cities of Kiev and Novgorod. Their founders were known as the 'Rus' – they were a mixture of Slavs from the east and Scandinavian Vikings from the west. The Russians were not a united people, but they did share a language and the Orthodox Christian religion.

▲ *Russia is a vast country, part of it in Europe, but most in Asia. It has huge forests and broad plains that extend as far as the eye can see.*

Over the next few centuries, Russia became a land of powerful city-states. These city-states were often at war with each other, but in the 1200s they faced a common threat from their east. In 1223, the Mongol armies of Genghis Khan swept into Russia from Mongolia to the east and conquered nearly all of the territory belonging to these city-states. The Mongols, known as Tatars to the Russians, ruled firmly, forcing Russian leaders in neighbouring lands to promise obedience to them. Most of Russia was ruled by the Tatars for more than two hundred years.

▼ *Red Square lies at the heart of the Russian capital, Moscow. To the right are the towers and high walls of the Kremlin, the fortress that guarded the royal palaces of the first tsars (rulers). The Russian word for the name of the square means 'beautiful', but the same word can also mean 'red'.*

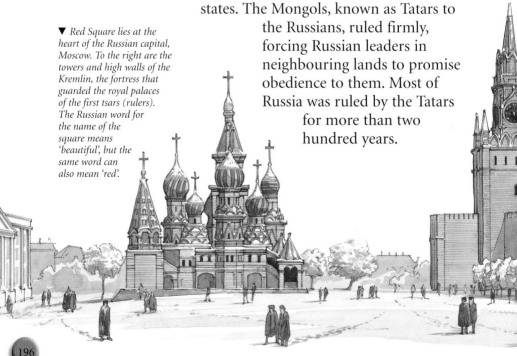

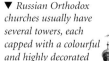

▼ Russian Orthodox churches usually have several towers, each capped with a colourful and highly decorated 'onion dome'.

THE RISE OF MOSCOW

Moscow emerged as the most powerful city in Russia. Its rulers kept good relations with the Tatars, and in 1326 they persuaded the head of the Russian Orthodox Church to move to Moscow from Kiev. Religious leaders agreed to call the rulers of Moscow princes 'of all Russia'. In the late 1300s, these princes led a series of successful revolts against the Tatars, and in the 1400s they extended their territories to include more of Russia.

HEIR TO AN EMPIRE

In 1453 Muslim Turks captured Constantinople (also called Byzantium), capital of the Eastern Roman, or Byzantine, Empire. Constantinople was the centre of the Orthodox Church, but now that it was ruled by Muslims,

▶ The Orthodox Church has been an important force in Russia for centuries. Orthodox priests supported efforts to end the Tatar rule of their country.

Moscow considered itself to be the new Orthodox capital. Grand Prince Ivan III of Muscovy (known as 'Ivan the Great') married the niece of the last Byzantine emperor, and the two-headed eagle of Byzantium was included in Moscow's coat of arms – it was regarded as the symbol of Holy Russia. In 1478, Ivan defeated the city of Novgorod, Moscow's main rival, and gained territories that extended from present-day Finland in the west to the Ural Mountains in the east. At this time the Tatars were becoming weaker and less united, so Ivan decided to free the Russian people from their rule. In 1480 he refused to pay the annual tribute to the local Tatar khan, or ruler. Russians see that date as the beginning of real independence.

EXPANSION

Once Ivan III achieved full independence, he set about expanding Russia by invading the neighbouring countries of Lithuania and Poland. He also established a code of laws and ensured that his heirs would follow him as tsar. His grandson was crowned Tsar Ivan IV in 1547. He was the first to use the title 'tsar', meaning emperor, from the Latin name 'Caesar'. Called Ivan 'the Terrible' because of the brutality he showed his opponents, he spent his 37-year reign making Russia stronger and still larger.

REVOLUTION

THE 1700s began with powerful European countries such as Great Britain, Spain and France ruling many colonies overseas. Slaves did much of the manual labour in many of the colonies, which sent goods such as sugar, cotton and timber back to Europe. At this time most of the European rulers were 'absolute monarchs' (rulers without any checks to their power). Increasingly, ordinary people began to feel that the kings were asking them to pay unfair taxes and were giving no benefits in return.

▲ *In 1773 a group of rebels, dressed as Native Americans, dumped a cargo of English tea into Boston Harbor, in what became known as the Boston Tea Party.*

▲ *Representatives from Britain's thirteen North American colonies signed the Declaration of Independence on July 4, 1776, thereby creating the United States of America.*

AMERICAN INDEPENDENCE

In the mid-1700s, settlers in the thirteen British colonies along North America's Atlantic coast began to grow restless at having to pay British taxes. In 1774 representatives of the colonies met at a Continental Congress. The British king, George III, saw this as an act of rebellion and sent soldiers to enforce the law. In April 1775 British and American troops fought at the towns of Lexington and Concord in Massachusetts. This led to outright war, and the thirteen colonies declared full independence from Britain on July 4, 1776. France sent soldiers and ships to support the American rebels. The war finally ended in 1781. Two years later Britain recognized an independent United States.

▼ *The British won the Battle of Bunker Hill, near Boston, in June 1775, but the closely fought battle strengthened the American will to fight on.*

THE FRENCH REVOLUTION

France became the next scene of revolution, as French involvement in the American Revolution drove the French monarchy into bankruptcy. In 1789, a meeting of the French parliament was called for the first time since 1614. The public began to overthrow symbols of hated royal power, and captured the Bastille, a famous prison in Paris.

▲ *In South America, Simon Bolivar led many attacks against Spanish troops in the early 1800s, as Spain's colonies fought for their independence.*

In 1792 the French declared their nation a republic (a country ruled by elected officials) and King Louis XVI was beheaded by the guillotine in 1793. Thousands of other people were also executed. France only settled down in 1799, when a successful young general, Napoleon Bonaparte, took control of the government.

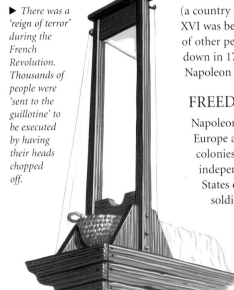

▶ *There was a 'reign of terror' during the French Revolution. Thousands of people were 'sent to the guillotine' to be executed by having their heads chopped off.*

FREEDOM FROM SPAIN

Napoleon's French armies advanced through much of Europe and invaded Spain in 1808. Spain's American colonies seized the opportunity to fight for independence, inspired by the newly created United States of America and France. Led by popular soldiers such as Simon Bolivar and Bernardo O'Higgins, the colonists threw off Spanish rule. By 1825, all of Spanish America, except Cuba and Puerto Rico, had established republics, and in 1822 Brazil became independent from Portugal.

THE RISE OF INDUSTRY

WHILE political revolutions in America and France changed the way countries were governed, a different kind of revolution in Britain changed the way people made their livings. In 1700 most people in Britain lived in villages, growing food. Most industry relied on farm produce, such as leather for shoes, wool for cloth and grain for bread and beer. By 1900 most British people lived in cities and worked in factories, using complex, fast-moving, steam-powered machinery and raw materials from abroad to make goods sold worldwide. It was the steam-engine more than anything else that powered these huge changes.

▲ *In a given time, one spinning Jenny (invented in 1764) could produce as much yarn as dozens of workers using traditional spinning wheels.*

THE POWER OF STEAM

Steam-pumps enabled miners to dig Britain's rich resources of coal and iron from deep underground. The iron was used to build, and the coal was used to fuel the steam-powered machinery that produced cloth and household goods in quantities and at a speed never seen before in history. From the 1820s onwards, steam-powered railways and ships changed the face of transport and trade for ever.

▼ *Weavers who used hand looms like this one lost their jobs when steam-driven looms were introduced from 1786 onwards. Traditional looms broke or wore out easily.*

VALUABLE RESOURCES

Britain became the world's first industrial country because it had coal, iron, copper, tin and lead, many rivers and a long coastline for shipping goods. It also had dynamic businessmen who were willing to try out new inventions. Britain even benefited from being involved in foreign wars that were fought overseas. These brought new colonies such as Canada and India, which provided new riches, such as furs, cottons and spices, and offered new markets for British-made products. Warfare also boosted industry with orders for guns, uniforms, provisions and ships.

▲ *In 1769, Richard Arkwright developed a water-powered spinning frame that drew cotton fibre into thread and twisted it onto bobbins.*

▼ *Thomas Newcomen developed a steam engine for pumping water in 1705. It was the first practical use of steam power.*

FACTORIES

The change to factory work meant long hours and unhealthy working conditions for many. Until about 1850 the new wealth from industry benefited the people who owned the factories, rather than those who worked in them. But from then onwards most people were able to dress better and live longer lives in more comfortable homes filled with more possessions. British businessmen and engineers spread modern industry round the world, first to neighbouring Belgium and France, then to Germany and the USA, and by 1900 to Japan.

▼ *Even before the arrival of railways in Britain, improved roads and canals made the movement of people and goods cheaper and faster. Great bridges, carrying roads and canals, spanned rivers and linked factory towns with the rest of the country.*

EUROPE AT WAR

NAPOLEON Bonaparte began as a brilliant young soldier who seemed to represent all the new ideas of freedom coming out of France. But once he had become Emperor, he used his power just as kings had done before him.

▲ Napoleon conquered countries across much of central Europe in the early 1800s, claiming them for the French Empire.

NEW PARTNERSHIPS

In 1793, Austria, Prussia, Britain, Spain, the Netherlands and the Kingdom of Sardinia formed an alliance (a partnership of countries) to fight revolutionary France. The alliance was called the First Coalition. In 1796 the French government gave a young general, Napoleon Bonaparte, the task of taking on Austrian forces in northern Italy. In less than a year, he had led his troops to victory over the larger Austrian army. The First Coalition fell apart. In 1798 Napoleon led an expedition to conquer Egypt, giving France a base for future attacks against British possessions in India. While Napoleon was in Egypt a new alliance was formed – the Second Coalition. This was composed of Russia, Britain, Austria, the Kingdom of Naples, Portugal and the Ottoman Empire (based in present-day Turkey).

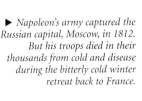

▲ Napoleon was a great leader and also a good judge of men. He would watch from a vantage point as his generals followed his orders and gained victories.

▶ Napoleon's army captured the Russian capital, Moscow, in 1812. But his troops died in their thousands from cold and disease during the bitterly cold winter retreat back to France.

IMPERIAL FRANCE

Napoleon returned to France as a hero in 1799 and was given control of the government. Knowing that the Second Coalition had won many battles against the French, he offered to make peace. They refused, so in 1800 Napoleon led a huge army across the Alps into Italy. There, and in Germany and Austria, the French won many important battles and gained more territory. In 1801 the Second Coalition fell apart, and fighting stopped.

Napoleon, who had been appointed by a revolutionary government, had himself crowned emperor in 1804. His rise to power in France was followed by further victories all over Europe. Britain's naval victory at the Battle of Trafalgar in 1805, however, denied Napoleon control of the seas.

LAST DAYS OF GLORY

The European powers formed yet more alliances over the next few years. But eventually Napoleon tried to extend his empire too far. In 1812, at the southwestern end of Europe, the Spanish and their British allies were trying to drive the French from Spain. Napoleon then decided to march against Russia, in the northeast of the continent. The French eventually captured Russia's capital, Moscow, but had to turn back because of cold, hunger and terrible losses. Nine-tenths of the French army was lost. France's enemies captured Paris in 1814. Napoleon was forced to leave France, but he was not quite finished. He secretly returned, organized an army and began more fighting. The French enjoyed brief success, but the end finally came on June 18, 1815, when the combined forces of Britain and Prussia defeated Napoleon at the Battle of Waterloo.

▲ *Napoleon's final defeat came at the Battle of Waterloo in June 1815. After a day of terrible fighting, his army was crushed by the combined forces of Britain and Prussia.*

RIVAL EMPIRES

A^{S EARLY} as the 1400s, Spain set up huge colonies in North and South America. Other countries, including France, Britain and Portugal, also settled in large parts of the Americas, Africa and Asia. Once these European powers had conquered the native peoples – whose weapons were usually no match for guns – they took the area's valuable items such as gold, silver, furs, spices or timber for their own benefit. But in the 1700s and 1800s, many colonies, beginning with those in North America, became independent. By 1825, Spain and Portugal had lost nearly all their American colonies. European countries began to use treaties rather than force to achieve their aims.

BELGIAN
BRITISH
FRENCH
GERMAN
ITALIAN
PORTUGUESE
SPANISH
INDEPENDENT

▲ *Many European countries claimed parts of Africa in the 1800s. Their conflict and rivalry there was termed 'the scramble for Africa'.*

▲ *British troops fought a series of battles against the Zulu people in South Africa to secure control of the country in the 1870s.*

▼ *Throughout the 1800s, European ports were full of great sailing ships arriving with goods brought back from foreign colonies.*

◀ This map shows the extent of the British Empire in the late 1800s. It encircled the globe, from Canada in the west to Australia in the east.

▼ From 1557 until 1999, the Portuguese leased from China a tiny enclave on the southern coast called Macao and ran it as a trade centre.

The map shows:
- RUSSIAN
- BRITISH
- FRENCH
- PORTUGUESE
- GERMAN
- BELGIAN
- SPANISH

With labels: CANADA, USA, RUSSIAN EMPIRE, AFRICA, INDIA, AUSTRALIA

INDUSTRIAL EMPIRES

By the mid-1800s, the leading European countries had become industrial powers. Their factories needed huge amounts of raw materials, such as cotton, copper and timber, to make goods. They also needed cheap food for their growing populations. Expanding their empires was one way to supply these needs. At the same time, many Europeans saw it as their duty to teach native peoples within their empires the European ideas of law, care of children and Christianity.

THE BRITISH EMPIRE

Britain led this drive for empire. Although small in area, Britain had the world's most powerful navy, which enabled it to send traders, missionaries (religious workers) and soldiers to Africa and Asia. By the end of the 1800s much of Africa, along with India, Malaya, Hong Kong, Canada and Australia had come under British control. It was said that 'the sun never set on the British Empire.'

▲ British officials were sent to govern India during what is now called the Raj – the period of British imperial rule in India.

TRADING RIVALS

France was almost as great a colonizing power as Britain. Belgium, the Netherlands, Portugal, Spain and Germany also ruled large empires. In 1898 the United States took control of Puerto Rico and the Philippines after fighting the Spanish in the Spanish-American War. Trade rivalry between colonial powers often caused tension, and later developed into outright war.

205

'A WAR TO END ALL WARS'

THE 20th century saw some of the worst conflicts in history. The two largest wars became known as World Wars, because they involved countries from several continents. New weapons such as machine guns, tanks, submarines and aeroplanes made these wars especially deadly. Millions of soldiers died, as did huge numbers of civilians – people not in the fighting forces.

▼ *Tanks were first used by British forces at the Battle of the Somme in 1916.*

EUROPEAN RIVALRY

The causes of the First World War, or World War I – which lasted from 1914 until 1918 – date back to the late 1800s. At this time, the major European nations of Britain, France and Germany had become jealous of each other's industrial power, and rivalry over establishing overseas colonies was fierce. Alliances were formed between these and other European countries. Although supposedly pledges of friendship, in reality they only increased existing fears. Both sides began building up their armed forces, and by the early 1900s tension was so high that one small incident was enough to spark off all-out war.

| Central powers | Neutral |
| Allied powers | Major fronts |

◀ *This map shows areas where some of the fiercest fighting took place during World War I.*

◀ *Big Bertha was a German cannon that could fire 1-tonne shells more than 15 km.*

THE FIGHTING BEGINS

The incident that started the war took place in Bosnia. A young Serbian killed Archduke Franz-Ferdinand of Austria-Hungary, who was visiting, in June 1914. Austria-Hungary declared war on Serbia, and because of their complicated alliances many other European countries were drawn into the war. Austria-Hungary was joined by Germany and Turkey. Together – and with some smaller countries – they were called the Central powers. Fighting against them were the Allied powers, led by Britain,

◄ Biplanes (two-winged aircraft) were the first powered aircraft to be used in warfare.

► First World War infantry soldiers: German (left) and British (right).

France and Russia. Altogether 32 countries were involved in the war, including troops from the United States, Canada, Australia, New Zealand and India. Vast numbers of people on both sides rushed to join up. Many people hoped that the war would soon be over, but fighting dragged on for more than four years. Soldiers spent months on end in cramped, muddy trenches (specially dug ditches). Both sides used deadly gas as a weapon. The Allies finally forced Germany's surrender, ending the war in November 1918. By then, more than 37 million soldiers had been killed or wounded. About 10 million civilians also died.

▼ In 1916, heavily armed 'dreadnought' battleships fought in the Battle of Jutland.

REVOLUTIONS IN EUROPE

In 1916 some Irish people rebelled against British rule, who had ruled Ireland for centuries. The uprising eventually led to Irish independence soon after the war ended. In 1917, the Russian Revolution overthrew the tsar, or Russian emperor, and set up a communist government. The war also broke up the empire of Austria-Hungary.

◄ Vladimir Ulyanov, known as Lenin, was a powerful speaker who emerged as leader during the Russian Revolution.

▲ Foot soldiers, or infantry, did most of the fighting during World War I, despite the development of modern weapons. As many as 1 million men were killed in just one battle, the Somme, in 1916.

THE GREAT DEPRESSION

THE Versailles Treaty, which marked the official end of World War I, forced Germany to hand back important industrial lands to France. Germany also had to pay large sums of money to the Allies, and give up its navy and air force. At the same time the United States was emerging as the world's most powerful country. Its economy (the amount of goods produced and sold) grew rapidly during the 'Roaring Twenties', as the lively, prosperous 1920s came to be known. Factories produced millions of cars, radios, refrigerators and other goods. People borrowed large sums of money to invest in (buy a part of) new companies. They felt rich as the value of these companies rose.

▲ Hollywood studios made many cheerful films in the 1930s to take people's minds off the Depression.

THE CRASH

On 'Black Thursday' – October 24, 1929 – the 'good times' stopped. A fall in the price of wheat led to a drop in the value of American companies. The same people who had scrambled to invest their money during the previous week now rushed to sell. Prices tumbled and many companies had to close down. People found it impossible to pay back what they had borrowed. They withdrew their savings, and the banks ran out of money. This huge 'crash' marked the beginning of the Great Depression,

▲ Hundreds of people in New York City spent long hours waiting for news of jobs or food handouts.

▶ Unemployed workers from Jarrow, in northern England, marched to London in 1936 to persuade the Government to find them jobs and raise wages.

which lasted for more than ten years. The 1930s were as difficult for people as the 1920s had been exciting. Millions of Americans lost their jobs, and the economies of other countries began to suffer, too, because they relied on selling to the United States. By 1930 the slump, or drop in trade, had spread to much of the world. Industrial countries were hit hardest. Governments stepped in to calm people's fear, and to provide work. President Franklin Roosevelt of the United States used taxes to pay people to build roads and dams, and gradually restored faith in the system of trade.

▶ *Benito Mussolini came to power in Italy in 1922. With the full support of his Fascist Party, he ruled Italy for more than 20 years.*

BRUTAL LEADERSHIP

During the Depression years of the 1930s, brutal leaders came to power in several European countries. They took advantage of their people's hardship and blamed the problems on the 'weakness' of the elected governments. Adolf Hitler became leader in Germany and by the mid-1930s the country was controlled by his Nazi (National Socialist) Party. In Italy, Benito Mussolini formed a similar government, led by the Fascist Party. In 1936 Spain suffered civil war after militay leader Francisco Franco rebelled against the elected Republican government. Germany and Italy sent forces to help Franco. In 1939 Franco defeated the Republicans and took control of Spain.

▲ *The three years of the Spanish Civil War (1936–39) saw terrible fighting in which tens of thousands of civilians died on both the Republican and Nationalist sides.*

▼ *The US President Franklin Roosevelt spent billions of dollars putting people to work on huge projects, such as building the Hoover Dam.*

WORLD WAR II

ADOLF Hitler claimed that the Treaty of Versailles (drawn up at the end of World War I) had forced his country to give up too much. He argued that the Germans had a right to get back what belonged to them. If it regained its former territories, Hitler believed Germany could be Europe's greatest industrial power. During the 1930s he built up Germany's army, navy and air force. Meanwhile Italy, under Mussolini, invaded Ethiopia in Africa and made it a colony, while in Asia, Japan attacked China.

▲ *The Messerschmitt was a German fighter plane, often used for 'reconnaissance' – surveying enemy areas.*

FULL-SCALE WAR

Other countries protested about the actions taken by Germany, Italy and Japan, but these countries stood firm. Then in September 1939 Germany invaded Poland, and World War II began. As had happened during World War I, countries joined sides. There were two opposing groups. Germany, Italy and Japan on one side were known as the Axis powers.

Opposing them were the Allies, led by Britain, the Soviet Union and the USA. The Axis powers had the advantage in the first years of the war. German forces swept through Europe, while Japan captured much of

▲ *British Spitfires were used to defend England during the Battle of Britain in 1940.*

Asia. By 1942, however, the Allies began to win more battles. The Soviet Union had pushed back a German invasion, Britain had survived prolonged raids by German bombers, and the United States had begun to defeat the Japanese navy.

▲ *Tanks like this German Panzer fought many decisive battles during the World War II.*

▼ *Submarines, called U-boats by the Germans, menaced enemy ships by coming up close to them underwater and shooting deadly torpedoes at them.*

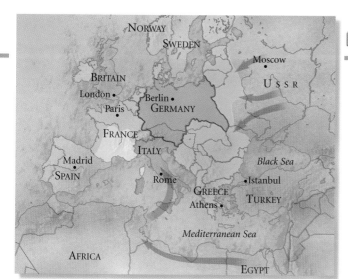

◀ *Germany occupied much of Europe during World War II, including France. From 1944, the Allies liberated them all.*

key
Axis powers
Allied powers
German-occupied
Vichy France
Neutral countries

In June 1944 the Allies launched a huge attack on France, which had been occupied by the Germans since 1940. They landed in Normandy on 'D-Day', and in less than a year freed all the countries that had been conquered by Germany. US forces also closed in on Japan and were nearing victory. The war in Europe ended in May 1945, and Japan surrendered three months later. More than 25 million soldiers and 30 million civilians had been killed.

▲ *The United States defeated Japan in the sea battle of Midway in June 1942, allowing them to regain control of the Pacific Ocean.*

▼ *The United Nations was founded as a force for peace in 1945, the year that World War II ended.*

LASTING NIGHTMARES

Two images from World War II still haunt people today. The first is of European Jews held captive in Nazi concentration camps. More than six million died in the camps – most of them brutally killed. This tragic chapter in world history is called the Holocaust. The second image is of the huge clouds made by the atomic bombs dropped by the USA on the Japanese cities of Hiroshima and Nagasaki in 1945.

▶ *Atomic bombs, used twice by the United States in 1945, forced Japan to stop fighting and surrender.*

THE COLD WAR

THE COLD WAR is the name given to the years of rivalry and distrust between the United States and the Soviet Union that lasted from 1945 to the break-up of the Soviet Union in 1991. The Cold War never led to a 'hot war' involving fighting between Soviet and American forces, but both sides supported armed conflicts between their allies in Asia and Africa. And there always seemed to be the risk of nuclear war between the two sides. The Cold War was also a contest between democracy and communism.

▲ *Fidel Castro led a communist rebellion in Cuba in 1959. After the Cold War, Castro kept Cuba under communist rule.*

'CONTAINING' COMMUNISM

The Cold War began with the break-up of the war-time alliance between the USA, Britain and the Soviet Union against Nazi Germany. Communist governments took over Eastern Europe and allied themselves with Stalin, the Soviet leader. Western Europe feared that Greece and Turkey might also come under communist control, so in 1947 President Harry S. Truman declared that the US would 'contain', or put a stop to, the further spread of communism. In 1948 he acted to prevent a Soviet takeover of Berlin. The US founded the North Atlantic Treaty Organisation (NATO) as

▲ *From 1961 to 1989 communist East Berlin was sealed off from the rest of the city by a wall (shown here being built). Dozens of people were shot dead trying to escape across the wall.*

▶ *In 1945, Winston Churchill (UK), Franklin Roosevelt (USA) and Josef Stalin (Soviet Union) met at Yalta in Russia to plan Germany's defeat and the founding of the United Nations.*

◀ On May Day during the Cold War years, Soviet troops paraded through the heart of Moscow to show off their country's military power.

▶ Both the USA and the Soviet Union built up huge stockpiles of long-range missiles. The US Minuteman missile, built in 1961, was able to aim nuclear weapons at targets 8,000 km away.

an anti-communist defence alliance in 1949, and supported South Korea against a communist invasion in 1950. The communist take-over of China in 1949 led the Americans to believe there was a world-wide communist plot to take over the world. This belief was only strengthened by the establishment of a pro-Soviet regime in Cuba in 1959 by Fidel Castro, right on America's doorstep. Soviet forces invaded Hungary in 1956, and Czechoslovakia in 1968, in their efforts to uphold communist rule.

THE COLLAPSE OF COMMUNISM

Cold War tension lessened following America's withdrawal from Vietnam, after its failed attempt to block a communist take-over there. But the Soviet invasion of Afghanistan in 1979 led to a massive US military build-up. The Soviet Union's attempt to match this led to the collapse of Soviet control. During the 1980s, people in the Soviet Union began to protest that communism was not working, and by late 1991 the communist governments in eastern Europe had been dismantled. The Cold War was over.

▼ US troops spent more than a decade in their failed attempt to prevent communist forces from winning in Vietnam.

NEW NATIONS EMERGE

THE end of World War II in 1945 not only brought peace, but it also changed the world map. Some new countries were created by the division of larger countries. Others that had been colonies of European countries gained independence as the colonial era gradually came to an end.

▶ *Representatives of 185 countries sit together to debate major international issues in the General Assembly of the United Nations.*

INDEPENDENCE

By the end of the 1800s, most of Africa and much of Asia were ruled by European powers. From the start of the 1900s, however, the colonies began to exert pressure on their European rulers to give them independence. India, a British colony, took the lead. It had one of the most active independence movements. People in other colonies followed the Indian example in pressing for a greater say in their own affairs. More and more people from the colonies were training as professionals – doctors, lawyers and teachers. Proud of their own countries' traditions, they believed that their countries could look after themselves without the help of a European power. During World War II, the European powers needed the help of soldiers from their colonies. Many of these soldiers returned home after the war with accounts of how people lived in other countries – and they wanted to see changes at home. But Britain, France and Belgium, which had been

Bahamas
1973

Cameroon
1960

Jamaica
1962

Dominica
1978

Gambia
1965

Angola
1975

▲ *Thousands of Jamaicans took to the streets of Kingston, the capital, to celebrate their independence on August 6, 1962.*

214

weakened by the war, had their own countries to rebuild and had little money to spend on their colonies. Starting with India in 1947, dozens of former colonies around the world achieved independence. Some, such as Vietnam and Algeria, gained independence only after bitter fighting and loss of lives. Others, such as Ghana and many Caribbean countries, became independent as a result of peaceful protests and talks with the ruling powers.

▲ *UN peacekeeping soldiers try to help civilians in regions that have been torn apart by conflict.*

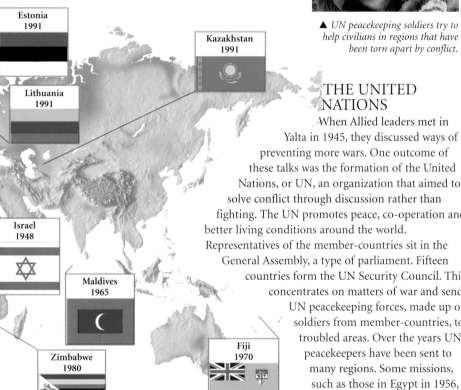

▲ *This world map shows some of the countries that have gained independence since the end of World War II. Many were colonies, ruled by European countries, before they gained independence.*

THE UNITED NATIONS

When Allied leaders met in Yalta in 1945, they discussed ways of preventing more wars. One outcome of these talks was the formation of the United Nations, or UN, an organization that aimed to solve conflict through discussion rather than fighting. The UN promotes peace, co-operation and better living conditions around the world. Representatives of the member-countries sit in the General Assembly, a type of parliament. Fifteen countries form the UN Security Council. This concentrates on matters of war and sends UN peacekeeping forces, made up of soldiers from member-countries, to troubled areas. Over the years UN peacekeepers have been sent to many regions. Some missions, such as those in Egypt in 1956, Haiti in 1995 and East Timor in 2000, have been successful. Others failed to stop widespread killing – for example in the former Yugoslavia, in Rwanda in East Africa, and in the Middle East.

POWER IN NUMBERS

The UN has grown as new countries have joined. In 1945, when it was formed, there were 51 member-countries. By 2001 there were 185 members. Some have little wealth or military power of their own, but within the UN their votes can make a real difference. They can press for medical and emergency aid, and for trade treaties.

A GIANT TRANSFORMED

THE RUSSIAN Revolution of 1917 created the Soviet Union (a united group of states) with a communist government. At first ordinary people thought the new system would give them greater freedom. But they quickly discovered that communist leaders dealt harshly with anyone who disagreed with them. After World War II the Soviet Union helped its East European neighbours to set up communist governments, and the pattern repeated itself in those countries, too.

▲ *By the late 1980s, the Berlin Wall – once a symbol of communist power – was covered with painted protests. The wall was torn down in 1989, as the communist government in East Germany also collapsed.*

VOICES OF PROTEST

During the Cold War, people living in the Soviet Bloc – the Soviet Union and its communist neighbours – did not dare to press for changes in government. Uprisings in Hungary in 1956 and Czechoslovakia in 1968 were crushed with military force. Then, in 1980, a trade union (an organized group of workers) called Solidarity was formed in Poland, with 10 million members – too many for the government to imprison. Over the next eight years Solidarity led many demonstrations in Poland, and news of the movement spread. The Polish government finally had to accept many of Solidarity's demands, including free elections. In 1989 Solidarity received a large number of votes in the first free election. It seemed the end of communism was in sight as huge anti-communism demonstrations were held in other countries.

▼ *Solidarity ('Solidarnosc' in Polish) became a symbol of how brave individuals could take on a powerful government – and win.*

THE BLOC BREAKS UP

By the end of 1989 the communist governments of East Germany, Poland, Hungary, Bulgaria and Czechoslovakia had been overthrown. In the Soviet Union, the communists were forced from power in 1991 and the Union – once made up of 15 republics – broke apart. The republics became independent countries, the largest of which is Russia. All of the former republics are trying to find ways to rule themselves modelled on the ways that Americans and Western Europeans have done for many years. The early years were difficult, and today many people consider themselves worse off since the fall of communism.

▶ *Russian troops, for decades linked by Western countries to Cold War tension, are eager to join in international peacekeeping efforts.*

LOOKING TO THE FUTURE

Today, one of the biggest causes of conflict is nationalism – people's desire to belong to one particular nation. Many groups believe that they are denied the right to speak their own language, govern themselves or worship freely. These concerns have developed into armed conflict in places such as the former Yugoslavia, Chechnya (formerly in the Soviet Union), eastern Turkey and southern Mexico.

▲ *The different nationalities making up UN peacekeeping missions have to learn to work with each other. They carry these lessons back to their home countries.*

▼ *A huge protest in Belgrade helped bring down Serbia's former ruler, Slobodan Milosevic, in September 2000.*

САВЕЗ ЗА ПРОМЕНЕ

QUIZ

1. What is the largest island in the world?
2. In which country are the Huang He and Chang Jiang (Yangtze) rivers?
3. Which country is the largest by area in the world?
4. Where in the world would you find gauchos?
5. On which continent are the great grasslands called savannahs?
6. In which country is Mecca – the most important city in the Muslim world?
7. What is the highest mountain in Africa?
8. Which country in Northern Europe has the largest population?
9. Where is the Murray–Darling River?
10. Which two American states are not connected geographically to any of the other 48 states?
11. Which country covers nearly half of South America?
12. How high is Mt Everest – the tallest mountain in the world?
13. Kazakhstan, Uzbekistan and Turkmenistan were all part of which country until 1991?
14. What is the name of the waterway that links the Atlantic and Pacific Oceans?
15. Which mountain range divides Northern and Southern Europe?
16. The Inuit are the native people of which part of the world?
17. Algeria, Libya, Niger and Chad all lie in which great desert?
18. Most people in Southwest Asia belong to which religious faith?
19. What is the name of the mountain range that runs down the entire west coast of South America?
20. Which two countries near China remain divided after a bitter war during the 1950s?

ANSWERS

1. Greenland
2. China
3. Russia
4. The pampas (plains) of South America – they are cowboys
5. Africa
6. Saudi Arabia
7. Mt Kilimanjaro, Tanzania, 5,895 m
8. Germany (82 million)
9. Australia
10. Alaska and Hawaii
11. Brazil
12. 8,848 m
13. The Soviet Union
14. The Panama Canal
15. The Alps
16. Arctic Canada and Greenland
17. The Sahara
18. Islam (they are Muslims)
19. The Andes
20. North and South Korea

ATLAS

IF YOU were to fly around our planet in a spaceship, you would look down upon large chunks of land (the seven continents) lying on an even larger expanse of blue (the oceans). All the land is divided up into more than 185 countries. Although no more than a third of Earth's surface is covered by land, there are huge differences between the continents. Apart from those people who live on the many islands scattered across the oceans, nearly all of Earth's population lives on six of the seven continents. World population soared past the 6 billion mark in 1999, and that figure continues to rise. People have learned to live in some of the world's harshest climates and landscapes, including scorching deserts, steep mountain sides and ice-covered plains.

NORTHERN EUROPE

MOIST air blows across much of northern Europe from the Atlantic Ocean, keeping the temperature moderate – it never gets really hot or cold. Forests cover the northernmost countries of Norway and Sweden, and farther south vast plains cross the heart of the region. The Alps, western Europe's highest mountain range, run through France, Switzerland, Austria and Italy.

Northern Europe developed the world's first modern factories, and today is one of the richest areas, thanks to a wide range of industries. Most of the countries belong to the European Union (EU). Member-nations aim to co-operate over issues relating to industry and farming.

FACT BOX
Highest mountain: Mont Blanc, France/Italy, 4,807 m
Largest lake: Lake Vänern (Sweden), 5,580 sq km
Longest river: Rhine, 1,320 km
Largest country (area): France, 551,500 sq km
Largest country (population): Germany, 82 million

▲ Porters in colourful hats carry huge cheeses such as Gouda to be sold at the famous Alkmaar cheese market in Holland.

▼ Minerals in the rocks give the dramatic peaks of the Dolomite mountains of Italy a pinkish colour in the sunlight.

▶ Amsterdam, the largest city in the Netherlands, is criss-crossed by a network of canals.

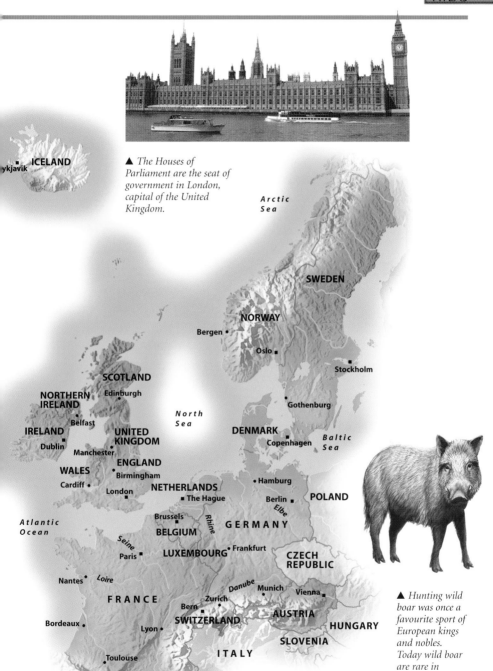

ICELAND
ykjavik

▲ The Houses of
Parliament are the seat of
government in London,
capital of the United
Kingdom.

*Arctic
Sea*

SWEDEN

NORWAY

Bergen •

Oslo •

Stockholm

SCOTLAND
NORTHERN   Edinburgh
IRELAND   Gothenburg
Belfast   *North
IRELAND   Sea*   DENMARK   *Baltic
Dublin   Copenhagen *Sea*
Manchester

WALES   Hamburg
Cardiff •   Berlin •   POLAND
Birmingham   NETHERLANDS   *Elbe*
London •   ■ The Hague
ENGLAND

*Atlantic   Brussels   *Rhine*   GERMANY
Ocean*   BELGIUM
Seine   LUXEMBOURG • Frankfurt
Paris •   CZECH
REPUBLIC

Nantes • *Loire*
Danube Munich   Vienna •
FRANCE   Zurich
Bern •   AUSTRIA
SWITZERLAND   HUNGARY
Bordeaux •   Lyon •   SLOVENIA

Toulouse •   ITALY

SPAIN
ANDORRA   Marseilles MONACO

*Mediterranean
Sea*

▲ Hunting wild
boar was once a
favourite sport of
European kings
and nobles.
Today wild boar
are rare in
Europe, but are
more commonly
found in parts of
Asia and Africa.

221

THE MEDITERRANEAN

SOME of the great early civilizations, including those of ancient Greece and Rome, developed around the Mediterranean. Today, the ruins of these civilizations attract large numbers of tourists every year. Millions of people also flock to Europe's many sandy beaches in summer. The Mediterranean area generally has dry weather, with cool winters and hot summers – ideal for growing grapes, olives and citrus fruits. Mountain ranges are found in many of the countries of southern Europe, and there are a number of volcanoes. Most of the natural woodland has been cleared, except in the north, where the Alps form a barrier with northern Europe.

▲ The Matterhorn, with its spectacular jagged peak, rises to 4,478 m in the Swiss Alps. A goal for skilled mountain-climbers, it was first 'conquered' in 1865.

FACT BOX

Highest mountain: Mont Blanc, France/Italy, 4,807 m
Largest lake: Lake Van, Turkey 3,763 sq km
Longest river: Kizil Irmak, 1,151 km
Largest country (area): Turkey, 779,450 sq km
Largest country (population): Turkey, 66 million

▼ Crowds of more than 50,000 people watched gladiators fighting each other or animals in the Colosseum, built nearly 2,000 years ago in Rome, Italy.

▼ Italy prides itself on its excellent culinary tradition. Popular dishes such as pizza and wines like Chianti are now enjoyed by people throughout the world.

▲ There are more than 2,000 Greek islands dotted across the eastern Mediterranean Sea. Tourists flock to the islands, but fishing also remains important.

SWITZERLAND

AUSTRIA

SLOVENIA

HUNGARY

Ljubljana ■ ■ Zagreb

■ Milan

CROATIA

ROMANIA

RANCE Turin • Po Venice • Rijeka •

Bologna •

BOSNIA
HERZEGOVINA

Belgrade •

SAN
MARINO

Sarajevo ■

ITALY

YUGOSLAVIA

BULGARIA

CORSICA

Rome ■

■ Skopje

Tirane ■ MACEDONIA

Naples •

ALBANIA

• Thessaloniki

SARDINIA

Cagliari •

GREECE

Palermo
•

SICILY

Athens ■

▼ Hagia Sophia is a huge and beautiful mosque in Istanbul, Turkey's largest city. Istanbul lies on the border of Europe and Asia.

MALTA

Iraklion
•

CRETE

▼ Chestnut, oak, olive and pine trees grow in coastal woodlands around the Mediterranean Sea.

EASTERN EUROPE

THE countries of Eastern Europe lie on a vast plain. Its rich, fertile soil makes good farmland, but farmers must harvest their crops before the bitter winter arrives. Unlike western Europe, this region has no mild ocean air to control the climate. Summers are very hot and winters very cold, with snow lying on the ground in some areas for up to five or six months. Huge forests cover most of the land that has not been cleared for farming.

Russia is the largest country in Eastern Europe. It is also the largest country in the world, extending into Asia as far as the Pacific Ocean. Until about 1990, many other Eastern European countries were controlled by Russia (or the Soviet Union, as it was called at the time). These countries are now independent.

FACT BOX

Highest mountain: Mt Elbrus, Russia, 5,642 m
Largest lake: Lake Ladoga, Russia, 18,390 sq km
Longest river: Volga, 3,531 km
Largest country (area): Russia (European part), 3,955,818 sq km
Largest country (population): Russia, 147 million

▼ Farming is essential to the economies of many Eastern European countries on the great plains. Crops include cereals, sugar beet and vegetables.

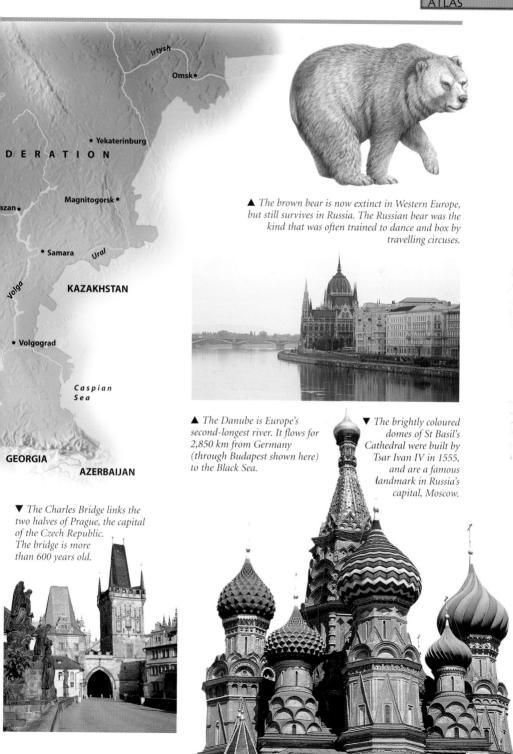

Irtysh

Omsk•

• Yekaterinburg

D E R A T I O N

Magnitogorsk •

azan •

• Samara   Ural

KAZAKHSTAN

• Volgograd

Caspian
Sea

GEORGIA

AZERBAIJAN

▲ The brown bear is now extinct in Western Europe, but still survives in Russia. The Russian bear was the kind that was often trained to dance and box by travelling circuses.

▲ The Danube is Europe's second-longest river. It flows for 2,850 km from Germany (through Budapest shown here) to the Black Sea.

▼ The brightly coloured domes of St Basil's Cathedral were built by Tsar Ivan IV in 1555, and are a famous landmark in Russia's capital, Moscow.

▼ The Charles Bridge links the two halves of Prague, the capital of the Czech Republic. The bridge is more than 600 years old.

SOUTHWEST ASIA

SOUTHWEST Asia, often called the Middle East, is bordered by Russia to the north and Africa to the south. Desert covers much of the region, although there is also fertile land, particularly between the Tigris and Euphrates rivers in Iraq. A number of ancient civilizations developed along the banks of these rivers. Southwest Asia also saw the birth of three great world religions – Judaism, Christianity and Islam. Most people are Muslims – followers of Islam, which developed in present-day Saudi Arabia about 1,500 years ago. The most important Muslim city is Mecca in Saudi Arabia. Many of the countries in the north of the region, including Kazakhstan, Uzbekistan and Turkmenistan, were once part of the Soviet Union. They became independent in 1991.

Istanbul
Izmir
Black Sea
Ankara
TURKEY
GEORGIA
Adana
T'bilisi
CYPRUS
Nicosia
Adana
ARMENIA
Yerevan AZERBAIJ
Ba
LEBANON SYRIA
Beirut
Jerusalem Damascus
ISRAEL
JORDAN
IRAQ
Baghdad
Tehran
Al Basrah
Esfah
KUWAIT
Kuwait
IR A
SAUDI ARABIA
Persian Gulf
Jeddah
Mecca
Dhahran
Riyadh
QATAR
Abu Dhabi
Red Sea
UNITED ARAB EMIRATES
M
Sana
OMAN
YEMEN
Arabian Sea

FACT BOX

Highest mountain:
K2 (Pakistan), 8,611 m
Largest lake: Caspian Sea,
378,400 sq km
Longest river: Euphrates,
2,815 km
Largest country (area): Kazakhstan,
2,717,300 sq km
Largest country (population):
Pakistan, 147 million

▼ *Modern hotels are built along the shores of the Red Sea in the coastal resorts of Israel and Jordan.*

RUSSIAN FEDERATION

Ishim

Irtysh

au

Astana

Karaganda ▪

KAZAKHSTAN

Aral Sea

Syr Darya

ZBEKISTAN

Khiva ▪

ENISTAN

Chimkent ▪ **Bishkek** ▪ **Almaty**

hgabat

Tashkent ▪ **KYRGYZSTAN**

Samarkand ▪

ashdad **Dushanbe** ▪

C H I N A

TAJIKISTAN

AFGHANISTAN

Kabul ▪

andahar ▪ **Islamabad** ▪

Lahore ▪

PAKISTAN

Indus

Karachi ▪

I N D I A

▲ *Beautiful temples and other buildings were carved straight from the rock in Petra, Jordan, nearly 2,500 years ago.*

▲ *Expensive cars are just one of the many luxuries that the people in oil-rich countries such as Kuwait and Saudi Arabia can afford.*

▼ *Burning waste gases from oil fields in Kuwait.*

◀ *A tiled minaret, or prayer tower, stands beside the dome of the great mosque of Samarkand, an ancient city in Uzbekistan.*

SOUTHEAST ASIA

SOUTHEAST Asia covers a huge area. It stretches from the Himalayas – the tallest mountain range in the world – southwards through the tropical rainforests of Thailand and Borneo to the long island chain of Indonesia. India is the largest country, with a population of more than 987 million. More than 70 percent of people there make their living from growing crops or keeping animals. Craft-making is also important. India is also the world's largest democracy – its government encourages everyone to vote in elections. Twice a year India and its neighbours experience monsoon seasons – periods of very heavy rain. Farmers rely on the rain to water their fields after the hot, dry months. Bangladesh often suffers serious floods as the heavy rains swell the rivers.

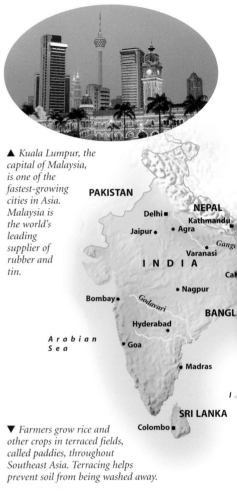

▲ *Kuala Lumpur, the capital of Malaysia, is one of the fastest-growing cities in Asia. Malaysia is the world's leading supplier of rubber and tin.*

PAKISTAN

Delhi■
Jaipur● ●Agra

NEPAL
Kathmandu■

Gange
Varanasi●

I N D I A

Cal

●Nagpur

Bombay● *Godavari*

BANGL

Hyderabad
●

Arabian Sea ●Goa

●Madras

I

SRI LANKA

Colombo■

▼ *Farmers grow rice and other crops in terraced fields, called paddies, throughout Southeast Asia. Terracing helps prevent soil from being washed away.*

FACT BOX

Highest mountain: Mt Everest
(Nepal/Tibet), 8,848 m
Largest lake: Tonle Sap (Cambodia),
6,475 sq km
Longest river: Mekong,
4,184 km
Largest country (area): India,
3,287,590 sq km
Largest country (population): India,
987 million

◄ *Most Indian women wear a sari, a long piece of cloth draped around them, often made of silk. Some also wear a round dot called a kumkum in the middle of their forehead, which is considered a mark of beauty.*

▲ *The island-country of Singapore is one of the most important business centres in the world. Skyscrapers tower over its busy harbour.*

Tai'pei
TAIWAN

CHINA

Irrawaddy

Mandalay
MYANMAR
LAOS
Vientiane
Chiang Mai
Hanoi
South China Sea
Manila
Hue
Da Nang
THAILAND
PHILIPPINES
Bangkok
CAMBODIA
VIETNAM
Phnom Penh
Ho Chi Minh City
Davao
Mekong

BRUNEI
Pacific Ocean
Manado
MALAYSIA
Kuala Lumpur
SARAWAK
SINGAPORE
BORNEO
SUMATRA
Pontianak
Padang
SULAWESI
INDONESIA
TIMOR
Jakarta
BALI
JAVA

▼ *The Himalaya range in northern India and Nepal is the world's highest mountain range. It extends for more than 2,410 km and separates the region from the rest of Asia.*

PACIFIC ASIA

CHINA is the world's third-largest country by area after Russia and Canada. More than one-fifth of all the world's people live there. To the south and west are the great mountain ranges of the Himalayas and Karakorums. A series of plateaux (high plains) and deserts lie in the centre of the country, while the east is crossed by the fertile valleys of the Huang He and Chang Jiang (Yangtze) rivers, which flow into the Pacific Ocean. Farmers grow wheat, maize and tea, but the main crop is rice.

China's neighbours include Mongolia, a land of deserts and plains, and North and South Korea. Once united, the Koreas split in the 1950s after a bitter war. Taiwan, in the Pacific, was once part of China. Japan (some 3,000 islands) is one of the world's leading manufacturing countries.

▲ At 3,776 m, Mt Fuji is the highest mountain in Japan. This dormant (inactive) volcano, known as the 'sleeping dragon', is near Tokyo, Japan's capital.

KAZAKSTAN

KYRGYZSTAN

Taklimukan Desert

PAKISTAN

Himalaya

NEPAL

Kathmandu

BHUTAN

INDIA

▼ The Forbidden City in Beijing was once the home of China's royal family.

FACT BOX

Highest mountain: Mt Everest
(Nepal/Tibet), 8,848 m
Largest lake: Qinghai Hu,
4,460 sq km
Longest river: Chang Jiang
(Yangtze), 5,520 km
Largest country (area): China,
9,396,960 sq km
Largest country (population):
China, 1.26 billion

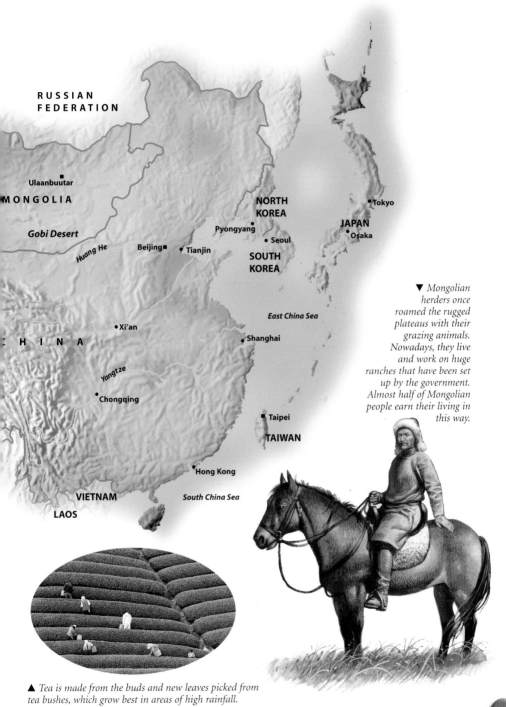

RUSSIAN FEDERATION

Ulaanbuutar

MONGOLIA

Gobi Desert

Huang He

Beijing■ •Tianjin

•Xi'an

Yangtze

•Chongqing

CHINA

NORTH KOREA

Pyongyang•

•Seoul

SOUTH KOREA

East China Sea

•Shanghai

■ Taipei

TAIWAN

•Hong Kong

South China Sea

VIETNAM

LAOS

•Tokyo

JAPAN

•Osaka

▼ *Mongolian herders once roamed the rugged plateaus with their grazing animals. Nowadays, they live and work on huge ranches that have been set up by the government. Almost half of Mongolian people earn their living in this way.*

▲ *Tea is made from the buds and new leaves picked from tea bushes, which grow best in areas of high rainfall.*

CANADA AND GREENLAND

ATLAS

Canada is the second-largest country in the world after Russia. To its east is Greenland, the world's biggest island. Around three-quarters of all Canadians live in a narrow band along the southern border with the United States. The rest of the country – like all of Greenland – is too cold to support many towns. The far north is a snowy Arctic landscape, which merges into a vast area of forested wilderness. Broad, grassy prairies cover the central south. Canada is made up of provinces and territories. In 1999 a new territory was created so that the Inuit could have a greater say in how their land is used. The territory is known as Nunavut – meaning 'our land' in Inuit. The Inuit also have a say in governing Greenland, which is partly controlled by Denmark.

◄ The Native Americans along Canada's Pacific coast traditionally made totem poles to record the history of their people.

UNITED STATES OF AMERICA

Gt. B

Mackenzie

• Whitehorse

Prince Rupert

Prince George

Edmo

Pacific Ocean

Calga

•Vancouver

Medici

Victoria

UNITED STAT

▼ Much of Canada's Atlantic winter trade passes through the port of Halifax on Nova Scotia.

FACT BOX

Highest mountain: Mt Logan, Canada, 5,959 m
Largest lake: Superior (USA/Canada), 82,414 sq km
Longest river: Mackenzie, 1,120 km
Largest country (area): Canada, 9,976,140 sq km
Largest country (population): Canada, 31 million

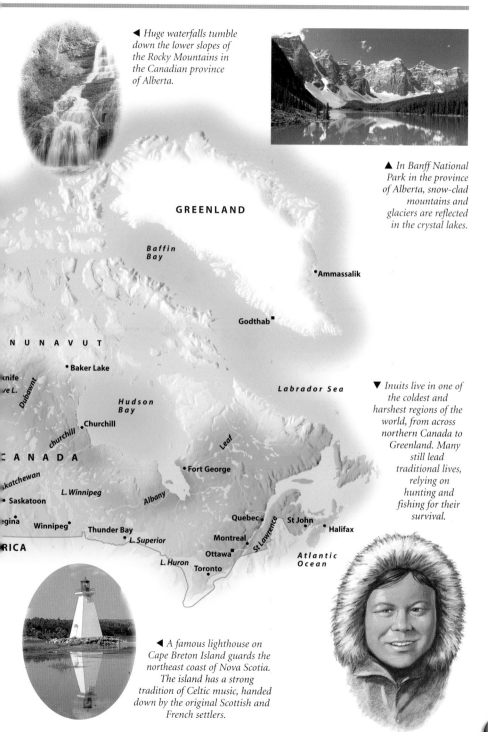

◄ Huge waterfalls tumble down the lower slopes of the Rocky Mountains in the Canadian province of Alberta.

▲ In Banff National Park in the province of Alberta, snow-clad mountains and glaciers are reflected in the crystal lakes.

GREENLAND

Baffin Bay

•Ammassalik

Godthab▪

N U N A V U T

knife
ve L.
•Baker Lake

Dubawnt

Labrador Sea

Hudson Bay

churchill •Churchill

C A N A D A

Leaf

•Fort George

skatchewan
•Saskatoon

L. Winnipeg

Albany

egina •Winnipeg•

Quebec•

St John

gina
Thunder Bay
•L. Superior

Montreal•

St Lawrence

•Halifax

RICA

Ottawa▪

L. Huron Toronto•

Atlantic Ocean

▼ Inuits live in one of the coldest and harshest regions of the world, from across northern Canada to Greenland. Many still lead traditional lives, relying on hunting and fishing for their survival.

◄ A famous lighthouse on Cape Breton Island guards the northeast coast of Nova Scotia. The island has a strong tradition of Celtic music, handed down by the original Scottish and French settlers.

233

THE UNITED STATES

THE United States is the world's third largest country by population and fourth by area. Its varied landscapes include the mighty Rocky Mountains, thick forests, deserts, tropical coastlines and fertile plains. Oil, coal and precious minerals have helped the USA become a rich and powerful nation. It is the leading producer of many crops and industrial goods. Forty-eight of the fifty US states lie in central North America. The state of Alaska is separated by Canada, and lies on the northwestern tip of North America. Hawaii is in the Pacific.

FACT BOX

Highest mountain: Denali
(Mt McKinley), 6,194 m
Largest lake: Superior (USA/Canada),
82,414 sq km
Longest river: Mississippi, 3,770 km
Largest country (area): United
States, 9,372,610 sq km
Largest country (population):
United States, 272 million

▼ *Hawaii is an island state some 3,800 km southwest of mainland America's west coast. Its captial is Honolulu. Millions of Americans visit the islands each year, attracted by their natural beauty and mild climate.*

CANADA

L. Superior

Duluth •

Fargo •

Minneapolis •

• Sioux City

Green Bay

Milwaukee •

Chicago •

L. Michigan

Detroit •

Toledo •

Cleveland •

Augusta •

Burlington •

• Portland

Boston •

Syracuse •

• Buffalo

• New York

• Trenton

Pittsburgh •

Baltimore •

Philadelphia

Washington DC ■

Missouri

Indianapolis •

• Cincinnati

Kansas City

ver

orado

Topeka •

• St Louis

Ohio

• Lexington

• Richmond

• Norfolk

T A T E S   O F   A M E R I C A

Springfield

Nashville

Atlantic
Ocean

Arkansas

• Tulsa

• Amarillo

• Oklahoma City

Mississippi

Chattanooga •

• Memphis

Birmingham

Little Rock

• Atlanta

• Charleston

• Dallas

Red

• Jackson

• Albany

Waco •

Mobile

Baton Rouge

Tallahassee

Pensacola

• Jacksonville

• Daytona

Houston •

New Orleans

Tampa •

• Orlando

Rio Grande

San Antonio •

Galveston

• Laredo

Gulf of Mexico

• Miama

Key West •

◀ Cowboys ride bucking broncos
at festivals of horsemanship called
rodeos. The cowboy tries to stay on
for as long as he can.

▲ New York
City, famous for its tall
skyscrapers, is the most
populous city in the
United States.

▲ The Colorado River has carved the magnificent
Grand Canyon in the southwestern state of Arizona.

CENTRAL AMERICA

CENTRAL America is the name given to the eight countries south of the United States. Mexico is the largest. South of Mexico the land becomes increasingly narrow, until it eventually joins South America. The Panama Canal in Panama cuts through the narrowest point in this land bridge, linking the Pacific and Atlantic Oceans. To the east lie the island-nations of the Caribbean. The largest are Cuba, Haiti, Jamaica and the Dominican Republic, which are independent. Many of the other small islands have links with Europe or the United States.

▲ Bananas and other tropical fruits are important export crops in Central America and the Caribbean.

UNITED STATES OF AMERICA

Tijauana•

Chihuahua•

MEXICO

• Monterrey

La Paz •

• Tampico

Pacific Ocean

Guadalajara •

Mexico City ■ Veracruz

Acapulco•

◀ *Guatemalans traditionally wear brightly coloured clothes and sell their goods at village markets. They are the descendants of the Maya people, who lived in the region from c.300 BC to AD 1500s.*

FACT BOX
Highest mountain: Citlaltepetl (Mexico), 5,700 m
Largest lake: Nicaragua, 8,029 sq km
Longest river: Rio Grande (Mexico), 3,030 km
Largest country (area): Mexico, 1,958,200 sq km
Largest country (population): Mexico, 100 million

▶ *Rastafarians are members of a religious and political movememt called Ras Tafari, which began in Jamaica in the 1920's. Rastafarians are best known for their music style, Reggae, and their ropelike hair called dreadlocks.*

▲ The 81-km-long Panama Canal links the Atlantic and Pacific Oceans, and is a vital route for shipping.

◄ The strikingly beautiful Quetzal is native to the rainforests of Central America. The Aztecs and Mayans once worshipped the bird as a god of the air.

BAHAMAS

■Nassau

Atlantic Ocean

TURKS & CAICOS ISLANDS

ANTIGUA & BARBUDA

of Mexico
Havana ■

CUBA

DOMINICAN REPUBLIC San Juan

GUADELOUPE

Camagüey ■

HAITI

PUERTO RICO

DOMINICA

ST KITTS & NEVIS

•Mérida

Port-au-Prince ■

Santo Domingo ■

ST LUCIA

ST VINCENT & GRENADINES

CAYMAN ISLANDS

■Kingston

BARBADOS

JAMAICA

GRENADA

Caribbean Sea

nopan ■ ■Belize City

Port of Spain ■

TRINIDAD & TOBAGO

BELIZE

HONDURAS
EMALA
emala City ■Tegucigalpa

■San Salvador **NICARAGUA**

VENEZUELA

SALVADOR
Managua ■

San José ■ Panama City ■

COSTA RICA

PANAMA

COLUMBIA

▼ The Mayas, an ancient people of Mexico and Guatemala, built the temple-city of Chichen Itza in eastern Mexico about 1,500 years ago.

◄ Mexicans celebrate the Day of the Dead (November 2nd) with toy skulls and sweets. It is a day for visiting family graves.

THE ANDES AND PAMPAS

THE Andes, one of the world's great mountain ranges, runs down the entire west coast of South America – for about 7,240 kilometres in all. The mountains rise up steeply from the Pacific coast and run through six countries. One of these, Chile, follows the course of the Andes southwards for 4,270 kilometres, but is only on average about 160 kilometres wide. There are many active volcanoes in the north, and glaciers in the far south. To the east of Chile lie Argentina, Paraguay and Uruguay. These countries are covered in vast grassland plains called pampas. Gauchos (South American cowboys) look after the huge herds of cattle that graze on ranches on the pampas. Other farms grow wheat, maize, oats and many kinds of fruit.

▲ *The artists' quarter of Buenos Aires, Argentina's capital, is a colourful jumble of brightly painted houses. Nearly one-third of all Argentinians live in or around Buenos Aires.*

◄ *The llama, a relative of the camel, survives in the harsh Andes mountains, where it forages for grass and is protected by its thick, woolly coat.*

▼ *The Atacama Desert in Chile is the driest place on Earth. Some parts of the desert have not had rain for more than 100 years, and in some areas rain has never been known to fall. The mineral-rich rocks are sculpted by the wind.*

FACT BOX

Highest mountain: Aconcagua, Argentina, 6,960 m
Largest lake: Titicaca (Peru/Bolivia), 8,192 sq km
Longest river: Paraná, 2,940 km
Largest country (area): Argentina, 2,766,890 sq km
Largest country (population): Argentina, 37 million

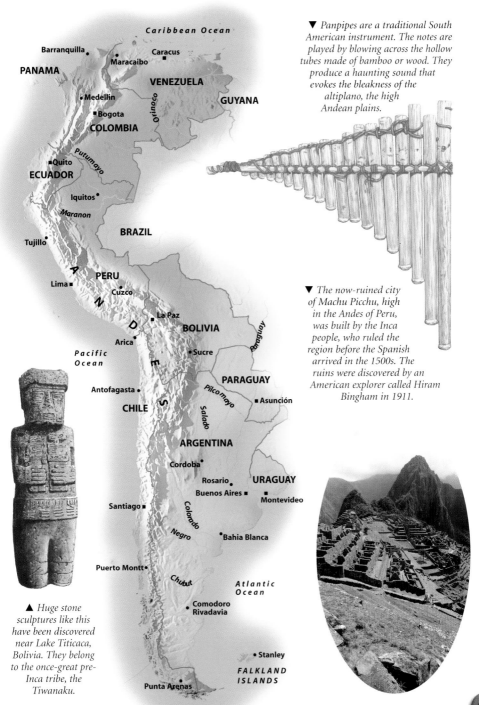

▼ Panpipes are a traditional South American instrument. The notes are played by blowing across the hollow tubes made of bamboo or wood. They produce a haunting sound that evokes the bleakness of the altiplano, the high Andean plains.

▼ The now-ruined city of Machu Picchu, high in the Andes of Peru, was built by the Inca people, who ruled the region before the Spanish arrived in the 1500s. The ruins were discovered by an American explorer called Hiram Bingham in 1911.

▲ Huge stone sculptures like this have been discovered near Lake Titicaca, Bolivia. They belong to the once-great pre-Inca tribe, the Tiwanaku.

Caribbean Ocean

Barranquilla
Caracas
Maracaibo
PANAMA
VENEZUELA
GUYANA
Medellin
Bogota
COLOMBIA
Orinoco
Quito
ECUADOR
Putumayo
Iquitos
Maranon
BRAZIL
Tujillo
PERU
Lima
Cuzco
La Paz
BOLIVIA
Arica
Sucre
Paraguay
Pacific Ocean
PARAGUAY
Antofagasta
Pilcomayo
Asunción
CHILE
Salado
ARGENTINA
Cordoba
Rosario
URAGUAY
Buenos Aires
Montevideo
Santiago
Colorado
Negro
Bahia Blanca
Puerto Montt
Chubut
Atlantic Ocean
Comodoro Rivadavia
Stanley
FALKLAND ISLANDS
Punta Arenas

239

BRAZIL AND NEIGHBOURS

BRAZIL is the largest country in South America, covering nearly half the continent. The great Amazon River runs east through the tropical north of Brazil, and is fed by thousands of smaller rivers and streams. The whole Amazon basin is covered by the world's largest rainforest. Brazil's many natural resources include diamonds, gold and vital minerals. Less than one-tenth of the land is farmed, but Brazil exports large amounts of coffee, orange juice, soya beans and cocoa. Factories in cities such as Rio de Janeiro make machinery, clothing and chemicals. A number of smaller countries border the Amazon rainforest to the north. The largest, Venezuela, is a leading oil producer.

▲ Some 275 cascades make up the Iguaçu Falls, which plunge for 60 to 80 m along a 4-km stretch of the border between Argentina and Brazil.

▲ Nearly 10 million people live in São Paulo, the largest city in Brazil – and in South America.

▶ The European Space Agency launches its rockets from a base at Kourou in French Guiana.

FACT BOX

Highest mountain: Pico Bolívar (Venezuela), 5,007 m
Largest lake: Maracaibo, 12,950 sq km
Longest river: Amazon, 6,275 km
Largest country (area): Brazil, 8,511,970 sq km
Largest country (population): Brazil, 168 million

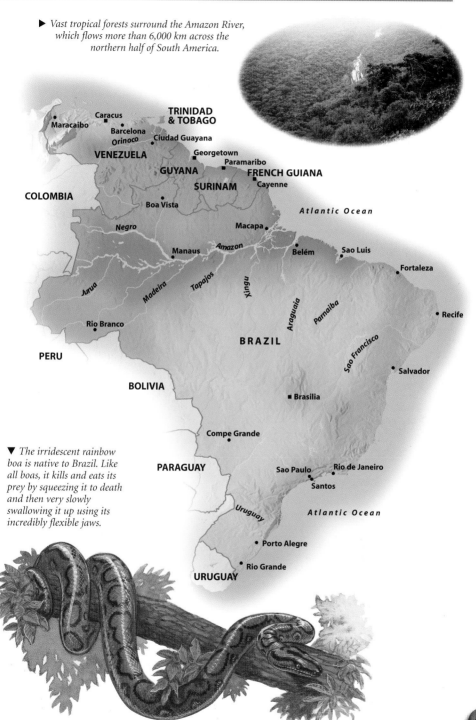

▶ *Vast tropical forests surround the Amazon River, which flows more than 6,000 km across the northern half of South America.*

Caracas
Maracaibo
TRINIDAD
& TOBAGO
Barcelona
Orinoco
Ciudad Guayana
VENEZUELA
Georgetown
Paramaribo
GUYANA
FRENCH GUIANA
Cayenne
COLOMBIA
SURINAM
Boa Vista
Atlantic Ocean
Negro
Macapa
Amazon
Manaus
Belém
Sao Luis
Jurua
Madeira
Tapajos
Xingu
Fortaleza
Araguaia
Parnaiba
Rio Branco
Recife
BRAZIL
PERU
Sao Francisco
Salvador
BOLIVIA
Brasilia
Compe Grande

▼ *The irridescent rainbow boa is native to Brazil. Like all boas, it kills and eats its prey by squeezing it to death and then very slowly swallowing it up using its incredibly flexible jaws.*

PARAGUAY
Sao Paulo
Rio de Janeiro
Santos
Uruguay
Atlantic Ocean
Porto Alegre
Rio Grande
URUGUAY

241

NORTHERN AFRICA

THE Sahara is the world's largest desert, covering more than 9 million square kilometres. It extends across northern Africa from the Atlantic coast in the west to the Red Sea in the east. Some of Africa's largest countries – Algeria, Libya, Niger, Chad and Sudan – lie in the Sahara. But they have small populations, because few people can live in the extreme desert heat. Most people in north Africa live along the coasts of the Atlantic Ocean and Mediterranean Sea, or by desert oases – fertile areas watered by springs. Many people still lead nomadic lives, moving their flocks of goats and sheep to seasonal pastures. The only north African country with a large population is Egypt. For thousands of years the Egyptians have farmed the land along the fertile banks of the River Nile, the world's longest river.

▲ The harsh, forbidding landscape of the Sahara Desert acts as a natural boundary between northern and southern Africa.

Atlantic Ocean

Tangier •   Al
Rabat ▪   Or
Casablanca •
MOROCCO

MADIERA

CANARY ISLANDS

ALGERI

WESTERN SAHARA

▪ Dakhla

S a h a

MAURITANIA

Nouakchott ▪

MALI

Tombouctou •

SENEGAL
Dakar ▪
GAMBIA
Banjul ▪   Bamako ▪   Ouagadougou •
▪ Bissau   **BURKINO**
GUINEA BISSAU   **GUINEA**   **BENIN**
Conakry ▪   **GHANA**
▪ Freetown   **TOGO**
SIERRA LEONE   Yamoussoukro •   Lomé ▪
Monrovia ▪   Por
LIBERIA   **IVORY COAST**   Accra No

Niger

N

Atlantic Ocean

EQUATO

SAO TO & PRIN

▼ In the Atlas mountains, Morocco, many houses have flat roofs as there is almost no rain to be drained off.

FACT BOX

Highest mountain: Jbel Toubkal, Morocco, 4,165 m
Largest lake: Tana (Ethiopia), 2,849 sq km
Longest river: Nile, 6,673 km
Largest country (area): Sudan, 2,505,810 sq km
Largest country (population): Egypt, 67 million

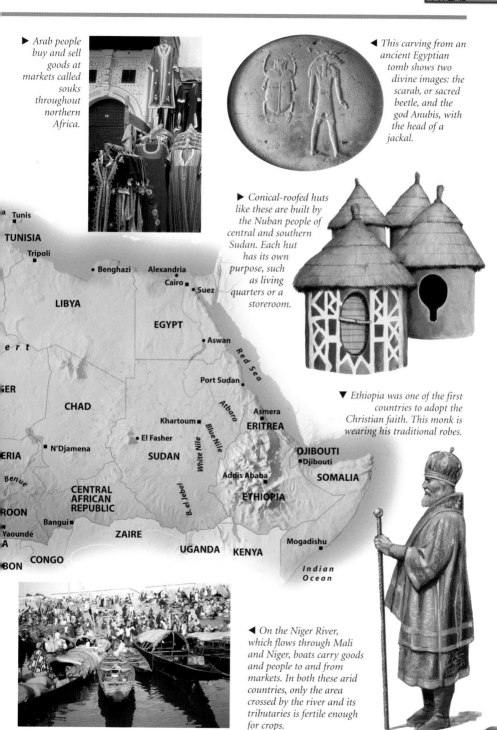

▶ Arab people buy and sell goods at markets called souks throughout northern Africa.

◀ This carving from an ancient Egyptian tomb shows two divine images: the scarab, or sacred beetle, and the god Anubis, with the head of a jackal.

▶ Conical-roofed huts like these are built by the Nuban people of central and southern Sudan. Each hut has its own purpose, such as living quarters or a storeroom.

▼ Ethiopia was one of the first countries to adopt the Christian faith. This monk is wearing his traditional robes.

Tunis

TUNISIA

Tripoli

• Benghazi   Alexandria
              Cairo •
                   • Suez

LIBYA

EGYPT

• Aswan

Red Sea

ert

• Port Sudan

GER

CHAD

Khartoum ■   Asmera ■
              ERITREA

Atbara

• El Fasher

■ N'Djamena

ERIA

SUDAN

White Nile   Blue Nile

DJIBOUTI
■ Djibouti

SOMALIA

Benue

CENTRAL
AFRICAN
REPUBLIC

Addis Ababa ■

B. el Jebel

ETHIOPIA

ROON

Bangui ■

Yaoundé ■
A

ZAIRE

UGANDA   KENYA

Mogadishu ■

BON   CONGO

Indian
Ocean

◀ On the Niger River, which flows through Mali and Niger, boats carry goods and people to and from markets. In both these arid countries, only the area crossed by the river and its tributaries is fertile enough for crops.

243

SUB-SAHARAN AFRICA

THE term Sub-Saharan Africa describes all of the continent south of the Sahara Desert. Most of this region lies in the warm tropics on either side of the Equator, but there is great variety in the landscape. Dense rainforests surround the Congo River and there are huge savannah grasslands to the east, while the southwest is desert. Many Sub-Saharan nations were once ruled by European countries. The path to independence has not been easy, and there have been many fierce conflicts over the past fifty years.

CAMEROON

EQUATORIAL GUINEA

Libreville

GABON

Brazzaville

Kinshasa

Luanda

Huambo

Naimbe

NAMIBIA

Atlantic Ocean

▲ The Victoria Falls have a 108-m drop. They are on the Zambezi River between Zambia and Zimbabwe.

FACT BOX

Highest mountain: Mt Kilimanjaro, Tanzania, 5,895 m
Largest lake: Lake Victoria (Uganda/Kenya/Tanzania), 69,463 sq km
Longest river: Congo, 4,666 km
Largest country (area): Democratic Republic of Congo, 2,345,410 sq km
Largest country (population): Democratic Republic of Congo, 41 million

▲ The Chimpanzee is an African ape, and is one of the most intelligent animals. It resembles human beings more closely than any other living creature.

▼ Table Mountain overlooks Cape Town, one of South Africa's largest cities.

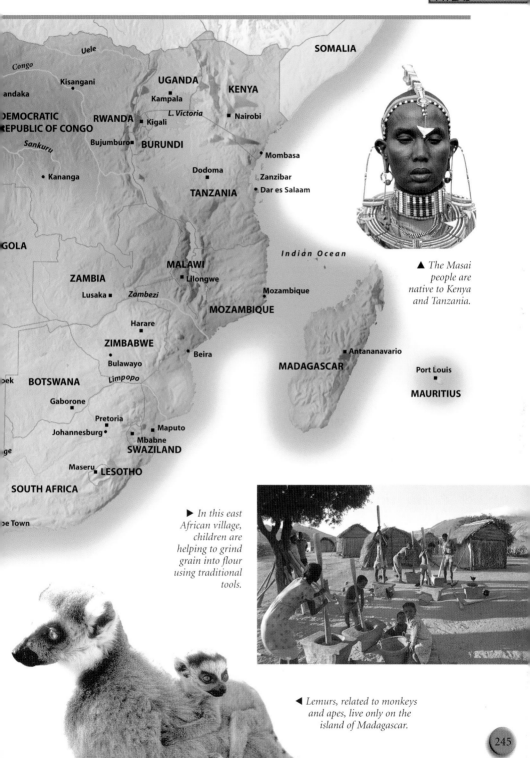

SOMALIA

UGANDA
■ Kampala

KENYA
■ Nairobi

Congo

Uele

Kisangani

andaka

DEMOCRATIC
REPUBLIC OF CONGO

RWANDA
■ Kigali

L. Victoria

Bujumburo■ BURUNDI

Sankuru

• Kananga

Dodoma
■

• Mombasa

Zanzibar
• Dar es Salaam

TANZANIA

GOLA

Indian Ocean

MALAWI
■ Lilongwe

ZAMBIA

Lusaka ■ *Zambezi*

Mozambique
■

MOZAMBIQUE

Harare
■

ZIMBABWE

• Beira

Bulawayo
•

■ Antananavario

MADAGASCAR

Port Louis
■

MAURITIUS

▲ The Masai
people are
native to Kenya
and Tanzania.

Limpopo

ek

BOTSWANA

Gaborone
■

Pretoria
■

Johannesburg •

■ Maputo

Mbabne
SWAZILAND

ge

Maseru
■ LESOTHO

SOUTH AFRICA

e Town

▶ In this east
African village,
children are
helping to grind
grain into flour
using traditional
tools.

◀ Lemurs, related to monkeys
and apes, live only on the
island of Madagascar.

AUSTRALIA AND OCEANIA

AUSTRALIA is the only country that is also a continent. It lies southeast of Asia, between the Indian and Pacific Oceans. Few people live in Australia, despite its size, because the heart of the country, the 'Outback', is very hot and dry – much of it is desert. Many of the lakes and rivers dry up during the hottest months. Most people live near Australia's coasts, where there is also rich farmland – Australia is the world's leading wool producer. Iron ore and coal are the main mineral exports. Sydney is the largest city.

▲ Coconut palms thrive in the hot, humid climate and are the main vegetation on many Pacific islands.

To the east of Australia is Oceania, the 20,000 islands in the Pacific. New Zealand and Papua New Guinea are the largest. The smallest are simply coral reefs or the tips of volcanoes that rise up from the ocean floor.

Perth •

◄ Melbourne, built on the Yarra River, is the capital of the Australian state of Victoria and is the second-largest city in the country.

FACT BOX

Highest mountain: Mt Wilhelm (Papua New Guinea), 4,300 m
Largest lake: Lake Eyre, Australia, 9,690 sq km
Longest river: Murray–Darling, Australia, 3,824 km
Largest country (area): Australia, 7,686,850 sq km
Largest country (population): Australia, 19 million

▼ The ferocious Tasmanian devil lives on the Australian island of Tasmania. It is a marsupial (pouched mammal) and is extremely strong for its small size.

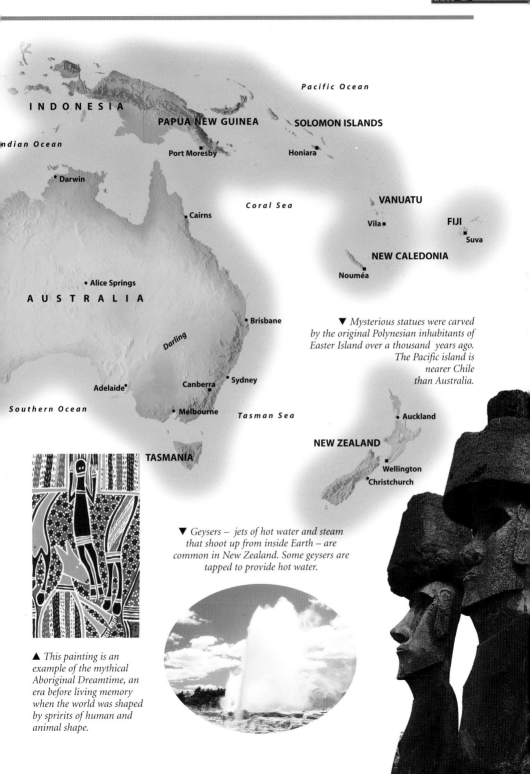

Pacific Ocean

INDONESIA

PAPUA NEW GUINEA

SOLOMON ISLANDS

ndian Ocean

Port Moresby

Honiara

Darwin

Cairns

Coral Sea

VANUATU

Vila

FIJI

Suva

NEW CALEDONIA

Nouméa

Alice Springs

AUSTRALIA

Brisbane

▼ *Mysterious statues were carved by the original Polynesian inhabitants of Easter Island over a thousand years ago. The Pacific island is nearer Chile than Australia.*

Darling

Adelaide

Canberra

Sydney

Southern Ocean

Melbourne

Tasman Sea

Auckland

NEW ZEALAND

TASMANIA

Wellington

Christchurch

▲ *This painting is an example of the mythical Aboriginal Dreamtime, an era before living memory when the world was shaped by spririts of human and animal shape.*

▼ *Geysers – jets of hot water and steam that shoot up from inside Earth – are common in New Zealand. Some geysers are tapped to provide hot water.*

INDEX

The publishers would like to thank the artists whose work appears in this book: Richard Berridge/Specs Art, Jim Channell, Kuo Kang Chen, Peter Dennis/Linda Rogers, Nick Farmer, Nicholas Forder, Mike Foster/The Maltings Partnership, Luigi Galante/Galante Studios, Alan Hancocks, Alan Harris, Richard Hook/Linden Artists, John James/Temple Rogers, Mick Loates/Linden Artists, Roger Kent/Illustration, Stewart Lafford/Linden Artists, Kevin Maddison, Alan Male/Linden Artists, Janos Marffy, Terry Riley, Martin Sanders, Peter Sarson, Mike Saunders, Rob Sheffield, Guy Smith/Mainline, Rudi Vizi, Mike White/Temple Rogers, Paul Williams

The publishers would also like to thank the following sources for the photographs used in this book:
Page 46 (B/L) Ralph White/CORBIS; 48 (T/R) Roger Ressmeyer/CORBIS; 51 (B/L) Wolfgang Kaehler/CORBIS; 56 (T/R) James L. Amos/CORBIS, (B/L) Wolfgang Kaehler/CORBIS; 58 (C/L) Jeffrey L. Ratman/CORBIS; 67 (C/L) Anatoly Kleschuk/CORBIS SYGMA; 80 (B/L) Jeremy Horner/CORBIS; 83 (T/R) Enzo & Paolo Ragazzini/CORBIS; 96 (B/L) Ed Eckstein/CORBIS, (T/R) Jerry Cooke/CORBIS; 97 (B/R) Steve Chenn/CORBIS; 111 (B/R) Laura Sivell/ Papilio/CORBIS; 112 (T/R) Eric and David Hosking/CORBIS; 113 (T/R) Lake County Museum/CORBIS; 114 (B/R) Philip Perry/ Frank Lane Picture Agency/CORBIS; 116 (T/R) Anthony Barrister/CORBIS; 108 (T/R) Science Pictures Limited/CORBIS; 142 (B) Yann Arthus-Bertrand/CORBIS; 146 (T/R) Lightstone/CORBIS, (B/R) Brian Vikander/CORBIS; 147 (T/R) Shama Balfour/ Gallo Images/CORBIS; 157 (C/L) Roger Ressmeyer/CORBIS; 196 (T/R) Dean Conger/CORBIS; 198 (B) Bettmann/CORBIS; 205 (C/R) Historical Picture Archive/CORBIS; 208 (C/L) Hulton-Deutsch Collection/CORBIS, (T/R) Bettmann/CORBIS; 212 (C/L) Bettmann/CORBIS; 213 (T/R) Yevgeny Khaldei/CORBIS, (B) Bettmann/CORBIS; 214 (B/L) Bettmann/CORBIS; 217 (C/L) Leif Skoogfors/CORBIS, (B) Reuters NewMedia Inc./CORBIS; 240 (C/R) Roger Ressmeyer/CORBIS

All other photographs are from MKP Archives